The Third Daughter
A RETROSPECTIVE

For my son Eoghan

The Third Daughter
A RETROSPECTIVE

Eileen O'Mara Walsh

THE LILLIPUT PRESS
DUBLIN

First published 2015 by
THE LILLIPUT PRESS
62–63 Sitric Road, Arbour Hill,
Dublin 7, Ireland
www.lilliputpress.ie

A CIP record for this title is available
from The British Library.

10 9 8 7 6 5 4 3 2 1

ISBN 978 1 8435 1 6 378

Set in 11.5 pt on 13 pt Garamond by Marsha Swan
Printed by GraphyCems in Spain
Index by Fergus Mulligan: www.publishing.ie

Contents

Illustrations follow pages 152 and 216

Preface and Acknowledgments

Dublin January 2011: Three score and ten, I had reached my biblical allotment of years. I was already five years older than either of my parents at the time of their death. My business life behind me, I was now embarked on an MA degree in modern English and was facing the task of writing a 20,000 word thesis with less than enthusiasm.

At about this time I encountered a couple now in their eighties who, as young people, had known my family in the 1950s. Entranced, I listened to their anecdotes, still fresh and warmly affectionate about both my parents; but their recollections of my father as a charmer, full of bonhomie, a joker and raconteur, intrigued and saddened me. It was not the father I remembered. An idea dawned gradually that once planted kept nagging until I realized that I was going to abandon the thesis and instead write my parents' story.

I would try to solve the mysteries and silences that had shadowed my childhood and trace the route that took a War of Independence exile and son of an opera singer to meet and marry an English socialist, erstwhile lover of Bertrand Russell. I would delve into my own memories of childhood in Limerick and adolescence in Dublin when Patrick Kavanagh paid my busfare home and my mother scolded Brendan Behan for putting his boots up on the kitchen table.

This is why *The Third Daughter* was begun. A coda worthy of Dickens coincided with its ending. In October 2014, as I walked through the restored Victorian buildings of the new DIT Campus in Grangegorman, a ghostly finger touched my cheek in valediction or remembrance of their previous incarnation: the desolate wards of St Brendan's Hospital, where my mother spent the last weeks of her life.

That this search for my parents has run away from its best intentions and become a chronicle of my own life as much as theirs is in no small part due to Paul Durcan, whose gentle but unrelenting persuasion drove the story ever onwards.

Eileen O'Mara Walsh
March 2015

*

The poem 'Portrait of the Artist' from *Cries of an Irish Caveman* by Paul Durcan is by kind permission of the author. The correspondence between Bertrand Russell and Joan Follwell is by kind permission of The Bertrand Russell Archives, McMaster University Library, Ontario, Canada.

Thanks are due to Dr Kenneth Blackwell, former archivist of the Russell Collection, for his courtesy to my mother in 1971 and to myself in 2014; to Eoin Purcell and Sine Quinn for their professional advice and encouragement; to Antony Farrell of The Lilliput Press for his faith in *The Third Daughter*, and to the unerring eye of his own daughter, Bridget; to Djinn von Noorden, for her editing skills and shrewd comments; to Mairead Breslin Kelly and Stephanie Byrne, friends and early critics; finally to my son Eoghan, to his wife Yvonne, to my sister Mary and to my extended O'Mara and Walsh families for their love and friendship.

The Third Daughter

A RETROSPECTIVE

1. *Listen with Mother*

LIMERICK 1941

The O'Mara family was typical of the wealthy Catholic merchant class that had emerged in Ireland from the middle of the nineteenth century. Thus it was Kate O' Brien's Limerick rather than the city of Frank McCourt where I was born in 1941, third daughter of the IRA son of an operatic tenor and Freeman of Limerick, and the Fabian daughter of a Salisbury socialist. In fact we had a close connection with Kate O'Brien, insofar as her sister Nancy was married to my father's first cousin, Stephen O'Mara, and lived in some grandeur at Strand House, only a short walk from the more middle-class redbrick of no. 4 Moyola Terrace on the Ennis Road where I spent most of my first ten years.

When I think of my parents, my mother always comes first to mind and is still a constant commentator, mentor and arbiter against whose taste, judgment, beliefs and prejudices I measure both myself and the world around me. Those early years in Limerick must have been golden ones for Joan Follwell, despite her difficulties as a foreigner, and an English convert at that, in the tight class structure and religious bigotry that characterized the Limerick of the 1940s and 50s. She was, according to all who knew her then, a beauty of the elegant, bony type epitomized by Hollywood legends such as Joan Crawford or Barbara Stanwyck, upon whom she quite likely modelled herself. She was the first woman to wear slacks in Limerick, her clothes square-shouldered and mannish except for the long housecoats, buttoned all the way down to the floor, which she wore in the evenings. She professed to despise jewellery and I never remember her wearing any except a string of pearls and an ornate signet ring of my father's. She was famous for her hats – or rather hat – as she always wore a variation of the same one, a turban, fashioned to her design by the modest local milliner-cum-dressmaker who made all our clothes. Indeed when we moved from the salubrious area of Moyola Terrace to the more working-class precincts of Crescent Estate, she was known, among the more daring of the local lads, as 'the Egyptian prime minister'.

In retrospect when trying to write about my parents, Power and Joan O'Mara, in their own context rather than simply as the progenitors of my important self, I find, whereas my father's story is vague and difficult to recreate, that my mother's early life comes effortlessly to the page. She had imprinted the images of her girlhood and youth so vividly on my memory I almost felt it had all happened to me, so if his voice is faint, hers is not. As Bertrand Russell suggested in one of the twenty-odd letters he wrote to Joan, she may well have had an undeveloped literary talent that expressed itself largely through her letters and through sporadic attempts at composition, both of prose and poetry.

Joan's father Edward Follwell was born of middle-class parents but his mother was widowed early and he went to work as an office boy at twelve years of age. This experience turned him into an early activist in the young British Labour Party and led him to identify all his life with Charles Dickens; so much so that he used to tour local halls and meeting houses and give readings of Dickens to earnest working men's groups. Joan's mother Maude's maiden name was Davis and she came from Bristol. She too died young and would have completely disappeared from family history but for her two sisters whose Christmas and birthday cards were awaited so eagerly in Limerick half a century later. Those red ten-shilling sterling notes represented untold treasure to their recipients, who dutifully wrote their thank-you notes to those unknown foreign species, 'Dear Aunt Mabs' and 'Dear Aunt Nell'. Edward Follwell married again, not to a cruel stepmother, but to a gentle lady known as 'Mater' by Joan and 'Grandma' by her Irish step-granddaughters. He married yet a third time, much to Joan's mortification, after Mater's death in the 1950s, to Phyllis who was half a dozen years younger than herself. The fact that Phyllis had a club foot slightly mollified her, together with the realization that her father, self-centred to the last, had ensured he would be looked after in his Salisbury home for the rest of his life.'

Joan's own words brings the child and later schoolgirl vibrantly to life:

> In those days we all wore sailor suits, boys and girls alike. Naturally the girls wore skirts and the boys were differentiated by sometimes having attached to their collars a silver whistle, held by a white cord. It was in such suits that we (my brother and I) were dressed by a kind friend of the family after our mother had been removed to the hospital where she afterwards died. The fact

that we had to be so completely fitted out brings home to me the poverty of our parents. We lived in Wood Green [London] in a dark flat of which I remember chiefly the texts on the walls, 'In all thy ways acknowledge Him and He will direct thy path.'

The first time I entered a Catholic church I was nine years old. It was somewhere in North London, a wild and stormy night. I was walking with my father and ahead of us were my mother and my little brother, he hanging on her arm and she wiping her nose through her veil. She was beginning to cry already and I knew what it would be like when we got home so I was glad when my father stopped before a building from whose half-open door light shone out. Inside it was brighter than anything I had ever imagined, people were standing and singing and we stood too, not singing but staring about us at the lights and the sweet-smelling incense that rose from the altar. When everyone sat down we sat too but when a bell rang and everyone knelt we continued to sit, my father disregarding with a smile the gestures that beckoned us to follow suit. I would gladly have knelt, felt painfully our conspicuousness as the bell rang again and all heads were bowed but ours. We came out again into the starry night while my father talked of Joseph McCabe, Boyd Barrett and the beauties of rationalism (so unlike Little Therese). When we reached home, my brother was in bed and my mother's lamentations were louder than ever before. 'When I am dead, you will be sorry.' My heart had broken already earlier in the evening when I had watched without seeing the comic film my father thought would cure my mother's grief – I knew then, sitting in the plush seat feeling in the darkness her agony, that we were doomed. In the morning she was gone. I never saw her again. After my mother's death my brother and I never spoke her name.

I was sent to St Gilda's Convent School in Yeovil, Somerset in 1916 when my mother became incurably ill and died soon after. I remember that my father deputed someone else to break this news to me and that all day I avoided by a show of high spirits being told what I already knew in my heart. Sister Superior I have described elsewhere but all my writings, my diaries, my letters were lost in the 'Blitz'. Her name in religion was Sister Ste Hermiland. She was very small, very dark; her skin was pock-marked and her lips the deepest most velvety red. At 'recreation' she would stand with her arm around me. This, I see now, accounted for the lack of popularity I so longed for and why school was not the least like those I had read about in the books of Angela Brazil.

We all wore black pinafores in the French fashion and for lack of looking-glasses we preened ourselves before the glass of the cloakroom door. We went for long walks in 'crocodiles' and were so hungry that we ate everything we could find. The taste of beech nuts and their shape remains with me still. Also sloes, which did things to one's mouth and of course, blackberries and even hips and haws.

The waking bell. Daily Mass was not compulsory, especially for non-Catholics, but I knew her eyes were fixed on me and even though the sweat came out on my forehead and strange bells rang in my ears I continued to kneel. To faint and die and receive Sr Hermiland's smile as I was carried out to recover on a cold tombstone was victory indeed. She was sad to see me go. She summoned me to her room and standing breast to breast (she was exactly my height) she pressed her velvety lips on mine while the wings of her coif enfolded both our faces.

Why Joan's father, a principled atheist, ever sent her there is obscure. Her resulting conversion to Catholicism was at first passionate, then lapsed into agnosticism, reviving again on her marriage but remaining idiosyncratic with leanings towards mysticism and ritual and a hatred for the dogmatism and prejudices of the Irish Catholic Church. Her account of boarding-school life holds huge resonances in our family history. Her husband, my father Power O'Mara and his younger brother Joe, who became a Jesuit priest, were both products of the Jesuit boarding-school system; both gentlemen and gentle men, but it may have sucked some essence, some vital spark from their personalities: 'Give me a child before he is seven and I will give you the man.' For Joan, the cloistered life seemed always to hold a romantic attachment. In her old age she wistfully spoke of ending her days living in a convent cell, with recourse to books, a plentiful supply of Sweet Afton and the occasional Baby Power.

Part of the ineradicable literary legacy she imprinted on the hearts and minds of her daughters Mary, Ruth and Eileen was her reading aloud; for instance, Antonia White's *Frost in May* was narrated with great relish to me, her youngest daughter, whilst her eldest, Mary, ironically raged and fulminated against her eight-year incarceration as a boarder in the Sacred Heart Convent, Roscrea. This life sentence had a deeply damaging, lifelong effect on that mother-daughter relationship. Yet Joan did not see, or perhaps refused to see, that her own version of sentimentalized convent life in First World War England brutally differed from the reality experienced by Mary in the Ireland of the Emergency and the implacable jansenistic sect that was Irish Catholicism. Her two younger daughters, Ruth and later myself, happily attended the Faithful Companions of Jesus Convent, Limerick, as day pupils.

The pains and perils of Limerick and Roscrea were far from the life twenty-one-year-old Joan Follwell was enjoying when she first encountered Bertrand Russell. She describes their first meeting in April 1927:

> When I was a young girl, living in Salisbury in the nineteen-twenties, my family were pioneers in the Socialist movement. We were all members of the I.L.P. [International Labour Party] and we played our part by giving hospitality to visiting speakers for the Cause. It was in this way that I met Bertrand Russell, or rather, that he met me, for me he was just another political guest (we had had Emmanuel Shinwell the previous week-end). As I waited for the bus at Harnham Bridge I felt a little more than the usual excitement and

anticipation that an important speaker normally aroused. I am sure this was not because he was 'Lord' Russell, it was because he was a writer and I had secret ambitions of my own. These I confided to him as we walked home. But I was dismayed and my parents were quite nonplussed when he asked after supper if we might be left alone together so that I could show him some of my 'work'! This work was practically non-existent – two chapters of an autobiographical novel, but he asked me to read it aloud to him. I had not proceeded very far when it became clear to me that he was far more interested in my mouth than in the words I was reading. So I said, with genuine feeling but with quite false naiveté: 'You are just like all the others!' And he admitted with the utmost gravity that he was.

Following that visit Bertrand Russell wrote:

31 Sydney Street, Londom SW

My dear Joan (may I call you so?)

I am telling the booksellers to send you a volume of Tchekov and also a tiny volume of my own. If you like the former, there are 11 more like it. I haven't much time as I go to Leicester today and Bristol tomorrow, but then my public jobs are done.

Saturday of next week I go to Cornwall for the whole summer – then to America for oct and nov. After that I shall live in Petersfield, where my wife and I are starting a school – but from there I shall come to London about once a week. If you think it worthwhile I should like to keep in touch with you by letter, so that when the time comes I can see you again. And I shall wish to know about your career, if you have time and inclination to tell me. Like other people I am not a free agent as regards where I live – but I shall keep the recollection of my visit to Salisbury, not without hopes for the future.

Yours

BR

Over the next two and half years, although they only met three times, Betrand Russell wrote her over twenty letters, becoming more enamoured and insistent as the correspondence between them flourished. The letters became a much-hinted-at, never-revealed and half-doubted secret throughout our childhood and youth until Joan produced the yellowing bundle in the late 1960s with a view to selling them after Russell's death to the highest bidder to provide some security for her old age. (The full text of the correspondence between Bertrand Russell and Joan Follwell is appended to this memoir by kind permission of McMaster University, Ontario, Canada, who also generously furnished me with copies of four letters in their Russell Archives from my mother to Lord Russell.)

When she parted with the letters in March 1971, she included the following note:

> Now after forty years and while these memories of Russell are still vivid in my mind and realising that I am uneducated in the academic sense, but having lived, loved, suffered and received certain intimations of immortality, I consider Russell's philosophy, as St Thomas Aquinas said of his own, 'so much chaff'. He believed to his dying day in the perfectibility of man; he believed that, 'if only' this and that, man might progress to a sort of heaven on earth. Even H.G. Wells recanted from this kind of thing when he wrote 'Man at the end of his Tether' and died in enlightened despair.
>
> Russell, I believe, will be read because he was a great writer and, if 'Le style c'est l'homme', he was a great man. As for mathematics, they are surely what makes the world go round – the stars in their courses, the music of Bach and great architecture. Russell glimpsed all this yet stubbornly refused to see the implications of his insights. He might be compared to Pascal, only Pascal was 'given' (I use the word advisedly for these graces are gratuitous) to see beyond logic and to experience the ineffable.

This then was the woman whom I knew simply as my mother. Her secret life, her regrets, her unfulfilled dreams, were unknown until I began to piece them together in this memoir. To be sure Bertrand Russell was a household name in the family, but as an almost mythical historical figure and not a very interesting one at that. Even when I finally read 'The Letters' in the late 1960s I was conscious of a faint disgust with more than a dash of pity for the naive girl being 'groomed' as Russell's objective in writing to her might be interpreted today. The fact that this period, in her eyes, was the pivotal experience of her life now arouses not only pity, but also a sense of anger. Anger at the society of the time, what Joan refers to scathingly as 'the bourgeois middle class of Ireland', which imprisoned her within its rigid rules of acceptable behaviour for married women. But also anger at Joan herself, who reflects through her sporadic writing and her confidences to me in later years – someone vain in her intellectual isolation who, as the years went by narrowed her horizons and confined her aspirations to communing, vicariously through her reading, with the ideas, philosophy and lives of contemporary and long-dead mystics, writers and poets.

Growing up I garnered the flotsam and jetsam of her inner life through the books on the shelves, the books I went in and out to Switzers Library in Grafton Street to exchange for her, and half remembered musings addressed to me, looking up from her book during shared evenings in Leeson Park in my teenage years. St John of the Cross, Thomas à Kempis and Simone Weil formed the backbone of her reading in mysticism, while Francis Thompson's *The Hound of Heaven* sat side by side with Tennyson and *The Secret Life of the Little Flower* by Henri Gheon on her bedside table. Isak Dinesen was much admired but Jean Rhys she thought of as a fellow pilgrim as she did Emma Bovary, reading Flaubert's French with some difficulty. She read Proust in translation as she did Colette's *Chéri* and *The Last of Chéri*, a slim Penguin edition inscribed to her by my cousin Hugh Carton. Fiction writers of her own era, Henry Green's *Loving*, David Garnett's *Lady into Fox* and *Man at the Zoo*, twinned in one volume (a rare one that I read and enjoyed myself at the time), Elizabeth Bowen, Elizabeth Taylor, L.P. Hartley, Graham Greene, one of the few who can still be found on library shelves. Her two heroes, most often read and most often quoted were Boswell's Samuel Johnson and Henry James although late in life she rediscovered with relish *Little Dorrit* and *Bleak House* and found spiritual comfort in Beckett. One of her last notes in 1970 after seeing a Gate production of the play typifies her lifelong sense of the divine:

> The clue to Beckett is in *Happy Days* and the clue in *Happy Days* is 'O Happy Chance'. This play is about the dark night of the soul and Marie Keane hadn't a clue but Ozzie Whitehead was wonderful. Dr Johnson hadn't the advantages of Beckett, for which he is to be honoured and pitied. His faith was blind and groping and he feared the wrath to come. In contrast Beckett's characters seem almost happy – they know Godot will come – they are souls in Purgatory and purgatory is a happy state reserved for the faithful soul, just as in *Happy Days*, Winnie, though up to the neck, is able to console herself with the long littleness of life because HE is there: 'once seen, never forgotten' O, the beauty of the ordinary phrase!

Sadly, always waiting in the wings but never valued in Joan's 'field of dreams' was her husband Power. Yet they stayed together, each faithful in their own way but unable to communicate. Joan summed it up:

> I read in Graham Greene's new volume of short stories: 'I could have explained that nothing is quite so bad as that at the end of what is called 'the sexual life' the only love which has lasted is the love that has accepted everything, every disappointment, and every betrayal, which has accepted even the sad fact that in the end there is no desire so deep as the simple desire for companionship,' It was like a knife in my heart.

That same knife must have also been embedded in Power's heart but he did not have Joan's gift of self expression and I can only paint the man, the husband, the father as he was seen by others, including his third daughter, myself.

9

2. Searching for my Father

Compared to my mother, my father had always been a shadowy figure, coming to life most vividly in memories of early childhood. I remember screaming with fright and delight when he threw me up in the air – pretending to miss on the way down but always just catching me in time. Like all fathers I thought him the most handsome man in the world. Randolph Scott was my first movie hero; I was convinced he resembled my father and wept loudly when a black-clad cowboy smashed his good gun hand during one harrowing showdown: fortunately he recovered in time to shoot down the baddie in a fair fight on one of those eternally deserted main streets of the black-and-white Western towns that were featured week after week of Saturday matinees at the Savoy Cinema on Bedford Row, Limerick.

For a special outing my father brought me to the O'Mara Bacon factory to see black puddings and sausages being made. It was a tour of Dante's *Inferno*: great black cauldrons full of liquid that looked, smelled and probably did consist mainly of blood – the stench was horrific and if there is such a thing as an aural memory I have it of squealing pigs wired up for slaughter. Another treat was to visit the shop and go up the ladder to the little glass box at the side where the lady sat and where the cash canisters came whizzing up the wires. She would unscrew them, take the money and docket out, put back in the change and send it whizzing back down to the shop man below.

Daddy had a gold watch and chain that had been given to him by his father, the great tenor Joseph O'Mara, one of the last relics of the carefree days before it was sold to alleviate one of our many financial crises. Other clear memories of my father are associated with Kilkee, where like all decent Limerick people (except for those few heathens who went to Lahinch) we spent as much as possible of the summer in temporary residence. Our preference was for the West End. We had a cottage on the Dunlica Road where a major event in our weekly routine was the placing of a big tin bath in the middle of the kitchen floor that was filled with kettles of boiling water heated on the range and cooled by cold water from the pump outside.

In the same kitchen I was the fascinated observer of the doctor bent over my sister Mary's bared bottom, extracting long black porcupine spines with some instrument of torture to the accompaniment of her shrieks and sobs. The porcupines were denizens of the Pollock Holes, natural swimming pools among the rocks at the bottom of the cliffs where Mary and Ruth had both learned to swim.

I remember being my father's sole companion on our hugely enjoyable visits to Scott's Bar, where there was a large oval mirror with a picture of two Scottie dogs, one white and one black. I was treated like a little Princess (his pet name for me) and put up on a high stool and given a tall glass of fizzy lemonade with ice cubes and tiny bubbles floating on top. He usually had a small glass of whiskey with some soda that I was allowed to squirt from the big bottle on the counter. On the way home, as a special treat, he would buy me a newspaper cone of periwinkles which had to be angled out of their shells with a pin. They tasted deliciously like snot.

Again as a small child, clutching Daddy's hand tightly crossing over Sarsfield Bridge in the dark. We were in the midst of crowds of people milling around: cheering voices, bright lights, torches held aloft and a mysterious fervour in the air. A band, rousing music, 'A Nation Once Again', 'Amhrán na bhFiann'. It was 1949, the celebration of the Declaration of the Irish Republic. What was in his mind, I wonder? I never recall him alluding to his early experience or making any claims of patriotic activity while others secured jobs and influence as freedom fighters for Cathleen Ni Houlihan.

Who was this father, beloved in my childhood, ever more distant as I grew up, who was born to the arias of Puccini at the dawn of a new century in London, and who died as quietly as he had lived in an anonymous hospital ward in the same city, just as the Beatles were sweetly and slyly revolutionizing popular music in the swinging sixties? It took me another forty years to find out.

James Power O'Mara was born in London on 21 May 1900. He was the second child and eldest son of Joseph O'Mara, a well-known tenor with a successful career on the operatic stage in London and as an international concert performer. His mother was Brid Power from Waterford and, as was often the custom, her maiden name was taken as Christian name by the eldest son. His grandfather James O'Mara had migrated from Tipperary to Limerick in the late 1830s and founded the O'Mara Bacon Company. Joseph O'Mara, the youngest of his thirteen children, was born in 1864 when the family business was already established as the leading bacon-curing company in Ireland and the family had rapidly climbed the social ladder to become leaders of the new Roman Catholic merchant class. By the early twentieth century O'Mara Bacon had subsidiaries and partners in the USA, Canada, Romania, France and Russia, where an elder brother of Joseph's, Jack O'Mara, had built a bacon factory in St Petersburg by commission of no less a personage than Tsar Nicholas II. The head of the family by then was Joseph's eldest brother, Stephen O'Mara, driver of the family's business expansion, and twice Mayor of Limerick, who had refused to host a civic reception for the visit of King Edward VII and thereby renounced a baronetcy. In 1900, a few years prior to the aborted royal visit to Limerick, his own son James was elected to Westminster as a Redmonite MP for the constituency of Kilkenny.

Joseph O'Mara appeared to break the mould by running off to sea at eighteen. Having got the wanderlust out of his system, and, on inheriting a small bequest from his godmother and secretly attending an audition in London, he announced at nineteen that he was going to study singing in Milan. His bemused parents apparently made no objections to this scheme and so his career was launched. Although leaving few recordings and reputedly disliking the embryonic technology, his quality as one of the foremost tenors of his age is well documented. He sang all the classic major roles in the leading opera houses of the day, including seasons in Covent Garden, touring extensively in the USA and Canada. He subsequently turned impresario as well as performer when he formed The O'Mara Opera Company in 1910. The family annals include letters from Nellie Melba, a contemporary and friend, such as the following undated note:

30 Cumberland Place

Dear Mr O'Mara,

I am afraid you took what I said 'au serieux' yesterday which was very wrong of you as I only said it for fun. I am one of your most enthusiastic admirers and I always say nice things about you to all sorts of people.

I am quite upset that you should have felt hurt because I did not mean what I said. Please drop me a line to say that you understand and please don't get huffy again.

Yours sincerely
Nellie Melba

P.S Come and see me

John McCormack, twenty years his junior, wrote to his widow after his death to say that Joe had been his guide and mentor, and telling how he had queued in the rain as a young man outside the Gaiety Theatre for the thrill of hearing O'Mara sing the title role in Gounod's *Romeo and Juliet*. Oddly, although McCormack was by then the better known, it was Joseph O'Mara who was invited to sing for the first transmission of Raidió Éireann on 1 January 1926.

In everything other than his unorthodox choice of profession, Joseph and Brid O'Mara remained true to their roots. Family life was conventional and retained all the traditional values of Catholic Ireland. For the first fifteen years of Power's life, they lived in England. Power and his younger brother Joe went to Stonyhurst College, the renowned Jesuit public school, and thereafter to Belvedere College, another Jesuit private school in Dublin when the family finally moved back to Ireland, presumably for reasons connected with the First World War, when overseas tours and opera performances in London were curtailed.

As a young man during those chaotic years in Irish history between 1916 and 1921 Power aligned himself firmly on the Sinn Féin side. Whereas his father Joseph showed no interest in the emergent Irish nationalist movement, the Limerick uncles and cousins were very much involved. It is from that branch of the family that Power gained his enthusiasm and association with the ever-hastening pace of political and revolutionary activity. His first cousin James O'Mara, who had resigned his South Kilkenny seat in Westminster, stood as a Sinn Féin candidate in the same constituency in 1918 and won a landslide victory. He is proudly featured in the classic black-and-white photograph of the meeting in the Mansion House of the First Dáil in 1919.

However, unlike his uncles and cousins so firmly committed to constitutional politics, Power O'Mara took the road of armed rebellion and secretly joined the IRA. An account of his involvement in an ambush of a British army armoured car during the War of Independence was given by his sister Eileen O'Mara Carton after his death:

> It was a foggy afternoon in November 1919; we were having tea in the drawing room when my brother Power came in looking for Joe who hadn't yet come home from school. I wondered why he seemed so restless and upset, even more so when at last Joe appeared, bursting with some tale of mayhem in Dorset Street, Power became suddenly infected with high spirits, grabbed Joe in a bear hug and galloped him down the room.
>
> Six months later I learned why: Power had secretly become involved in the War of Independence. On that November day, he had been stationed at the corner of Findlater Street waiting for a convoy advancing from O'Connell Street. At the very moment he flung the Mills bomb towards a passing Saracen car, he saw his brother Joe on his bicycle crossing the intersection on his way back from lunch to nearby Belvedere College. It wasn't until Joe walked into the room four agonising hours later that he knew whether or not his brother had survived.

However, a few months later another skirmish resulted in Power being wounded, which brought his subversive activities to the ears of his shocked parents and his hurried departure to a new life in Canada. Whether or not he was a willing or reluctant exile is not known. It was a period of his life he never spoke about, and, until this memoir, the twenty-year gap between his exile to Canada and return to Ireland in 1940 was never explored or explained. He was taken in by another first cousin in the innumerable O'Mara clan, one Joe O'Mara, who had settled in Canada some years before to manage another offshoot of the O'Mara bacon empire in Palmerston, Ontario. This cousin – the family entrepreneurial flame well alight – also established a rubber-tyre factory, K & S Tire and Rubber Goods Ltd in Toronto, where Power was working in early 1926, according to a long and affectionate letter to his parents about this time. Had the rubber business flourished Power might well have remained in Canada for the rest of his life but in the late 1920s British control of the rubber plantations in Asia pushed up the price of rubber in the US and Canada and the business failed. He returned to Ireland briefly to register the death of his father in Dublin in October 1927.

The next official record is of his marriage in 1932 in Salisbury, England, to one Winifred May Follwell (her old-fashioned Christian name long rejected in favour of Joan), born in Bristol on 13 May 1906. Her wedding on the same day twenty-six years later provoked headlines in the local newspaper: *SALISBURY BRIDE DEFIES SUPERSTITION,* referring to the double jeopardy of marrying on her birthday, dressed in green. The same newspaper clipping describes the occupation of the groom as 'Factory Manager, Melksham', the only clue to where and how they met, as Joan's last letter is written on headed notepaper from the Avon India Rubber Company, Melksham. Given Power's recent employment in the rubber business in Canada, it is not unreasonable to suppose they met each other through work, but whether he is the lover Joan refers to in her correspondence with Russell remains an unanswered and intriguing question.

Whatever the gamble, it appears their first few years of married life were both happy and prosperous as evidenced by the salubrious neighbourhoods of their first homes, in Cheadle Hume, Manchester, and Richmond, Surrey. But the outbreak of World War Two changed all that. In 1940 Power, a pregnant Joan, with their daughters, Mary Elizabeth and Ruth Winifred, aged seven and five, dressed in 'siren' suits with labels round their necks, were evacuated to Ireland. All their possessions were lost in the London Blitz apart from an old travelling trunk containing the family silver and precious memorabilia of Joseph O'Mara's operatic career. Both his parents were dead, Joseph in 1927 and Brid in 1935, so it was the more distant Limerick family of uncles and cousins, deeply embedded in the family tradition of business and civic duty, who offered asylum to the refugees from war-torn Britain.

In Limerick Power took up a position with the family firm, the O'Mara Bacon Company. Their third daughter, myself, Eileen Thérèse, was born there on 15 January 1941. Nineteen forties Ireland was radically different to the revolutionary fledgling republic Power had left twenty years before. De Valera's neutral Free State was a closed society where Church rather than Empire held sway over a rigidly conservative and economically protectionist political system. The re-entry seemed to have been a painful transition for both Power and Joan and they endured a peripatetic life for the first year, largely apart. Several loving letters from a lonely Power, working for far-flung O'Mara outposts in Claremorris, County Mayo, and Letterkenny, County Donegal, attest both to his love and loneliness.

He was torn between having to work away from home – 'if only I could get a settled job someplace' – and his worry about Joan, who was moving from Limerick to remote Kilkee, apparently in escape from family pressures. Another letter speaks volumes of both his homesickness and the sexual mores of the day.

> I am longing to see you and will take the first opportunity of getting away for a weekend. A rather embarrassing question if we are to start this 'Rhythm' business you will have to let me know when I can make love to you. I doubt if I could withstand the temptation otherwise. Are you still nursing Eileen once or twice a day or is she on the bottle altogether now. Isn't she lovely in the enlargement?

A telegram sent from Letterkenny on 13 May 1941, the ninth anniversary of their marriage, says it all: 'Many happy returns heartfelt gratitude past nine years. Love Power.'

Some months later he finally landed that 'settled' job as manager of the O'Mara retail store Rays Limited. Limerick was to be their home for twelve years, beginning in hopes for a new life, a new job, a new child, the first to be Irish-born. The city proved a harsh introduction to the Ireland of saints and scholars for Joan, erstwhile lover of Bertrand Russell, unredeemed socialist, unorthodox convert to Catholicism. When the family moved to Dublin in 1953 she, at least, was not unhappy to shake the dust of Limerick's shibboleths from her elegant ankles as she left for a shabbier but more contented life among the left-wing literati of Dublin town.

3. At Home

The basement – a cavernous kitchen and scullery, the vast black range and red flagged floor; bread and dripping, delicious if you were allowed to dig down to the beefy jelly at the bottom of the bowl; sticky spoons of Cod Liver Malt to make you strong; golden syrup – the green and gold tin had a picture of a lion on it with the words 'out of the strong comes forth sweetness'. The first banana ever tasted, a bit slimy – strange but delicious. Apart from the ceremonial stirring of the Christmas pudding when I was allowed to drop in silver thrupenny bits with the little rabbit on them and scrape the bowl afterwards, I have no recollection of my mother ever being in the kitchen at all. Later recall of a vast dog-eared tome entitled *Mrs Beeton's Cookery Book*, which followed us from house to house leads me to believe that Mother did in fact cook but, as it was in her eyes a chore rather than a pleasure, meals, other than grand Sunday lunches, never took on an aura of nostalgia.

The kitchen stairs led up first to the hall return where the playroom led out to the wooden landing and rickety stairs down to the back garden – featureless like every garden our family had apart from a swing constructed on strong timber stakes and the two lilac trees at the far end, which flourished against all the odds, their fragrant purple blooms hanging just within range of your toes on the upmost arc of the swing during the long spring and summer evenings. A couple of shallow steps up from this grown-up-free zone lay the dining room. Here was the brilliance lacking in the kitchen: all gleaming mahogany, table, sideboard, serving trolley on wheels, the family silver laid out, carelessly opulent, carefully polished with all the reluctant effort of the Silvo-stained fingers that took on the mammoth task in sibling disharmony. Because they so suddenly disappeared from my ken, my visual and tactile memory of these symbols of prosperity that adorned the sideboard is still vivid. A great serving dish with entwined handled lid, the soup tureen and ladle, sat on the large silver tray inscribed with the family crest, a winged bird of prey with the motto 'Opima Spolia' over the script: TO BRIDE AND JOE, FROM FATHER, JUNE 1896. On the smaller more ornate tray nearby lay the silver service of tall coffee pot and round tea pot, milk jug and sugar bowl with tongs, all resting on lion-headed, clawed feet. The table itself was covered in white, sometimes embroidered white cloth where my father presided, all bonhomie and jokes, armed with the large bone-handled carving knife and fork; he always made a ceremony of sharpening the knife on the steel with much flourishing before tackling the joint of beef or even roast chicken for special occasions. *Pièce de résistance* of the feast were the roast potatoes served last from a big china bowl, to be lathered with rich brown gravy from the gravy boat.

The drawing room was at the entrance of the house to the immediate right of the front door, which opened on to a long flight of granite steps, a shrine to scraped knees and scenes of great lamentation when my mother was seen departing in one of her elegant suits and turban hats. The heart of the house lay here, certainly not in the dungeon kitchen. It was large, comfortable and untidy. A big sprawling settee ('sofa' was non-U); two deep armchairs and a couple of worn leather poufs; a glass-fronted cabinet with its precious and long-gone collection of Crown Derby and hand-painted fruit dishes. Bookcases, also with glass doors, each with a tiny key; the books seemed very dull and heavy with no pictures: 'and what is the use of a book' thought Alice 'without pictures or conversation in it' although there were some rows of slim red and white Penguin paperbacks that seemed more like my own fastgrowing Puffin collection. The mantelpiece had my favourite delicate Dresden monkey-headed shepherd alongside his shepherdess. I can see her exquisite pink-figured looped gown to this day – they met an awful fate smashed on the fireplace in another house one grim day a few years later. Lastly, a handsome round mahogany sewing table, whose top opened into compartments overflowing with darning wool, reels of cotton, odd socks and knitting of various colours and dimensions.

Three pictures informed and enthralled my budding visual consciousness: an old beshawled crone, sitting upright on a wooden rocking chair – it was by William Conor, given away in later years by my mother as a wedding present because she had no money to buy one; a glowing silver and black 'Frozen Pond' by George Campbell – this too became a wedding gift to my sister Ruth in 1971. The third was an impressionist view of the backs of houses at Ennistymon by Grace Henry. I was convinced as a child that a human leg was hanging out of one of the windows until I saw the selfsame picture at an Adams auction fifty years later and realized it was part of a line of washing.

The bedroom interiors are vague, perhaps because I never inhabited any of them except when sick with measles or pneumonia when I was upgraded from my attic abode to my mother's bedroom. I remember tiptoeing past its closed portals in the mornings so as not to disturb her before the sacrosanct cup of tea was imbibed in the shadowy dimness of that holy of holies, where even my father trod quietly. Sometimes I would be called into the darkened room before leaving for school to give Mummy a kiss. I hated the gloom and Mummy's face, shiny with Nivea and bloodless lips, so unlike her daytime soft powdered cheeks and bright lipsticked mouth.

Up again lay the attics, plural as there were several partitioned-off rooms within that spacious roof space. Years later, driving down the Ennis Road as an Irish Tourist Board recruit en route to Paris, I could still distinguish the house by the wooden bars on the front attic windows. A Christmas Eve in the 1940s: I wake up in the dark, a beam of grey moonlight coming through the skylight shows a limp stocking hanging on the end of the bed. I hear footsteps coming up the stairs and squeeze my eyes tight shut in case Santa would discover I was awake and leave the stocking empty, the latch lifted, stealthy sounds followed, the door shut quietly and when I got up the courage to look – lo and behold the stocking was bulging with interesting shapes. I was able to maintain with the absolute conviction of the true believer that Santa did exist long after my friends had lost their own more precarious faith.

There were eight years between myself and my eldest sister Mary, who was two years older than Ruth. To all intents and purposes it was a generation gap. Mary was away at boarding school in Roscrea from the age of eight, and early memories of her are fraught with strange events and whispered secrets. I was four when she was sent home from school in the middle of term and in disgrace – Mary had told the nuns she had swallowed a safety pin and not being sure whether it was open or shut she was sent home so that her family would have the dubious pleasure of examining her bowel movements for several days after the event. No evidence was ever found but Mary got an extra week's holiday for her trouble. But however difficult her reputation at home or at school, Mary was my protector and as glamorous as a film star. When I too was sent away to Roscrea at the ripe age of seven, she became my one beacon of hope, the only certainty in a world of black-robed warders, mocking co-prisoners, strange rituals and inedible food.

Although I recall my soujourn in Roscrea as interminable, I had only to endure the two-month summer term of 1948 to prepare for my First Holy Communion. My mother's more ascetic form of spirituality found the showy and materialistic celebration of children's first communion in Ireland when neighbours' children visited their friends and relations on the big day to be given half crowns at least, vied with each other and boasted of their wealth, quite shocking. It was anathema to the English ex-Protestant, still devout convert with a particular devotion to the spare mysticism of the Little Flower. So she determined that her youngest daughter would go to the altar unsullied by the paganism rampant in the Holy Confraternity City of Limerick. I survived to the glorious day in June, when, arrayed in my cousin's borrowed long white bridesmaid's dress and veil, I kneeled, with only one other, on priedieux at the steps of the altar. My only conscious prayer was that I wouldn't faint and have to come back for a rerun. All was sweetness and light afterwards with tea and cakes in Reverend Mother's parlour. My horror when she bent down to pinch my cheek and tell my mother how good I was and how I must be let come back again next term – was there a pause or did my mother see my imploring, desperate eyes? In any event my sentence was over. Mary had two more years to serve.

Where was Ruth in all of this, the middle sister, the quiet one, the solid citizen, not wild like Mary, not a princess like Eileen? In my eyes Ruth was 'she who must be obeyed'. I longed to be allowed play with her, or better still have her play my games – playing 'house' was my passion, a continuing saga involving complicated role-playing. The playroom on the return in Moyola Terrace was the terrain. Pushing the trestle tables around to form various rooms, journeys were undertaken with bundles of rags stuffed into pillowcases known as 'burdens', which had to be carried up and down stairs, a tribute perhaps to *Pilgrim's Progress*. Playing house must have been real agony for Ruth because she was the quintessential tomboy: her best friends were boys and she read only boys' books.

My debt was largely repaid by frequent trips next door to borrow Louis' comics. As well as *The Hotspur*, there was *The Champion*, *The Rover* and of course *The Dandy* and *The Beano*, so I escaped the saccharine doings of *Girl's Crystal* and *School Friend* for the much more thrilling adventures of Rockfist Rogan, Desperate Dan, Wilson, the Boy Runner, and Ginger Nutt, the Boy Who Took the Biscuit. Later I graduated to *Biggles* and *Just William* and I am grateful for this apprenticeship in male sportsmanship before I fell under the spell of Enid Blyton, the Chalet Girls, and Angela Brazil, whose jolly hockey sticks never held quite the same mystique for me as *Teddy Lester, Captain of Cricket*. This robust fare mixed happily in my imagination with my mother's diet of the *Green, Yellow* and *Red Fairybooks* with Andrew Lang's beautiful illustrations, the *Water Babies, The Princess and the Goblin, The Did of Didn't Think* and the Victorian tear-jerker *Froggy's Little Brother*.

She was an expert tree climber while even then I was scared of heights. If I got stuck Ruth would get into trouble if adults had to be called on to rescue me. I must have been a serious pest. She had to take me out for walks too – one time we went as far as Barrington's Pier and back along the river, a lonely windy path, me with the doll's pram and Ruth pulling me along faster and faster because of the funny man who kept walking alongside us and whispering or whistling, I'm not sure which. He had a long raincoat and then he had his trousers open with his willy hanging out. Ruth never said a word, just went faster and faster until we got to Rose's Avenue and he went away. We never said anything about it at home.

Next door was like going into *Alice Through the Looking Glass* country, the same rooms back to front but occupied by the Keane family. I was always made very welcome but had to brave the fearsome 'Manger', the big Alsatian dog, who lurked behind the kitchen door and growled sullenly as I edged by. Reputedly, Manger – or more likely Major – loved children, and although I pretended equal affection when led up to pat his head, his yellow eyes and raised hackles sent me a very different message. Unlike some of our other neighbours the Keanes were not posh but presumably rich because they owned a motor car and used to bring me to Kilkee for the day, an expedition of forty miles there and back. We always stopped en route at Fanny O'Dea's for red lemonade where I would gaze wonderingly at the big hearth where I was told the fire had been lit one hundred years ago and never gone out since. I sat on Marie's knee in the back of the car, which was better than sitting on Father Scanlon's knee. He was fat and jolly with a red, perspiring face and often came for tea on Sundays in the Keanes' drawing room where Marie played the piano as he led the singsong. These occasions joined the Manger-type of pitfalls to be avoided if at all possible. How to avoid sitting on his lap became a study in juggling politeness and obedience with discomfort and embarrassment. When the former won, I perched stiffly on his knee while his stubby fingers edged inside the elastic of my knickers and touched my 'botty'. I always jumped down as soon as I could, but never told anyone; it would have been too rude.

4. The Outside World

Across the road lived the Cross, Sexton, O'Malley and Duggan families, a little further along the Harrises and the Treaceys. For some time Grace Cross was my best friend. She lived in the corner house opposite, beside the cross-roads. My earliest effort at English composition went thus: 'Grace Cross at Union Cross is very Cross.' She was a fearsome little girl with blond curly hair and bright red cheeks. When we first met she was three to my five but she was always much stronger and bossier than I and took complete charge of our playtime together. On one occasion she would not let me go home and straddled her front doorway on her fat little legs, arms akimbo, defying me to pass. We used to play doctors and nurses in the old shed at the back of her garden, taking a great forensic interest in our bottoms and tummy buttons. I fancy this must have been at my suggestion as I got a nurse's outfit one Christmas complete with apron, cap, bandages and red ink iodine with which we painted each other's arms and legs.

The other families within our immediate neighbourhood had less impact on my own small world. Their children were older, closer to my sisters' age, but certain vignettes remain with me still. The Sextons all had red hair and Rosemary Sexton was at my school and died. I report this baldly because it is all I was told; the horror mixed with awe that someone I actually knew was dead. The O'Malleys were a distant presence: there was a Jane O'Malley whose uncle Donogh was a friend of my father's. He became a popular Minister for Education in the 1960s and is credited with bringing in free secondary-school education for all. He died young and I remember being introduced to him in a pub in Molesworth Street as a teenager by my father. He had been instrumental in getting my father his IRA pension when family fortunes were on the downward slide. My mother's few remaining papers include one from the relevant authority refusing to continue the pension payment of £2 a week to her after his death in 1967. Next came the Duggans, reputedly very rich but vulgar, not quite approved of by the more genteel if less well-off neighbours. The Treacys, whose daughter Marion was in my class in Laurel Hill and whose tawny, curly hair and pert pretty face I admired enormously was the reincarnation of Rosie Redmond in *What Katie Did Next*. The Harrises seemed to be all boys, – large, wild boys. One of them was my sister Mary's particular friend, the first boy who ever kissed her, Dickie Harris, known in later life as Richard Harris. How she impressed her English granddaughters when she confided that Professor Dumbledore, was her first boyfriend!

Although also on the Ennis Road, Strand House. home of the head of the family Stephen O'Mara, and his wife Nancy, seemed quite a long walk from our house towards town, although a nostalgic retracing of the same route fifty years later hardly took five minutes door to door. It was here that De Valera was staying when he received news on the signing of the 1921 Treaty in London. The large house was of a warm yellow hue with a terracotta tiled roof and jutting eaves. Going to tea there on summer afternoons lives in the memory like a scene from a Merchant-Ivory movie: the conservatory with cane cushioned chairs, china tea set and delicately cut bread and butter, scones with jam and cream and, oh bliss, chocolate finger biscuits. Uncle Stephen was much older than Daddy, with thick greying black hair, dressed always in tweeds. Aunt Nancy was gracious and elegant with gentle blue eyes and long hair beautifully arranged in a chignon. Their adopted grown-up son Peter, was a great admirer of my mother. They became soul mates in the intellectual desert that was Limerick at the time and swapped books of poetry and banned novels, of which there were many. Sometimes Nancy's sister Kate O'Brien was there – according to whispered family legend she was Peter's real mother, severe in comparison to her feminine sibling.

But it was the gardens rather than the humans that were the true delight; to reach them you had first to pass the lily pond with stone lions at either end and peer under the perfect ivory and yellow blossoms floating on their green-petalled crafts, to catch a flash of the swift gold and crimson fish darting about beneath. Then out to the carefully controlled wilderness of the kitchen garden, picking strawberries and gorging on their sweet juiciness, gooseberries too, all bristled and plump yellowy green; the first and last time I ever saw or picked peaches from a vine trailing up a sunny wall.

I thought I had imagined or perhaps invented those peaches until I read

Patricia Lavelle's recollection of Strand House in her biography of her father, James O'Mara:

> There was a paddock of several acres between the house and the high boundary wall that cut out the road from the river. There was a kitchen garden with peach trees growing on a nine-foot southern wall. There were glass houses with melons and grapes and plenty of stabling.

The first external stimulus was the radio – the handsome polished brown Pye wireless with all the twiddly knobs and mesh front. *Listen with Mother* at 1.45 pm was not to be missed: 'Are you sitting comfortably? Then I'll begin…' Great anticipation awaited the derring-do of my hero, Dick Barton, Special Agent, who came on at 6.45 pm – the plot was never quite grasped but the awful doom that befell Dick and his brave mates Jock and Snowy at the end of Friday's episode was always miraculously averted by the following Monday. Lunchtimes in summer meant Dad rushing in demanding the Test score.

Devoted as I was to the wireless, the cinema offered even more alluring delights – delights being perhaps not quite accurate as my earliest memories are filled with more painful emotions. Only scenes remain with me: a city street in the rain … black umbrellas … a dark-haired little girl, face tilted up, tears mingling with rain on her cheeks. The next was an even briefer moment: a long row of men in army uniform being ordered to dig by another group of soldiers holding guns. When this task was completed the soldiers with guns shot the other men who fell backwards into the holes they had just dug. I must have been brought clandestinely to these films by Theresa or Lily on their day off. But Walt Disney was the cause of even greater anguish when I had to be carried out in screams of terror engendered by the Wicked Queen's ghastly green visage in *Snow White*.

Finally there was theatre, a rare and special event in Limerick or any Irish provincial city in those days. The impact of live performance versus the silver screen won hands down. I sat spellbound before Cyril Cusack and Siobhán McKenna in *The Playboy of the Western World*, unforgettable, unsurpassable. I saw both of them many times in later years as well as many productions of *The Playboy* but the slim, wiry, conniving Christy as played by Cusack and the glorious red-haired termagant that was Siobhán were creatures from another place, an Ireland I had never heard of. My mother told me years later how shocked she was by the play. She failed completely to understand how or why the audience could laugh at what her English sensitivity saw as a brutal, savage portrayal of a pagan peasantry devoid of human sympathy.

The other theatrical legend was Anew MacMaster who would now be considered totally OTT – but I never viewed *The Merchant of Venice* again without the same absolute conviction that Shylock was the true victim, totally justified in his claim against Antonio and the sneering band of complacent

Gentiles. I finally got to meet my idol Siobhán McKenna in the Gresham Hotel, Dublin, in the 1950s when my father introduced me to her between the matinee and evening performance of Shaw's *Saint Joan*. She had smoked-salmon sandwiches and a glass of red wine, which seemed to me the epitome of glamour.

Mrs Condell ran the small Montessori School at the end of Roses Avenue that I attended at the age of four. She was the Frances Condell who was later to become the first woman Lord Mayor of Limerick, famous for her gracious and distinguished reception of John F. Kennedy during his legendary 1963 visit to Ireland. Mrs Condells' meant colouring pictures with crayons and a small fat boy named Winston who always had a snotty nose and wet his pants. It was a gentler and more tranquil place than the Salesian Convent I attended later, where I learned copybook writing painfully assisted by a ruler rapping my knuckles whenever I veered above or below the lines. Not quite as frightening however as the bendy cane which swished down when you were told to hold out your hand for six slaps for not saying the words of the catechism right. 'Who made the world?' 'God made the world.' I always thought the next question should be 'Who made God?', but it was 'Who is God?' 'A heavenly Being who cannot be seen with bodily eyes.' The words 'bodily eyes' fascinated me – I made no connection with the word 'body' and imagined bodily eyes to be giant jellyfish-type orbs floating around space. Never did the Chinese millions learn their *Little Red Book* with more enthusiasm than I absorbed our penny catechism. My mother's tolerance for the Salesian nuns and theirs for her came to an abrupt end when I returned home one day with a large bruise on my forehead, the result of Sister Mary Aloysius throwing the wooden blackboard duster, not at me, but at another unfortunate whom she managed to miss.

I moved on that September to big school at the Faithful Companions of Jesus Convent, Laurel Hill, truly a garden of roses after the rigours of the regime in Roscrea. In fact gardens are what is most memorable about schooldays there. What has left an indelible impression was their outward displays of devotion and religiosity, many of which involved walking round and round the gardens wearing either black or white veils, depending on the season, and saying the Rosary. Advent, Lent and the month of May were the seasons around which the year turned and each of them had their own particular momentum and mood. Advent was solemn but not as laden with doom as Lent, and shorter, lasting only the four weeks before Christmas. Lent, on the other hand, seemed endless: lists were made at the beginning of all the pleasures we were going to give up, starting with sweets and going on to bananas or sugar in one's tea. Then came the penances to be undertaken in honour of the suffering souls in Purgatory, such as a hundred aspirations on your knees at bedtime: 'Jesus, Lamb of God, forgive me my sins' … 'Mystical

Rose, Tower of Ivory, pray for me'. Some hardy souls would include items of physical deprivation like not wearing gloves on the bike to school, holding a finger over a flame, picking a nettle or putting a stone in your shoe. Scapulars became a popular and smelly item of clothing. I had a brown one that supposedly contained some relic of great holiness and was kept pinned to the inside of my vest for months until my mother finally managed to 'lose' it when the hot weather came in. Next in the religious calendar was the Marian Month of May. Coinciding as it did with springtime, we seemed to spend all our time out of doors, 'processing'. We had a procession on May the first for Our Lady, Queen of Heaven, another on the thirteenth for Our Lady of Fatima and the final one on 31 May in honour of The Visitation. These processions were looked forward to firstly for getting us out of class, secondly for the wearing of our flattering white veils and thirdly for the hymns: 'Hail Holy Queen', 'I'll Sing a Hymn to Mary' and 'Bring Flowers of the Fairest' as we paced solemnly round the convent's gravelled garden paths, to the Grotto with its ubiquitous statue of Mary in the white gown with blue veil and rosary clasped in her hands. Years later at a riotous party in Rathmines, Dublin, I was half horrified when Patrick MacEntee, a noted barrister, gave a perfect rendition of 'I'll Sing a Hymn to Mary' in a fine tenor voice.

One year I became very holy indeed. It was probably in the May of the year I made my confirmation. My religious fervour reached its pitch when I insisted on building my own May Altar in the back garden with grass sods dug up from the field. I decorated it with my shell collection and a big picture of Our Lady of Lourdes cut out from a magazine stuck onto cardboard in the middle, plus a number of satellite Holy Pictures. A tasteful posy of daisies and buttercups stood on each side in clean Baby Power whiskey bottles with the labels washed off. When June and the summer holidays came, I went off the whole idea and the altar and decor reverted back to the soil in an ecologically correct fashion ahead of its time. Little did I know that I would later be hoisted by my own petard of overweaning sanctity. That Christmas, apart from getting a record eleven books, I was intrigued by a mysterious box I had seen hidden in my mother's wardrobe shelf. I found it wrapped in red crinkly paper under the tree. It was a miniature version of the statue of Our Lady, in the same blue and white apparel, I had admired so much six months previously. In my first act of true heroism I said it was just what I wanted and I think my mother believed me ... it stood on my mantelpiece for years, like an accusing presence. My fondness both for the Virgin Mary and the rituals of the Catholic faith never regained their former intensity thereafter.

Ballet became the next obsessive passion. Irish dancing lessons were already a fixture of autumn and winter afternoons after school. I became the proud possessor of a medal for the slip jig and performed a mean hornpipe with taps on the toes of my old school shoes. How did the hornpipe transmute itself into the *double entrechat*? Mrs Lloyd had no difficulty in extending her repertoire to classical dance and I became an ardent devotee, acquiring a pair of pink satin ballet shoes with block toes. Madame, having completed a few practice movements with us, blithely put us on pointes and taught us the rudiments of the discipline. Being slim, with long legs and arms and my mother's beautiful hands, I was soon the leading light of our small school, which was nothing if not ambitious. The music of *Swan Lake* still swells with the memory of my debut as the wicked Odette in a version staged in the Savoy as part of the Christmas pantomime. The adaptation must have been particularly free because at some point I transformed into a witch with a cackling laugh who drove the frightened swans into a fiery furnace. My ballet career was brief. It ended abruptly when my mother found me hiding the bloody bandages I had wrapped round my offending toes for fear they might stain the pink satin shoes. The dream however lived on a little longer. My mother was persuaded I had some genuine talent and brought me on a sad visit to Cork to meet Joan Denise Moriarty, Ireland's sole professional ballerina. She was formidable – tall with red hair, like Moira Shearer in *The Red Shoes*. She was kind but devastating – yes, I had a certain natural grace, especially my hands and arms, but I was totally unsuited to take up dance seriously. I was too tall, my feet had been ruined, I had dropped arches and would probably walk badly for the rest of my life. I returned home subdued and turned my attention to drama, although Nadia Nerina, Beryl Grey and Margot Fonteyn remained on my walls until their places were taken over by Marlon Brando who shared his wall with no one.

5. The Fall

In the summer of 1950 Joan and I were in England on holiday, a first introduction to my maternal relations and the cathedral city of Salisbury where she grew up. Grandpa, with the funny accent, sporting a navy blazer with a crest on the pocket, proudly took me to his bowling club and showed me the wooden plaque on the wall with his name etched out in gold letters: Mr Edward G. Follwell, President 1948–1950. Grandma too was kind but kept much in the shadow of Grandpa's domineering personality. Our bounty of Limerick bacon, sausages and Irish creamery butter was a major contribution to the family larder in post-war ration-book England. In return they had saved up all their 'sweetie' coupons for me to spend among the fairly depleted stocks of the local sweet shop. I also met our Christmas angels, Uncle Edgar, Aunt Mabs and Aunt Nell in Bristol, but I remember best the donkey ride on Bournemouth Promenade and Uncle Edgar's fearsome grey and green parrot that scuttled down the long stick I held in mortal fear of his polished sharp-edged beak.

No hint of any untoward upheaval in the comfortable domesticity of Moyola Terrace can be gleaned from the devoted letter from our then maid Lily to Joan:

> Dear Mrs O'Mara
>   Received your beautiful letter last Saturday many thanks for same. Every line was a thrill and a joy to me. I'm so glad both yourself and Eileen

are having such a good time I also received Eileen's post card. It was kind of her to write so soon. Thanks for your kind enquiries of Nancy she is improving every day. D.V. Still as you say I think it will take some time before she is really herself again. Dear Mrs O'Mara I certainly felt lonely after you left. I miss you more and more each day.

The weather has been quite warm for the past week here so I hope it is the same at the moment in Salisbury. And wasn't it a thrill for Dear Eileen to meet her nice new friends on the mailboat. I don't wonder the American girl thought Eileen so cute. She is a child with a personality all her own and could be easily loved. But that is natural for her when her Mother possesses the same sweet charm.

You can rest assured I am looking after Mr O'Mara knowing how he certainly must miss you. Now you will get bored with this letter so I will finish up with all the best to you and Eileen. I hope the weather will be favourable for the rest of your holidays. May God bless you and bring you safely home so I may once again have the pleasure of beholding the joy of gazing into those kind brown eyes that makes life a little happier for me and all concerned.

Sincerely as ever
Lily

The fall in our family fortunes occurred between that holiday in June and August when Mary wrote home from her au pair position in a French château. 'Have you moved into the new house yet?' with the somewhat ominous follow up: 'A pity it's so far from the bus stop, now Daddy hasn't got the car any more.'

In my memory there is a seamless passage from luxury in Moyola Terrace where Power is a popular member of the O'Mara business clan, and Joan the elegant leader of fashion and the intelligentsia, to our family being ensconced in a raw three-bedroomed semi on the edge of the city. Whatever transgression Power committed in Limerick all those years ago, no record remains and can only be a matter for conjecture. I still find it hard to accept that the truth was withheld even from Mary, his eldest and favourite daughter, and wonder if some sort of self-induced amnesia has kept her early memories of him unstained and his humiliation erased. That it was humiliation I have no doubt; that unique kind of humiliation visited on the middle class who must keep up appearances without the wherewithal to do so.

A young family friend who stayed in Moyola Terrace for a couple of months just prior to the move remembers being aware of tensions in the house, the usually genial Power silent, Joan withdrawn and nervy, but not a hint of what was going on was disclosed by either of them. The change in our financial circumstances was not dramatic, at least for me and the move from the Ennis Road to Crescent Estate was the only outward signal of trouble afoot. Ruth and I continued in the private education system at Laurel Hill although Mary had left boarding school after the Inter Cert, two years earlier than the norm.

Crescent Estate was a new housing development on the outskirts of Limerick. Number 4 was one of four houses at the extreme end of the estate, behind and beyond which lay straggly fields also destined for cheap housing. My mother hated it – it was bare and unfinished with plastered breeze-block walls and small rooms that looked out on a muddy vista of rough ground stretching towards a bleak and treeless horizon. Everything was cheap; none of the large furniture survived the move except for the drawing-room settee and armchair now squashed into the chilly front room. Both Joan's long mahogany looking glass and dressing-table-mounted looking glass were retained and lasted as long as she did herself, which is indicative of her clinging to her own standards of gentility. Her heavily ornamented silver hand mirror I still have and holding it in my own hand looking at its now bleared glass brings her briefly back to life. The paintings survived for a time and helped to make the sitting room more familiar as did the ornaments and bookcase but the magnificent sideboard was gone and with it the largest of the family silver collection. The tea set and cutlery were wrapped carefully in old sheets and kept in what became known as the silver chest, along with the Joseph O'Mara memorabilia and of course the Bertrand Russell letters. These became a mysterious, often jocose subject of family folklore, never actually seen and not quite believed in.

If Crescent Estate represented a snake in the O'Mara family board game, for one member at least it was a ladder to another life of freedom, fun and friends. Gone was the musty formality of life on the Ennis Road, the barriers between upstairs and downstairs – no maids here to block access to an adored mother who was wonderfully available and hardly ever went out anymore. Best of all I was no longer dependent on Ruth or cross Grace to play with and found myself suddenly the centre of a host of friends who came to the door to ask 'can Eileen come out to play' and out I simply went. Out to the safety of the street, which had no traffic, only the occasional delivery van, bike or slow family car that were rare as hens' teeth in that small wilderness of newly built houses.

Children of all ages were in plentiful supply and we ran blissfully wild, out in the fields kicking ball with the boys, playing hopscotch on the pavement and, best of all, ball games up against a gable wall. Equally intricate were the skipping-rope games, with two people turning the rope and the rest skipping in and out to chanted refrains:

> My mother and your mother were hanging out the clothes,
> My mother gave your mother a puck on the nose,

Did she mean it or did she not ?
What was the colour of the blood that came from her nose?

The chief difference in family life was the change in my parents' social life and the shift in authority within the family from Power to Joan. The marital bedroom became a thing of the past. Ruth and I shared, and Mary was an au pair in a French château. A letter from Power to Joan, dated 9 March 1951, while she was staying with his sister Nora (my godmother) and her country doctor husband Billy Cussen, survives with a note in Joan's handwriting:

Dear Joan

Just a short note by the early post so that you may have the family news on Sat. Nothing exciting to report. Ruth and I enjoyed 'Treasure Island' immensely on Wed night and got home just after 9 o'c. I went down and fetched Mary. Yesterday was cold so I gave myself a treat and went to bed for the afternoon and had a bath before tea. Mary was on late again so I went to the pictures and fetched her home. All of them are in good form and Lil doing her stuff every day. Told her to order a joint for Sat. And we will repeat last weekend's menu. Hope you are having a good rest with some little diversion. Weather cold here but no snow or rain.

Give my love to all – wish I was in Cardiff for tomorrow. Suppose Billy will be glued to the wireless.Love Power

Joan's note on the back of the letter reads:

It is a truth yet remaining to be recognised that the last stage in the mental development of each man and woman is to be reached only through the proper discharge of the parental duties. And when this truth is recognised it will be seen how admirable is the ordination in virtue of which human beings are led by their strongest affections to subject themselves to a discipline which they would else elude. (Herbert Spencer: Moral Education)

This could have been referring to Joan's disillusioned feelings towards Power, now fulfilling a solely parental rather than conjugal role in her life. It could also be a reference to the increasingly difficult relationship with her eldest daughter Mary, lately returned from France at eighteen with a job in Cruise's Hotel, and in full revolt against authority and maternal authority above all. The pent-up anger of those Roscrea years at the Sacred Heart Convent manifested itself in outbursts of rage at any attempt of control or supervision. She was earning her own money, emotionally hungry and attracting the Limerick young males like bees around a honey pot. Tensions at home became extreme. Joan, always an insomniac, lay awake for hours waiting for the key to turn in the hall door. One scene is like a still from a Hitchcock movie: a dark hall and stairs where I was crouched in my nightie, the lighted sitting room, the tiled fireplace and mantelpiece; Mary, scarlet-faced, tongue characteristically clenched between her teeth, towering over a weeping Joan; the graceful Dresden figures held high for a moment, then smashed down on the beige and white tiles; the hall door slammed, and silence.

Mary left Limerick for good in 1952 to take up nursing in Truro, Cornwall, a short-lived career followed by a series of exciting jobs ranging from selling encyclopaedias to American troops in Germany to becoming the first CIÉ rail hostess before settling in London where she immersed herself in left-wing politics. At least some of Joan's influence had borne fruit. An odd codicil to family history occurred in 1959 when, joined in the latter stages by myself, a less enthusiastic supporter of the cause, she marched from Aldermaston with the Campaign for Nuclear Disarmament CND and we both listened to an apparently immortal Bertrand Russell speaking in Trafalgar Square.

No letters, notes, or anecdotes explain what actually triggered the final break with Limerick, but Power's position in the family firm was clearly under threat and their last years there must have been increasingly fraught with anxiety. He finally left the family business in summer 1953 and the family moved to Dublin that September. Although Joan rarely referred to the parting of ways, she remained bitter towards the Limerick O'Maras, especially *bon viveur* Uncle Jack, my godfather, whose influence on my father she often spoke of with disapproval. Joan's own role must also have contributed to the growing estrangement between the families. Always outspoken in her opinions and never exactly a pattern of an Irish-Catholic matriarch, several instances of her independence and growing isolation were recounted to us in later years: her active intervention to encourage our maid Theresa to marry the father of her child and escape from her disgrace as a 'fallen woman' while she was apprenticed out to us on a short leash from the Good Shepherd laundry; her public espousal, through a wartime letter to the *Limerick Leader*, of the Jewish community and warning of a revival of the 1920s anti-Semitism; and her equally public support for the notorious and, in the eyes of the O'Mara social circle, disgraced Minister of Health, Dr Noël Browne whose letter to her in May 1951 foretells another chapter in Joan's life.

> *Dear Mrs O'Mara*
> *I would like to say how very much I appreciated your very kind and thoughtful act in bothering to write to me following my resignation.*
> *Your very gracious and encouraging letter has given me confidence in my belief that I acted correctly in taking the step I did. It has also helped to re-affirm my belief that throughout the country there is a general appreciation by thoughtful and conscientious people that our Health Services should be further improved and extended and that they should be easily and readily accessible to all, irrespective of means.*
> *Yours very sincerely Noël Browne*

Little or no contact was retained with the Limerick family after the move to Dublin apart from the large, canvas-wrapped smoked ham that arrived regularly every Christmas and stopped abruptly the year of Power's death, as did the annuity of £350 he received after leaving the family business. What can be read into these remaining links with Limerick? The most charitable interpretation is that he was not totally *persona non grata*, but never quite achieved acceptance within that Confraternity City where the O'Maras reigned supreme. Certain hints by Joan in later years suggest he left under a cloud and that he was heavily in debt, Uncle Jack reputedly leading him to live beyond their modest means, and to drink and gamble on poker and horses.

In the months following the family move to Dublin, Power became an increasingly vague, apologetic and absent figure. I could find no trace or call up any memory of where he worked in the immediate period following our arrival in Dublin until searching among some papers in the family trunk I came across a large, Browne and Nolan 1954 cardboard-bound page-a-day business diary on which I fell with delight, hoping to find details about my father's activities during that mysterious period. But apart from a couple of pages full of figures and cryptic notes in Power's minute handwriting, it mainly contained Joan's composition of her boarding-school memories during the First World War, followed by scrawled drafts of my own thirteen-year-old English essays. 'My Favourite Book', for instance, on the subject of Baroness Orczy's deathless *The Scarlet Pimpernel*.

However I did pick up one or two vital clues, two long pencil-written columns listing prices, presumably for comparison purposes. One was headed 'O'Mara', the other 'Clover Meat'. The entry for 1 January that year reads like an aide-memoire and eye for sharp business practice:

> First Steps: Inspect factory Meet personnel Stocks – Debtors Ledger – Bank Position – Pig Killing – How obtained – Farms Collections – Gate – Pig prices % total Stock & Factory Insurance – Costings – Yields – Tests. 10sh – 15sh below Limerick – wet – poor selection – excessive claims – 3 long deliveries for week – poor trade – fishy returns – excessive credit – salesman (Peter Byrne) 1 ½ % comm.

These sketchy notes place Power as the newly appointed manager of Clover Meats, a competitor to the O'Mara Bacon Company, but what happened to end this career move is not recorded. In any event Power re-joined the family in Dartmouth Square. Our Limerick past gave way to the Dublin of the 1950s where poets, players, painters and proletariat, seedy, shabby, warm and gregarious – shoved over to open a place for Power and Joan within its many coated, multi-layered circle. They had landed, for a few years at least, on their feet in friendly territory.

6. Dublin and Adolescence

The family migration to Dublin in the autumn of 1953 signalled the end of childhood and the beginning of adolescence. Life for the O'Mara family became peripatetic once more. Another tall redbrick house reminiscent of Moyola Terrace, 62 Dartmouth Square, became our first home in Dublin – this time we were not spread carelessly over its three storeys but squashed into four rooms on the top floor. It was certainly a genteel address, as were all three flats we lived in before I left school in 1958: 66 Fitzwilliam Square succeeded Dartmouth Square, in turn succeeded by 28 Leeson Park, which was to remain the family home for twenty years.

My own entry into Dublin society was inauspicious from the first. I was enrolled after the start of term in Second Year at the Dominican Convent, Muckross Park, in Donnybrook – an ordeal in itself to be ushered into a strange classroom and a sea of strange faces. With the egoism of childhood I took no interest in how food was put on the table. Thankfully we wore uniforms to school – a shapeless green tunic with deep hems and a black and silver blazer bought in 1953 that saw me through the Intermediate Certificate examination in 1956. Clothes were often second hand and my Dublin Carton cousins passed on winter coats. Mary, an exotic if distant figure in London, was an excellent seamstress who made me greatly appreciate dresses from time to time, unlike poor Ruth, working in a quantity surveyor's office and handing up most of her wages to supplement the family budget, who saved to buy me a second-hand bicycle for Christmas, which I tearfully compared to Meriel-next-door's shining new blue and white model. Mine was not a case of the ugly duckling being changed into a swan, but the reverse process taking place. As in all the best fairy tales, the change occurred in the twinkling of an eye. One day I was the star of Crescent Estate, Limerick, Overnight, it seemed, I was transformed into a lanky, clumsy creature with old-fashioned plaits and skimpy clothes, named Bobby by the boy next door, unerring in his jibes of the new girl on the block who had inadvertently drawn ridicule by telling a story about a bear called Bobby Blackberry to his six-year-old sibling.

My Bobby persona did not fit in with the teenage youth of Dartmouth Square, the reigning queen of whom was one Sally Ann Egan, she of the perfect Protestant skin, short curly black hair, blue cardigan and navy pleated skirts, a replica of boy/girl George of Enid Blyton's *Famous Five*. Her adjutant, Ann Richardson, was more like Darryl, Head Girl of *Mallory Towers*, tall and willowy and auburn haired. Both were sporty – hockey in winter, tennis in summer. Our next-door neighbour Meriel, though not quite up to the calibre of the amazonian duo, joined us occasionally. She too was tall and blue-eyed, with wavy blonde hair, but more interested in clothes than sport. Two small boys sometimes tagged along: one was Ann's young brother John Richardson, the other a nearer neighbour of mine at number 57, Paul Durcan, who became the noted poet and played a pivotal role, unknown to himself, in my life fifty years later. John Richardson was tall and bony with red hair and tore around the square on his bike. Paul was smaller with blond hair over his eyes and fair skin, which gave him a more angelic look. He was equally wild but although they were cheeky and rough spoken, I would have far preferred to be a member of their gang than suffer the mocking innuendos of the girls.

I got away with the sporty facade during the first winter months through evincing great interest in Munster Women's Hockey (after all I was a 'blow-in') but summer and the nearby Mountpleasant Tennis Club loomed ever nearer and my ineptitude in all ball games inevitably came to light in one cringe-making afternoon on the courts. Thereafter I became a hopeless case, the butt and buffoon of all outings. Nobody, least of all myself, saw anything wrong with this natural order of the universe until Joan was confronted one day by a blotchy-faced thirteen-year-old who sobbed, 'Oh Mummy, why am I so ugly?'

It was during the second year in Dublin that Bobby slowly faded out of the picture and I re-emerged as Eileen, albeit a chastened shadow of my former self. I made other friends unconnected with the Dartmouth Square elite and the Dominican Convent at Muckross Park became the much-loved incubator for a natural inclination for languages, Irish and French, while history and English provided fertile ground for my omnivorous reading and even some courageous debate. Domestic science and the despised sewing classes were thankfully discarded in favour of Latin. Only maths, specifically algebra and geometry, remained a largely neglected and impenetrable territory. Curiously, and to Joan's faint concern, I excelled in the intricacies of religious knowledge, loving the logic of 'First Cause' which Sister Dominic asserted was unanswerable by pagans, communists or even extreme Darwinists, and the subtle definitions and delineations of Transubstantiation, the Real Presence, the Immaculate Conception and the Virgin Birth.

It was about this time that I met and fell in love with two groups of people, very different each from the other. Their influence was enormous and ran in parallel right through my teenage years and beyond. Anne Leahy was small, pale and at first sight undistinguished, but her clear grey eyes and quick tongue made her a popular figure in our third year in Muckross Park. Having outgrown the ringletted blonde Meriel and thrown off the yoke of my early servitude to the Dartmouth Square tennis buffs, I was ready for more intellectual companionship. Like me, Anne hated sports and loved reading and the cinema so we gradually set up a mutual alliance against all games and shared a dreamworld of fruitless longing to be 'grown up'. When we moved flats, the friendship became closer still as Anne and I used to meet daily in Baggot Street, she from Pearse Street, I from nearby Fitzwilliam Square, to catch the Number 10 bus to Donnybrook. So it was that I entered into the Leahy family circle.

The Leahys lived above the shop on the corner of Erne Street and Pearse Street. Mr Leahy was a widower and spent his days, in his flat cap and cardigan, behind the counter of his tiny tobacconist's, doling out Woodbines in packets of ten, five, and even in ones and twos. He also dealt in sweets, chocolate and some basic foodstuffs such as tins of beans, quarter-pounds of tea and Marietta biscuits, just in case the neighbours ran out of essentials after the local grocers had shut for the evening. The family were often sitting round the kitchen table when the hall-door knocker would summon someone out to get the begged-for article from the shop and so satisfy some local domestic emergency. It gradually dawned on me that the shop was more of a pastime than a source of income sufficient to cover the expenses of bringing up seven children, all of whom were going to fee-paying schools.

Mr Leahy, from Toornafulla in east Limerick, owned not only the corner block the family lived in but also several large shabby houses in and around the Pearse Street area. His home premises included the newsagent's on Erne Street and Conefrey's, the chemist shop, adjoining his own small emporium. On the opposite corner of Pearse Street was Moroney's public house, home to the twelve Moroney children who were the Leahys' best friends. Summers would see various members of both clans, with me in tow, spending long, lazy afternoons in Merrion Square, mysteriously in possession of a large black key to that coveted inner-city green space, the private property of Archbishop John Charles McQuaid, although we never saw even the hem of his purple robes on its not-too-well-tended lawns.

I was often bemused at how casually and warmly I was accepted into the Leahy family circle. My mother always had to know in advance if I was bringing anyone home for tea so that she'd have the good china out and something special prepared, but it never seemed to matter what time one arrived at 136 Pearse Street. The stained steel teapot was always on the gas ring, sometimes a fairly black brew 'you could trot a mouse on' as Auntie Madge Leahy would say. Someone would start slicing bread, there was always ham and tomatoes to hand, a block of orange cheese or ripe yellow bananas for sandwiches and Oxford Lunch fruitcake for afters. The cake was Anne's elder sister Nora's staple diet, not that she actually ate the cake, she simply picked all the currants out and left the rest. I thought all the family were fascinating but Nora was plain weird. She was very tall, white-faced with a haughty patrician demeanour. Her thinness I can now recognize as verging on anorexia, while her compulsive hand-washing and nervous body-hugging were, possibly, all symptoms of incipient obsessive-compulsive disorder. She was the only one of the siblings with a room of her own, a tiny coffin-shaped space with both door and window always left wide open because, Nora explained, 'if the robber gets in the window I can run out the door and if he comes up the stairs I can escape from the window'. No one ever remarked on these eccentricities. She spent most of her evenings with the sewing machine, paper patterns and mysterious lengths of cloth spread out on the kitchen table. We never saw the results of all this industry as, apart from her school uniform, Nora was never seen in anything other than a brown shop coat that she wore in the house at all times. She was older than Anne and I, coming between gentle Margaret and acerbic Phil, who, combining an unconscious carrot- and-stick method, kept her in check, and she managed to get through to adulthood in one piece.

Patrick was the eldest and when I arrived on the scene he was already grown-up, a trainee with Kennedy Crowley, Dublin's major accountancy firm, and engaged to Una. He was tall and handsome with sandy curly hair. The Crowley family thought so highly of him that he was the youngest and first outsider to be appointed as partner. His father, sisters and two young brothers, Tommy and Aeneas, adored him and, when he was killed in a car accident on the Naas road in 1964, he took his father's heart with him. Today, Nora, in her old age and suffering from dementia, talks to him constantly, often in Irish.

Being a Limerick man Mr Leahy had enormous respect for the O'Mara name, not only because of their business reputation but also because of their political and patriotic renown in the annals of the national fight for freedom. He too had been active during the War of Independence' and was a strong supporter of De Valera in the subsequent Civil War. He had been part of the East Limerick flying columns and for all we knew had encountered my father in his forays in that area.

One evening he came in from the shop chuckling to himself. 'That's a good one,' he said. 'I was standing behind the counter not ten minutes ago when in came this gentleman looking for twenty Players. When I was giving him back his change I said to him: "You don't recognize me do you?" "No," he said, looking straight at me. "The last time I saw you," I said, "was through the barrel of a gun." The man was gobsmacked – it was David Neligan, and I knew him, as true as I stand here. We had orders to set up an ambush on the road from Newcastlewest to Abbeyfeale and this vehicle came along with two Free Staters in it. They had to stop the car and I came out onto the road – I recognized Neligan as soon as I saw him; I knew he was a decent Limerick man so I let them go and I haven't seen him from that day to this. 'What did he say?' We were agog. 'Arragh, we both laughed, had a good old natter, shook hands and he left.'

Mr Leahy was a staunch Fianna Fáil man all his life, until Charlie Haughey and the Taca men offended him in their vulgar display of wealth and power. He finally followed Desmond O'Malley into the newly formed PDs (the Progressive Democrat Party). It was around the Leahys' kitchen table that I first became aware of the delights and dangers of political debate. The fact that Noël Browne had made the eccentric choice to run for Fianna Fáil in the 1954 election gained me inclusion to the august discussions of my elders although my own budding socialism was swept away before the tirades of the various Leahy siblings entirely devoted to internecine Fianna Fáil Cumann rivalries. At least I wasn't a Blue Shirt, and anything else did not enter their radar and I was tolerated just as if I were an unfortunate misled follower of Islam. The cut and thrust, downright personal invective, and strident verbosity all bludgeoned my own woolly thoughts into articulate speech. The love of argument for its own sake has stayed with me, with a rueful awareness that what I have considered mere friendly chat about some issue of the day has been described by my interlocuters as unnecessarily confrontational. If indeed so the blame must be laid foursquare on that kitchen table in 136 Pearse Street fifty-five years ago.

Some six or eight miles south as the crow flies from down-at-heel Pearse Street lived the Sheridan family in the newly minted suburb of Kilmacud, also teeming not with sharpfaced citizens of Dublin but with the rosy, noisy spawning population of young families recently installed in these Groves, Avenues, Dales, and Gardens of the expansion of 1950s Dublin. The Sheridans were prototypes of Bohemia transplanted to suburbia. Martin, then attached to the *Irish Times* as a journalist, was thin, nervous of speech and temperament, an intellectual with a dry, if not downright caustic, turn of phrase. His wife Patsy Madden was a Galway woman from the Claddagh, who had trained with Siobhán McKenna in the Taibhdhearc, and, until marriage and a rapidly growing family intervened, had made a successful transfer to the

Abbey stage. Like Jack Sprat's wife, Patsy was plump and in my eyes very beautiful, with long black hair usually drawn back into a heavy chignon. A fascinating husky voice à la Marlene Dietrich and mellifluous Galway accent completed the picture of a Gaelic femme fatale. I was their devoted admirer and babysitter for most of my teenage years.

My mother had met Patsy shortly after coming to Dublin through a mutual Limerick friend and I soon found myself on the 64A bus from Leeson Street on my way to its terminus in far-flung Kilmacud, a bus route that no longer exists. My first purely social visits soon turned into a mutually agreeable arrangement whereby I would babysit the young Sheridan siblings for a generous ten-shilling fee while Patsy and Martin caught the selfsame bus to St Stephen's Green and its nearby hostelries, in particular O'Neills in Merrion Row, also frequented by my parents and a mixed bunch of *Gaeilgeoirí* and leftwing intellectuals. Very often I would arrive in Redesdale Estate early for family tea and Patsy would regale me with stories of Galway and her glamorous stage career. I loved watching her get ready to go out, making up carefully in a tiny mirror propped up on the kitchen window, applying the panstick makeup, mascara and scarlet lipstick, sweeping up her hair into its high bun and prodding it with long black hairpins. I remember her mainly in black or red. As they never had any money to spare, Patsy's stratagems for evening attire were often innovative, including a front window's lace curtain dyed black, which became an extremely fetching evening blouse. Over it all she draped a truly magnificent black Claddagh shawl with heavy fringing whose carefully mended signs of wear and tear suggested it was already an heirloom of a bygone age.

I learned so much from Patsy during those afternoons in the Sheridan kitchen, including the facts of life, as Patsy must have had at least two pregnancies during those babysitting years. I will never forget her graphic description of labour when I tentatively asked if the pain was very bad or the experience very embarrassing. 'You could be in Switzer's shop window in the middle of Grafton Street and you wouldn't give a tinker's curse if the whole of Dublin was looking on, and you screeching and roaring at the top of your voice.' I also received some clear intimations of the realities of married life and the finely wrought sexual tension between Martin and Patsy. It was a tempestuous pairing. Martin, ever dapper and particular, Patsy, a housekeeping disaster; Martin playing Beethoven LPs at deafening levels, Patsy coping with screaming babies and milk turned sour in the fridgeless kitchen. Two images come to mind: the hardening remains of an egg splattered on the wall of the kitchen as a silent reminder of Patsy's missed aim, and the splintered bottom panel of the front door where Martin's foot witnessed both the shoddiness of the house builder and the rage of a locked-out spouse. Need I say the marriage was happy and certainly fruitful.

Whereas my storytelling career in Dartmouth Square was painfully short, it blossomed within the Sheridan clan. Michael, Anne and a toddling Gráinne were my first charges, followed within a couple of years by Christine. John and David, bringing up the rear, missed out entirely. A certain desperation of what to do to entertain or pacify three small children under eight was the initial spur to my storytelling persona but in retrospect it is easy to see that I was instinctively reliving my own not too distant childhood, already imbued with nostalgia in the face of the new reality of Dublin life. I did not actually read to the children, or very rarely – it all had to come out of my head. I began with nursery rhymes, and then went on to the simple tales of Hansel and Gretel and The Wolf and the Seven Little Kids. I soon graduated to the more complex fairy stories that I had pored over in the treasured Green, Red and many-coloured fairy books of Andrew Lang: 'Catskin', 'Rumplestiltskin', 'The Tin Soldier', 'The Little Mermaid', 'The Little Matchgirl' and many more. When I ran out of those I graduated to *The Phoenix and the Carpet, Little Lord Fauntleroy, The Secret Garden* and on to *The Railway Children, What Katy Did,* and *Little Women*. I even attempted *Jane Eyre* and *David Copperfield* but I missed out on *The Wind in the Willows* and *The Lion the Witch and the Wardrobe,* which I only came to when the cycle started all over again with my own son in the late 1970s. As the children were young, some of the stories, even though bowdlerized in the telling, must have seemed long and overcomplicated but I could make them last a few weeks and we created a little magic circle of our own where storyteller and listeners mesmerized each other into suspension of disbelief, time and place.

When I eventually ran out of stories I began on films. I was by then an addict, my mother my first guide and fellow enthusiast. Soon Anne Leahy and I were allowed to go to the Green Cinema on St Stephen's Green on Saturday afternoons, great value for one and three pence, even if one had to move seats a couple of times to get away from the trembling knee nudging and the heavy breathing of the man sitting next to you. So whatever I saw on Saturday had to be regurgitated the following Friday for the delectation of the Sheridan children. *The Man from Laramie, High Noon, 3.10 to Yuma, The Tin Star* were particular favourites, as were those great tear jerkers, *The Magnificent Obsession* and Lana Turner's *Madame X*. The evening I recounted the gothic horror *House of Wax,* with Vincent Price, the first film in 3D, stands out. It was winter and the fire was lit in the sitting room; Patsy and Martin went out with the usual instructions of bed by nine o'clock. If they were home in time, I would catch the last bus home, otherwise I'd put Gráinne into bed with Anne and then go to bed myself. They eventually arrived home about midnight to find an apologetic babysitter with their stouthearted eldest son Michael who, wide awake on the sitting-room couch, had flatly refused to go back upstairs, having woken screaming about melting skeletons hiding behind his bedroom curtains.

As I moved through my mid to late teens, my visits to the Sheridans gradually diminished, though not my affection for them. I became awkward and self-conscious in the storytelling role and the spell was broken. This coincided with my morphing into a kind of Lolita nymphette in the eyes of many of my parents' male friends Nothing overt ui threatening ever took place and I have nothing but the fondest memories of their changing attitude towards me. It usually manifested itself in teasing, or condemning my efforts at more sophisticated attire, make-up or hairdo. There was a certain wistful interest in my opinions coupled with perhaps a subconscious attempt to inculcate me with their own overriding passions. With Martin it was music: he would peremptorily order me to sit down and listen while he gave a running commentary on his favourite conductor's rendition of a particular concerto. Tomás de Bhaldraithe, the Gaelic scholar, tried to interest me in Aogán O Rathaille, while Bob Bradshaw, that unrepentant republican, fixed me with his unblinking blue-eyed gaze while reminiscing about his years on the run and the pusillanimity of erstwhile comrades, all of which went completely over my head. My apparent interest hid the conviction that my parents' friends were boring at best and half mad to boot. Like all teenagers before and since, these figures lived on the margins of my existence, etchings on a frieze that bordered the centre of the universe, my important self.

7. Pubs, Ploughs and Players

It was when we moved from 62 Dartmouth Square to 66 Fitzwilliam Square in the spring of 1955 that I first became conscious of the role the pub played in my parents' lives. Their favoured hostelry then was O'Neills of Merrion Row under the lofty stern ownership of Mr O'Neill. My mother held him in some dread as he did not approve of women in his establishment unless they were respectably lodged in the snug. The women who frequented O'Neills were not of this ilk, they boldly accompanied their spouses, or, it must be said, gentlemen who were sometimes other people's spouses, and sat with them at tables or at the bar, equal participants in debate and consumption of alcoholic beverages. Mr O'Neill's puritan heart daily struggled with his pecuniary instincts and fortunately for the ladies, the latter won out; My mother was proud of her acceptance by Mr O'Neill as an individual in her own right if ever she ventured in to seek friends and company for her ritual glass of stout and occasional Baby Power to take away.

There was a strong element of *Gaeilgeoir*ism among the clientele of O'Neills, many of whom would be found after closing time wending their way back to nearby Fitzwilliam Square with the sacrosanct brown paper bag under the arm. Quite how my parents became part of the group I never knew. My Stonyhurst-educated father and Sassanach mother had nary a word of the vernacular between them but our sitting room often echoed with fluent, flowing Irish discussion and strong personalities demanding the floor: gentle, bespectacled Tomás de Bhaldraithe of UCD locked horns with TCD's bumptious, opinionated David Greene; podgy little Tomás O Laighin, a senior civil servant, said very little but seemed highly respected by all. He was like the Dormouse in *Alice in Wonderland*, generally comatose with drink but perking up now and then to put in some deliberately worded remark. Proinsias Mac Aonghusa was a young Labour activist and Val Iremonger a respected poet who earned his living as a diplomat in the Department of External Affairs. Brian Ó Nualláin (Flann O'Brien) was an infrequent member of the group: recollections of him then are confused with later memories of the early sixties, when he was a morose, black-clad, black-hatted figure on a bar stool, always alone. Some late-night visitors to Leeson Park were not so welcome. Joan was not impressed by Brendan Behan's swearing and Dublin gurrier pose. Finding him asleep with his muddy boots resting on the dining-room table was the last straw, he was asked to leave and did so, according to my sister Mary, with good grace but came back banging on the door half an hour later looking for his bottles of Guinness.

The artist Nevill Johnson was a floating member of this milieu, always a semi-detached, slightly amused observer of events. His impressions of the Dublin of that time are evoked with sympathetic insight in his memoir *The Other Side of Six*. Dublin's impressions of him, through the eyes of a curious fifteen-year-old adolescent, were of a large, blue-eyed, grey-haired gentle giant of a man. Instinctively I felt his attraction for women in our circle, as an Englishman, an unbeliever, an outsider. Unaware of the shibboleths of rela-tionships between the sexes in Ireland, he treated women as equals, as friends and occasionally as lovers, simultaneously safe and sexy.

My mother, a fellow Englishwoman, shared his outsider/insider status though she, trapped from within, envied his mobility and rolling-stone persona. He was always welcome in our flat, unusually so as Mother did not practise the casual 'drop-in' form of Irish hospitality. He borrowed her *New Statesman* and it may have been retrieving that badge of left-wing solidarity that initiated my own daring 'dropping in' to his studio and flat in a small lane off Hatch Street. This casual errand became a fixture on Sundays after 12 o'clock Mass in University Church – Newman's Church on nearby St Stephen's Green. Although never spelled out, I knew that Nevill and Sally were not married. It never struck me as odd or immoral: to the contrary, I thought Sally, usually still in bed when I arrived, gorgeous in her grubby but glamorous silk dressing gown, lazily sipping her cup of morning tea while Nevill worked. The studio contained all the paraphernalia of domesticity: the big bed by the window, the timber table half full of crockery, pushed aside to make room for a large jar of various-sized paintbrushes, a couple of kitchen chairs and a rickety sofa in front of an open turf-burning stove (the smell of turf, mixed with turps and linseed oil remained with me for years and became one of my strongest triggers to the past). Canvases primed, partially finished and, to the neophyte eye, completed, lined the walls; the easel standing on sheets of paint-smeared newspaper, in pride of place, took up at least a third of the space. What appealed to me was the normality, the ordinariness of it, in barefaced contradiction of all the tenents of my orthodox Catholic vision of living in sin.

Three years later, in 1959, aged eighteen and tentatively spreading my wings in London, I had the nerve to telephone Nevill, then living in Chalk Farm. He was delighted to hear an Irish voice and I received a warm invitation to visit. But the flat was a poor shadow of his Dublin eyrie and Nevill appeared diminished against its dreary backdrop. Even Sally looked plain and somehow older. Suddenly, as if to conjure up a genie, he told me to close my eyes, and I heard the sound of a cupboard opening and a rustle of newspaper. 'Abracadabra!' I opened my eyes and there on the table lay an oblong parcel of newspaper. He unwrapped it carefully and lying there was a sod of turf. He picked off a shred and ceremoniously lit it while we sat around the table breathing in the odour like incense and the magic returned, albeit briefly.

It was the last time we met. I think of Nevill as my 'first' artist because Nevill Johnson's Dublin studio kept recreating itself as I grew from adolescence to adulthood. Hatch Street morphed into Avenue Kleber, which in turn was transposed into the Rue de Vaugirard before I finally met my 'last' artist in Baggot Street. Today a painting of Nevill's entitled *Orpheus*, depicting a half blind Grecian head with a faint figure of Euridice in the background, holds a special place facing out onto green trees in my twenty-first century Dublin suburban apartment.

There were also formidable female members of O'Neills' inner circle. They were of necessity formidable to gain entry in the first place to what was an entirely male-dominated society. Patsy Sheridan, former Abbey actress, was always welcome – she was beautiful, witty and spoke Irish – what more could she need? The sculptor Hilary Heron was not only a fine artist but she put up with the boorishness, at least in one observer's eyes, of her husband, Trinity professor, David Greene. Máire McEntee arrived sometimes in the company of David Greene but as time went on she replaced him with a fascinating young diplomat named Conor Cruise O'Brien. Eileen O'Brien, daughter of the 1916 veteran, Professor Liam Ó Briain, was another regular visitor, also encountered at the Sheridan home, tall and thin with an attractive horsey face, a journalist on *The Irish Times*.

I met a lifelong friend of my mother's around this time, Norah O'Neill, a tawny-haired beauty whose heavy club foot never interfered with her enjoyment or her obvious attractions for the opposite sex. She was a civil servant who, as she never married, survived the marriage ban to become one of the first women to head a government department. She was a staunch member of the Labour Party and it was their joint devotion to the cause of Noël Browne that brought her and my mother together. Her acknowledged lover at that time and for all the years until his death was another Socialist activist but their relationship remained unrecognized by society and when he died, her grieving also went unrecognized. My mother often spoke about the sadness of a woman in her position and warned me, unavailingly, against falling into that trap. I used to visit her in her basement flat in Marlborough Road after my mother died. She adored Michael O'Leary who was her last boss as short-lived leader of the Labour Party and Minister for Labour in the 1970s coalition government. She became custodian and founder member of the Irish Labour History Society (now housed in the regenerated Beggar's Bush Barracks) and remained unfailingly cheerful and as passionate about politics as ever, even after she had to take to the wheelchair. At any party or function she attended in old age, the wheelchair was soon surrounded and she became the pivot of attention in the room. Young people in particular were immediately attracted to her and she to them. In the 1990s, no longer able to cope on her own, she became a reluctant inmate of the Maryville Nursing Home in Donnybrook. How she loathed the obligatory daytime format of the armchaired semicircle of elderly people facing the silent gyrations on a silent television screen. I sometimes, though not often enough, called in at lunchtime from my nearby office to wheel her round the grounds and bring her up to date on political news and gossip. I returned from a business trip abroad to find her dead and buried, one of the unsung heroines of the mid-twentieth century feminist and labour movements.

The common link between the O'Neills' patrons was their left-leaning credentials. It was around this time in our Fitzwilliam Square flat that the name Noël Browne entered into my egotistical teenage consciousness. I did not actually have much option because my mother became part of the editorial team which published *The Plough*, a radical broadsheet that took the extreme left ground on social issues and championed the then out-of-office Noël Browne. Our flat became a regular meeting ground: young turks like Justin Keating, Proinsias MacAongusa and Roy Johnston, whose much warmer wife, Mairin, I came to know in later years, joined the workhorse team of my mother, Maisie McConnell, May Keating, wife of the artist Sean Keating, and others. For an intense period of time building up to the general election of 1957, our sitting-room floor and all available surfaces were littered with small brown envelopes which a team of enthusiastic supporters were industriously filling with election folders for the great man's re-entry to the Dáil. I was relegated to the back windowless bedroom where I fumed in silent indignation at the invasion of my privacy. Noël Browne seemed to attract a slavish loyalty from his supporters. He was certainly charismatic and women, including my mother, were devoted to him and followed him blindly through the many vicissitudes of his later political career, from standing for Fianna Fáil in 1954 to the Labour Party and out again to become an Independent T.D. along with his faithful disciple Jack McQuillan. Perhaps I was an early cynic in political matters but I felt his attitude to my mother and the other women in his life was condescending and he viewed them *de haut en bas*.

Many years later I met Justin Keating at a social function and spoke about those early memories. He treated me and an aghast circle of listeners to a tirade against the great man. He railed against his overweening egoism, lack of party loyalty, and how divisive and manipulative he had been, impossible to work with. He went as far as suggesting that the claims Noël Browne made for the eradication of TB were much exaggerated: he happened to be in the right place at the right time when the advance of medical science had introduced effective drugs against the disease. Not knowing anything about their personal or professional history, this was an eye-opener, although recent biographical work has endorsed some of his views. It was my first glimpse into the *realpolitik* of what lay behind the solemn facades of Leinster House and its environs.

I connect this era with my late onset of puberty, which happened in that same back bedroom in the Fitzwilliam Square flat. All my friends were already jaded experts in the field of sanitary belts, safety pins and proud possessors of perky or in some cases ripely rounded breasts. My own development in that area was non-existent, yet another proof of my paltry claims to feminine attraction. My mother – true to her progressive views – had told me all about where babies come from, that is to say I knew they grew in ladies' tummies but quite how they got there in the first place, I was less than certain. Either Joan had glossed over the awkward bits or, to be fair, I had found it too embarrassing to take in. I knew in principle that a man's penis, that completely flaccid appendage as portrayed in classical art, had a role to play at the outset but it was not until I personally felt the somewhat pressing nature of male desire that the logistical process began to make sense of the story my mother told me at an earlier stage: 'You see, dear, the mummy has a machine inside her that makes babies and the daddy has the starting handle that makes it work.' Although the onset of womanhood made no appreciable difference to that longed for bosom, I did gradually grow out of those plain-Jane years and by the time we had moved to our third and final family home in Dublin, if not quite a swan, the ugly duckling showed some signs of transformation at last.

A fixed point in these years of moving flats and wildly swinging fortunes was Mother's lode star, Switzer's Lending Library, occupying the entire top floor of Switzer's department store in Grafton Street, the annual subscription paid gladly even if it meant cutting down on the Sweet Afton or getting another season out of the shabby winter coat. Here she took on a different persona, not a mere wife, not the mother of three girls, not a down-at-heel matron, but a confident, erudite and literary woman who updated weekly her order list of newly published novels, poetry volumes, biographies and theological studies from the review pages of the aforementioned *New Statesman,* another piece of self-indulgence. It was a truly wonderful service – often Mother would gleefully arrive home with a book that had not even yet been displayed in the window of Hanna's Bookshop in nearby Nassau Street. It certainly put her ahead of the posse in O'Neills of Merrion Row and later McDaids of Harry Street where she would compete with John Jordan on the merits of the latest Anthony Powell or Edmond Wilson's essay on *Lolita.* (I pride myself with smuggling in a copy of *Lolita* from London as her Christmas present when it was dropped from the list of banned books in England in 1959.)

In the spring of 1957 the family moved yet again, this time to a much more pleasant garden flat in 28 Leeson Park at the challenging rent of £3 a week. The move witnessed my father's improved prospects and a new stage in our lives. Quite literally a stage, because he had been appointed the previous year as business manager of the young, ambitious Globe Theatre Company in Dublin and with the new job he regained some of his lost confidence and love of life. If not exactly a sinecure, it was a job that gave him a regular income and some standing in the community of intellectuals and literati he and my mother were now part of. A sliding door opened between the magical make-believe world of his youth, where his father strode the Gaiety stage like a colossus, and his own new life in the theatrical profession where he struggled to make a going concern of a neophyte troupe of young actors in an upstairs pocket theatre in Dun Laoghaire.

The Globe Theatre Company began in the tiny theatre above the Dublin Gas Company showrooms in Dun Laoghaire where this young, vibrant group of actors set out to challenge the established theatrical coterie of Dublin with its innovative productions of modern, British and American playwrights. They came together sharing a possibly prejudiced view that the Abbey, still under the despotic sway of Ernest Blythe, would never accept them, either because of their non-Irish-speaking capabilities or their aspirations to stage contemporary drama. The alternative national theatre company, the illustrious Gate, under Lord Longford, was largely in the hands of MacLiammóir and Edwards and it was said cattily by the younger theatre crowd that this was a closed shop unless you were either over fifty or a beautiful youth like Patrick Bedford.

The Globe Theatre Company, like many a radical young arts group before and after, courageously set up their own ensemble and went on to become the leading actors of their generation. In between selling programmes and serving coffees among the gas ovens and fires, I would stand at the back of the tiny theatre gazing at the celestial beings on stage with awe and admiration. The couples who formed the backbone of every production's cast-list: Godfrey Quigley, married to willowy blonde Genevieve Lyons; Milo O'Shea, married to sexy Maureen Toal; Norman Rodway married to *coloratura* Pauline Delaney; ably abetted by character actors Donal Donnelly, David Kelly, Anna

Manahan and Jim Fitzgerald, later an outstanding director of RTÉ Drama but volatile, with a fatal inclination to alcoholism. I swooned over a black-bereted Genevieve Lyons in Christoper Isherwood's *I am a Camera,* who could give Liza Minnelli a run for her money any day, albeit without the music of its successor *Cabaret.* Other productions I remember include Jacqueline Ryan (daughter of Phyllis Ryan), invoking both chills and pangs of jealousy in my heart in her evil-child role in *The Bad Seed*; comedy by budding playwright Hugh Leonard, *Madigan's Lock*; the gothic drama of *The Sons of Bernardo Alba*; and much later Godfrey Quiqley in Ireland's first production of Arthur Miller's *A View from the Bridge*, where, horror, he kissed another man on the lips, another first for Dublin theatre audiences.

The Abbey, housed in the old Queens Theatre, had neither the elegance of the Gate nor the blowsy opulence of the Olympia and seemed boring and old fashioned to my critical young eyes. The Gaiety, however, held a special place in our family affections. The stage left Dress Circle Box was known as the Family Box where in my father's youth aunts and cousins gathered for the first nights of the O'Mara Opera Company season during World War One. A particularly fierce aunt used to settle herself firmly in her seat, immediately on stage right, turn to the others and say 'How do we look from the front, girls?' In memory of those heady days of the early twentieth century the tradition was reinstated after the family moved to Dublin in the 1950s, when we saw every Jimmy O'Dea pantomime from 1953 until his death in 1965 and thereafter when Maureen Potter took over his mantle. His wicked leer and ribald *extempore* jokes seemed sometimes directed right at us. Best of all was the year I saw Micheál MacLiammóir play King Rat, the name of the panto long forgotten: who could forget MacLiammóir with crimson grin, evilly swinging a long sinewy tail, while he strutted his stuff in diabolically well-endowed ballet tights and scarlet cloak? I was introduced to both himself and Hilton Edwards when my father brought me to Jammet's back bar during the Holy Hour to drink a bowl of rich French soup. I was taken aback and frankly shocked to see he was wearing makeup, not too carefully applied at that.

By the late 1950s my sister Ruth had also taken up theatre as a profession. Between her's and my father's experience, I gained more than a glimpse into the highs and lows of that precarious milieu. I was at once fascinated and repelled by what I managed to observe from the margins, first as a gawky teenager, and then as a young adult whose critical faculties were beginning to take over from the starstruck girl. The fascination was, and is, for the magic these sometimes silly, often fragile, always self-centred people managed to create, moving about a small square of space, speaking words written by somebody else, in front of a silent, dark auditorium of strangers. Nowadays I only see the magic. Groome's Hotel often provided the backdrop for these excursions. For years it operated as a glorified green room, for the Gate Theatre in particular, but for all other Dublin theatres as well, and a bone fide public house, where the favoured elite and their hangers on would drift into the back lounge at closing hour at 11 pm and remain there until the wee small hours. The owner-manager was Joe Groome. As a dyed-in-the-wool republican and long-term executive member of the Flanna Fáil party, he was probably impervious to the law, but due deference was paid to the rules of engagement, and the back room remained open while the public bar was duly closed for business. Clear snapshots and moving pictures on the memory screen etch the fluid groups of actors, authors and back-stage workers mingling, merging and parting like figures in a formal gavotte; the intensity of greetings, embraces and rapt attention given one to another until the run of the show is over; the players exiting to be replaced by another theme song and a new set of performers.

The excitement in getting to see a new play was made even more thrilling if I also managed to tag along to Groome's, to stand around unnoticed when the actors, not always minus their stage makeup, made their way across the road after the show. I got to meet them, as my father's daughter, or Ruth's little sister. A beaming smile, 'How did you enjoy the show?', but answer came there none or came too late, the great one having moved on, and the process often repeated itself next time we met. I lost some illusions but gained some insight. I was no longer stagestruck and decided against acting as a career. I saw not only glitz and glamour, but the brave front of those who had been 'resting' for too long. I saw the fickleness of some friendships, the loyalty of others. Above all I came to see it as a tough way to earn a living and feared for my father and for Ruth. Power and Ruth were made of the same stuff. They had the same virtues and failings in their psychic make-up and dealt with life in much the same way. They were both dreamers, both gentle and self effacing, both hopeless with money, and both attracted, and perhaps subsumed, by stronger personalities than their own. They were also loyal, faithful and stoical about their own troubles.

My father was first to leave the theatre world. The Globe was stretching its wings beyond the confines of the Dun Laoghaire gas cookers and wanted more dynamic management than Power was able to offer. At sixty he was redundant to requirements. A year later when all resources had dried up and with no chance of a job in Ireland, Power, without fuss, moved to London to work in an anonymous office job. I had already left home and in 1960 was working in Paris. Typically, my parents kept their private lives to themselves and I exhibited scant concern for what must have been yet another period of anxiety and stress for both, apart from a brief reference to the news in one of my letters home:

> Has Daddy gone to London yet? I do think it's the best thing; you and Ruth could manage alright somehow ... How are you going to manage? I'll try and send something next month.

In the meantime Joan, in Leeson Park, kept the family flat going for whichever member of the family chose to come and perch for a few weeks, or a few months, depending on their circumstances at the time. Her income was Power's pension from the O'Mara Bacon Company, £350 per year, of which rent on Leeson Park was £150. Power sent over what he could, and this was supplemented with irregular contributions from her daughters. The separation was never intended to be final, but Joan and Power never lived permanently together again apart from the much-anticipated holidays, when Power would slip back into Dublin life for a few days or weeks, as quietly and unobtrusively as he had left it.

8. *Ruth*

Of the three O'Mara girls, Ruth always saw herself, quite philosophically, as the least important and valued. High-octane Mary, the eldest, Daddy's favourite, was by the 1950s an immensely attractive woman leading a varied career. I was the little princess, spoiled rotten (according to her elder sisters), my mother's favourite and largely sheltered from the realities of the family's lost fortunes.

Ruth was short, barely attaining five foot and somewhat square of build. The fact that she had beautiful creamy skin and the finest eyes in the family, deep grey with long black lashes, rated little in her own self estimation. Maths and draughtsmanship were her strong suits at school and she could have excelled in university in any of the sciences or applied arts. But naturally stoical and loyal, she quietly took on the role of main family support after the move from Limerick by getting a good job with Fearon & Company, quantity surveyors. She uncomplainingly handed up most of her wage packet to supplement Power's sporadic earnings in those early Dublin years. Her sense of inadequacy hid under an apparent disregard for the usual trappings of femininity. The tomboy grew into a young woman who dressed in whatever came to hand as long as it was shapeless and dull. She wore her hair cut short with a fringe hiding those lovely grey eyes. A single photograph circa 1954 when she was nineteen gives the lie to this self-portrait. It shows a beautiful heart-shaped face, full lips, huge wide eyes with strongly arched eyebrows under a cap of short brown hair, à la Siobhán McKenna in *St Joan* or Jean Seberg in *A Bout de Soufflé*. She is wearing an off-the-shoulder white dress showing that lovely neck and shoulders. It was her first dress dance on the arm of her boyfriend Colm. No smile, however, I don't think she enjoyed herself as Cinderella at the ball, and soon went back to the more comfortable baggy skirt and jumper of everyday life. But I treasure that photograph of Ruth, the real princess.

Ruth became enamoured of theatre life more or less in tandem with Power's new career. She emerged from the dusty surveyors' offices of Fearon & Co blinking into the footlights leaving steady boyfriend Colm Fearon, son and heir to the family firm, behind her. Ruth had been living an independent life since she moved into another Dartmouth Square flat, Number 4, with girlfriend Roz, who had joined Madame 'Toto' Cogley's Acting School and Studio Theatre in Upper Mount Street. Roz and her boyfriend, the exotically named Sydney Lazarus, introduced Ruth to another abiding passion, poker. Her third and fatal passion, alcohol, made its innocent first appearance in the occasional glass of wine, which went completely unremarked in the alcohol-soaked culture of the era – she may well have taken the glass of wine to avoid being noticed for the extremely odd behaviour of being a non-drinker. Ruth's foray into the acting profession was thankfully short-lived as she showed no talent whatsoever in front of the curtain. Her first and only role was that of the gormless maid in Noel Coward's *Blithe Spirit* where Marie Conmee was also making her debut as Madame Arcadie and stole the show. When Ruth met Marie Conmee she fell under her spell and her influence, unfortunately to her cost. Her gentle, diffident soul could never withstand Conmee's domineering personality and wayward charm. Her ambivalent sexuality always troubled her and may have been the cause of her growing alcoholism. Her drinking began at this point and crept up almost unnoticed. She became a fixture in Neary's back bar, on the long seat just inside the rear exit, which led to both the gents toilet and the Gaiety stage door across the alley. So quiet and self-effacing with her gin and tonic, cigarettes and paperback crime novel, that on many occasions the barmen closed up for the Holy Hour without her presence being perceived by anyone.

Ruth's logical mind, coupled with an excellent memory for detail and innate good sense, soon manifested itself in the role of stage management, a term which at the time encompassed everything that went on backstage to mount a successful production, from sets and lighting to props and wardrobe. She became in much demand by many of the independent Irish theatre companies and made a comfortable living for a number of years in that volatile profession. An undated newspaper clipping with photograph mentions her as working on an exciting new play, *The Field* by John B. Keane when it opened in the Cork Opera House in 1958. By 1960, when Power retired from his job with the Globe, Ruth was forging ahead in her career, not only in stage management but also with a try at direction with the new Gemini

Productions. A letter from her to Joan, who was in England on a visit to her brother Eddie, dated 20 August 1960 shows her enthusiasm and ambition:

> On Thursday night both Godfrey [Quigley] and Norman [Rodway] came down to the Pike to see me, to know if I was interested in doing their Festival plays. I said I was of course and I went down to the Gate to settle the details yesterday. They want me to take over 'Rollo' which opens on Monday after the 1st week. If I do that it'll save them paying 2 S.M.s. I haven't discussed salary yet but I'm going to hold out for £10. They need me badly and I'm worth it to them. I'm very pleased, to say the least of it, because it means 5 weeks work and also an 'in' with the Globe. I haven't heard anything from Hilton yet but it's not so important now.

Of the many companies she worked for she most enjoyed her association with the Edwards-MacLiammóir company. 'The boys' treated her as a bright child, approved of her lineage and vaguely welcomed her into their entourage. She became firm friends with Patrick Bedford, then Hilton's lover. She and Patrick, known as Paddy, may well have been lovers themselves for a short time. Both were bisexual, with the homosexual rather than heterosexual side to their natures dominating. They had a true and lasting friendship that survived even when Ruth had finally lost the trust of Dublin's theatre management through her growing alcoholism and finally moved to London in 1969. Highlights of her career include the notorious *Rose Tattoo* at the Pike, where she was a trainee ASM, sent home before the show was closed down by the gardaí; MacLiammóir's bizarre depiction of Hitler in *Roses Are Real*, which featured a wildly executed portrait in oils of the leading lady by a young artist named Owen Walsh and transferred to London's West End for a three-month run; and the first production of Brian Friel's *Philadelphia Here I Come* with Patrick Bedford as Gar Private and Donal Donnelly as Gar Public in 1964 at the Gaiety. Unfortunately all her papers together with the George Campbell painting disappeared after her death, so actual records other than personal memories of her life are sadly fragmented.

Ruth's slow descent into alcoholism is associated in her siblings' minds with her sexual relationship with the actress Marie Conmee. They had known each other since the mid fifties when Ruth first flirted with theatre life, and by the mid sixties they were living together in a flat above a shop at 101 St Stephen's Green (the whole building long since demolished). Marie was a larger than life personality in more ways than her broad girth. She was a Jekyll and Hyde character, hugely charming and full of life, who could quickly turn nasty, with a vicious tongue. She had a successful career playing character parts and drank heavily but could always hold it better than Ruth – she was a binge drinker rather than a steady imbiber, capable of staying sober when a good part demanded it.

By the end of the sixties Ruth's afternoons in Neary's sipping gins and tonics had become a quiet addiction that affected her work, requiring as it did meticulous preparation and faultless timing. A mutual friend described an occasion where the curtain in the Gaiety failed to come down because she had fallen asleep in the wings. The work in Dublin dried up and Ruth moved to London, finding a bookkeeping job with the Post Office. This led to an unexpected quirk of fate when she met John Brown. He was a working man with a mysterious but colourful past – he looked like an ex-boxer or maybe sailor, complete with broken nose and tattooed arms, and he too was an alcoholic. But he adored Ruth, admired her 'posh' accent and superior intellect, treated her like a precious fragile creature and showered her with the most ridiculous gifts such as a cigarette lighter that tinkled *Für Elise*. She responded in kind, looked on him as her *parfait chevalier* and married him. A couple of pages full of proud delight remain of a long letter to Joan written during the summer of 1970 announcing their engagement:

> *One thing you won't like, as I mentioned to Eileen, he's a divorced man. He married at 20 and the first spot of bother he got into (about a year later) she left him. The only thing that affects us is the Catholic view point and with divorce now sanctioned in Italy, maybe it's not all that serious. At least he's determined to marry me and not do an Owen or a Ken (that's rather bitchy so don't show it to Eileen or Mary. I told Eileen that you'd probably let her read this so for God's sake, censor it). Eileen mentioned in her letter that she might get over for a long weekend and would like us to meet her. We could easily do this, work permitting, as John drives a Jaguar (which he's talking about selling because he thinks we need the money) but it's the love of his life and I'd starve sooner that let him do it. Not that I could stop him if he made up his mind! ... I don't think I've any more to say anyway and I'm getting writer's cramp and an impatient John. I enclose £1 to drink our health with, sorry it's not more... All my love Ruth ... P.S. He has tattoos on his left hand and arm, possibly of previous girl-friends, but he says it's his sister ... ROM*

On the back of this page John wrote:

> *Dear Mrs O'Mara first of all I must ask you to excuse my writing as I have not written anything, let alone a letter for years. As you knew – my name is John and I'm the one who is very much in love with your daughter and I hope I am the one who is going to marry her. I would very much like to meet you and all of Ruth's family and freinds and get there approval and we will do our best to do so. I suppose Ruth has told you our plans (she stopped me reading over her shoulder so you will know more than I)*
> *All the Best John*

They lived happily ever after (even if the ever after was cut short and the happiness sometimes seen through a haze, it suited them both) in a speck-lessly neat flat in North Ealing, in a house owned by an elderly Irish emigrant building worker who also drank heavily. They kept regular hours and went to work every day. Ruth, tranquilly drinking sherry from a Thermos flask on her lunch breaks, home at night to more sherry with their favourite curry reheating on the stove. They made several trips back to Dublin where Ruth fondly introduced John to her theatre friends. He was instrumental in getting me through my driving test by selling me for £50 the ponderous 1950s Austin Cambridge he had arrived in on one of their visits. I was then living in a flat in Herbert Place beside Huband Bridge. Always leaving the car parked facing Baggot Street, I learned to drive by dint of driving up the canal to Baggot Street Bridge, turning left and left again into Haddington Road and there-after left and left again until finally reaching home again, never having been obliged to venture into the middle of the road to turn right. Ruth and John enjoyed a great holiday on the £50 and I, safe and secure in my veteran tank, took the road like a rally driver.

9. *Skiving and Jiving*

Something occurred between sitting the Inter Cert in June 1956, passing with the expected flying colours and the beginning of term the following September. In June I was an enthusiastic student, beloved babysitter, dutiful daughter. Deceit and subversion came on like the measles on returning to school for the autumn term – not that I was an out-and-out rebel, more a subversive fifth columnist. Fifth year, post Intermediate and pre Leaving Certificate was traditionally undemanding, but it was the double Latin that finally did it. Anne Leahy and I endured the torture of two Latin classes back to back on a Tuesday and Thursday afternoon up until Christmas. Then, one grey January afternoon sometime after my sixteenth birthday we met on the number 10 bus after lunch and, wordlessly, stayed on the bus as it passed the Marlborough Road stop. We got off at the Donnybrook terminus and boarded another just leaving, sailing past Marlborough Road again, we carried on back down Baggot Street, round the Green, down Grafton Street, past Trinity College, across O'Connell Street Bridge, finally alighting at Nelson's Pillar.

This became an almost weekly routine – how we got away with it for so long I do not know. We got braver and more brazen as time went on, regularly raiding my mother's handbag for two-shilling and half-crown pieces. We developed a varied programme of amusement to while away our afternoons of illicit freedom. I have a composite impression of regaling ourselves on Knickerbocker Glories in the Palm Grove on O'Connell Street, or coffee and chocolate éclairs in the trendy Coffee Inn on Anne Street (coats carefully buttoned over green school tunics). As spring came on the zoo in the Phoenix Park at the other end of the number 10 bus route became an occasional option. Best of all, finances permitting, were the pictures. Vista Vision had just been developed – how eagerly I watched that snowy capped peak rear up on the screen of the Capitol, our cinema of choice for cheapest seats in the gods. It was a golden age of cinema, with great Westerns (*The Man from Laramie, The Searchers*), musicals (*White Christmas, The Student Prince, Guys and Dolls*), Hitchcock cliff-hangers (*To Catch a Thief, North by North West*), comedies (*We're No Angels, The Lady Killers*) and thrillers and romance (*The Desperate Hours, Sweet Smell of Success, An Affair to Remember, Anastasia*). We indiscriminately devoured them all and tolerated each other's foibles: Anne's devotion to newcomer James Dean's mumbling red-jacketed *Rebel Without a Cause* versus my loyalty to Brando, repaid a thousand times in *Sayonara*, when I heard him utter the immortal line in perfect southern drawl: 'Eileen's coming to Kobi … Eileen's coming to Kobi' – I sat through the film twice just to hear him say it again.

Discovery was inevitable. The Leahys had a phone and Margaret and Nora, as recent past pupils, got a tip off. Retribution must have been mild or has simply paled into comparison with our later Brussels debacle. Ostensibly we returned to the fold, only risking rare outings thereafter, but the rot had set in and school was now a daily penance to be got through before real life could begin. Real life, meaning boys, was beginning to impact. Dances or 'hops' as we called them, were the rage and our last year at school became a battle-ground of just how far we could stretch the limits both at school and at home. How innocent those limits were, largely consisting of getting out of the house wearing our normally limp skirts and getting into the 'hop' with added layers of heavily sugar-starched petticoats lifting those same skirts and transforming them into calf-length tutus, on which our arms could rest outstretched from our waists. We distributed our custom over a wide field, depending on current heart-throbs of the time, always a collective heart-throb: I certainly never had one of my own, after a horrendous back-seat cinema tryst with a boy named Cyril who inexplicably and disgustingly forced his tongue into my mouth and almost choked me.

The 'hop' was confined to rugby-playing schools. GAA schools never featured. The much-despised Mountpleasant Tennis Club was also on the map but it was our venture into the forbidden precincts of Sandford Park School that set the cat among the pigeons. Up till then the nuns tolerated these out of school activities, apart from warning us about 'occasions of sin', which apparently had something to do with getting a crossbar home. Boys from nearby Gonzaga College and St Mary's were often invited to our year-end musicals but somehow neighbouring Sandford Park never had a look in. On this particular Saturday night rumour had it that there was a particularly good band, or a particularly yummy fellow, going to be there, so three or four of us dressed up to the nines and presented ourselves at the dance. The evening stands out from the rest for two reasons. I was asked to dance by a grown-up, a dazzlingly handsome, red-headed rugby hero by the name of Tony O'Reilly, and because the straps of my bra – padded carefully with balled-up stockings – snapped in the middle of a hectic jive number, I suddenly found myself with four 'chests', as Jack Lemmon would famously say a few years later, two of which were sticking out below the boned cups of the bodice of my borrowed green taffeta dress. A tattered veil of amnesia cloaks my rapid departure from the dance floor but when news of our evening out reached Muckross Park, the veil was truly rent in twain. Two days later all fifth- and sixth-year girls were called to assembly, where the parish priest of Donnybrook Church, Father Kiely, gave us a serious lecture about the inherent dangers of mixing with Protestant members of the opposite sex who did not have the same religious scruples or moral standards as Catholic boys, and whose respect for Catholic girls was extremely doubtful. Crestfallen, if not convinced, we retired to lick our wounds. My mother was furious and wrote a scathing letter to Reverend Mother stating her daughter's activities outside school hours were no business of anyone other than her parents and that she had their full permission to attend social functions run by any religious denomination or none.

This is one of the few occasions that I can remember any sense of religious bigotry being overtly expressed at school although we were imbued with a dread and fear of communism and all its works and pomps. We offered up rosaries for the recovery from hiccups of Pope Pius XII and the release of the saintly Cardinal Mindszenty from his 'capitivity' in Budapest. We saw flickering newsreels of the brave rebels of the Hungarian Revolution, a huge treat for the nuns, for the Dominicans were an enclosed order and they never went beyond the front or back gates of the school. For all that, they were a worldly and pragmatic group of women, intensely engaged and interested in all matters outside their own narrow confines. Sister Patrick and Mother Hilary were particular favourites of mine. Sister Patrick was short, fat and red faced, with an irrepressible enthusiasm for the Irish language and history, any interest in either being singularly lacking at home. The 1916 leaders were, for her, saintly martyrs sacrificed on the pyre of heroic patriotism and, as our history book ended in 1921, we never pondered on the results of their legacy. Pearse's 'the beauty of this world hath made me sad, this beauty that will pass' seemed to me unutterably pathetic and I gave a very affecting performance as the Mother in the same writer's *Eogheanin na nÉan*. The red-covered *Filiocht na Gaeilge* in the old Gaelic script became a treasured memento of the 'aisling' love poems for many years.

Mother Hilary, on the other hand was a more subtle purveyor of knowledge. English and History were her subjects. She allowed and encouraged debate, a rare opportunity in the rote-based education of the time. I think she secretly favoured me as I had already been indelibly infected by Victoriana at home and produced a first-class composition on the Brontës at the end of fifth year, which won me the class book prize, a small Everyman edition of Jane Austen's *Emma*. My essay was largely culled from Elizabeth Gaskell's biography of Charlotte but it was a brave effort nonetheless. I also became enamoured of the French Revolution and Napoleonic period and defended Napoleon's territorial acquisitions with bravura and conviction. My love affair with Marlon Brando was then at its zenith and his portrayal of Napoleon in that long-forgotten movie *Desirée* helped colour my view of the historical figure. The same actor innocently became the subject of a heated class debate on *Julius Caesar*. Mother Hilary, who although she never actually saw any movies, took a great interest in the medium, castigated the very idea of an American daring to attempt Shakespeare. I rallied to his defence and rightly lauded his faultless Oxbridge accent in rendering 'Friends, Romans, and countrymen'. It took quite some time to mend that breach between us.

Most of all, the Dominicans allowed us develop as independent-minded (apart from theology) young women, fully expected to go out into the world as equal members of society. Not that there were ever any what might be called 'feminist attitudes' or ideas. Our-male dominated society was not alluded to, nor were we ever told there were limits to what we might do with our lives. Marriage and children were out there among other choices to be made. As this coincided very much with what I saw and heard in my domestic milieu, it never occurred to me to question or fear what lay ahead. All I wanted was to fly away and experience real life. I believe the nuns did have expectations for me. I learned later that they had waived fees for me in my last year at school and wanted me to apply for a university scholarship. Apart from university fees, putting a daughter through college was out of the question for my parents, so the scholarship never arose.

10. *Floundering in Flanders*

In September 1958, after an unexpected honours Leaving Certificate result and little prospect of a job, an opportunity arose through those much-maligned Dominican nuns. Some mysterious process of cross-party networking within religious orders saw Anne Leahy, myself and another schoolmate Oonagh set off on a great adventure. We had been offered places in the Ursuline convent at Tildonk in Belgium as what were disingenuously termed 'pupil teachers'. We were to receive room and board and lessons in the French language in exchange for English conversation plus some supervisory duties with the student boarders. We set off blithely with little or no information of where or to what we were heading. The fact that Belgium – or rather Brussels – was host to the 1958 World Fair only added to our excitement at this opportunity. No website, no TripAdvisor to consult. The nearest point we could identify in the large school atlas was Louvain, a more graceful-sounding name than Tildonk, with its strong historic links with Ireland through its Irish College and Jesuit House, where my Jesuit Uncle Joe O'Mara was then residing. Our first shock was the grey featureless village of Tildonk itself, then the looming darkness of the convent, entered only through a single *portière* in the high stone walls that surrounded the entire conglomerate of school, church, convent, dormitories and outbuildings.

In those first two months I rarely saw either Anne or Oonagh who were relegated to different duties in different parts of the school. The first shock was that hardly anyone spoke French – either English or Flemish was the *lingua franca* of the school, Tildonk being situated in the Brabant district, where French speakers were despised almost as much as were Flemish speakers by the Walloons of Brussels. Thus we picked up the intricacies of Belgian history. History of a more modern era was also rapidly thrust upon us. All those French girls we had hitherto expected to be our schoolmates turned out to be either local Flemish girls attending the day school or the daughters of English and American troops stationed in Germany as part of the NATO Allied Forces. Thus in the wake of my sister Mary, recently travelling from barrack to barrack selling British encyclopaedias, I struggled to keep order among the darling daughters of those same officers. The vow of poverty taken by those pure-minded nuns did not extend to the eschewing of profits on behalf of their Mother House as the cost of hiring qualified teaching staff was reduced threefold by the acquisition of their Irish intake of pupil teachers. Each of us had a full timetable of classes and supervisory duties, including dormitory supervision. We may well have been the convent's first venture into this enterprising scheme of below-cost labour, as the private-school network in Ireland, being an even smaller society than it is now, had not spread any reports from grateful (or otherwise) past recipients of the Tildonk educational system. We were certainly the last.

Only two of my teaching experiences come to mind, both distinguished by the hopelessness of my delivery of the required competence to my pupils. The first was on the games pitch, where first efforts to put a hockey stick into my hand for hockey practice failed and had to be passed to the better qualified Oonagh. Lacrosse sticks proving unknown utensils to all three, I was put in charge of rounders, and rounders I played on that muddy field Monday after Monday, attempting to herd groups of equally reluctant fourteen-years-olds into something resembling teams. The second was teaching the history of the British Isles to the 5th formers, who were approximately my own age. I was briefly instructed to read the chapter for next day's class beforehand, set three questions at the end of the chapter for study work and correct these in accordance with the information contained therein. Nothing simpler. It did not, however, take into account any questions that might arise in those keen young minds during the session, nor indeed the queries that arose in my own young mind when I read accounts of the 'Irish Question', which cropped up with boring regularity and differed quite fundamentally from my own recent immersion in that same period. I made valiant efforts to correct the balance of historical accuracy, which at least took up time and went some way to disguising my almost entire ignorance of British domestic history. I know it left me with an abiding fear of standing on a podium to speak in front of an audience, and to this day I have a recurring nightmare of finding myself up there without a script and with no idea of the topic to be addressed. I made one net gain from the experience: I can still reel off the English monarchs from the Wars of the Roses to Elizabeth II.

We were miserable, lonely and trapped inside those high stone walls. Uncle Joe came to visit one Sunday and all three of us fell on his neck with tears of joy – he immediately and generously became my friend's uncle too but could do little or nothing to alleviate our plight. He did not take it or us too seriously, having spent most of his own life interned in similar institutions, but he was kind and cheery and his gentle Irish voice reminded us of home; and homesick we were. After some time we were allowed out for a few hours on Saturday afternoons and soon found our way by bus to Louvain ten miles away. We received about £1 a week pocket money from the nuns, which we spent on delicious Belgian pastries and hot chocolate; my first taste of *pain au chocolat* was in Louvain. Even better, we met some American students, and so for several weeks we looked forward to Saturdays as the one spot of light in an otherwise drab existence. But, inevitably, one Saturday we failed to get back to Tildonk by nine when the *portière* was closed and we were out of bounds and stranded outside those high walls. Loath to get into trouble by ringing the big brass bell we spent a virtuous if squashed night on the floor of Andy's *studio/ coin cuisine* the French equivalent of a bedsitter – back in Louvain. Innocently thinking we wouldn't be missed until after breakfast we slipped back in next morning to a gale of recriminations. Not only were we missing all night, but one of the English girls had given Mère Agathe a garbled version of our activities with our American friends' medical student, Max, who had found us willing guinea pigs to practise his study of hypnotism for his psychology degree, to greater or lesser success. By the time this had reached Mère Agathe's ears it had taken on all the horror of a black-magic ritual, with the three Irish girls as willing participants.

Scandalized missives were sent off to Dublin where our parents were informed that we had been taking part in séances of an immoral nature and that from then on we would be confined to the convent and grounds until Christmas, as the nuns could not otherwise accept responsibility for our behaviour. It was in early December when we were permitted at last to join the school day outing to Brussels, including a sightseeing tour of La Grande Place and the Mannekin Pis with the afternoon free for Christmas shopping. We three walked around Le Bon Marché department store with our eyes out on sticks and little or no money in our pockets. It was the most beautiful department store we had ever seen, stunning displays of merchandise laid out on open counters throughout a series of vast, brightly lit halls, floor after magnificent floor.

A kind of *folie à trois* came over us and with no exchange of words but with a single mind, we began, at first surreptitiously, but then flagrantly, picking up and hiding all sorts of items under our coats, in our pockets and into our handbags. We ended up dishevelled, giggling helplessly in the ladies' loo with a statue of a little ballerina, a brass version of the Mannekin Pis, a sparkly evening bag, several scarves and a pair of lacy knickers Then, the sensation of my stomach falling away, as the door opened and a large grim-faced security guard entered. The rest is a series of grainy pictures: marshalled out to an office, crying and lying in broken French; by car to a police station, waiting in a cell together for hours. One kind policeman brought us thick, dark hot chocolate to drink. Then Mère Elizabeth and Mère Agathe arrived. It might have been midnight. They said not a word, neither did we, afraid to meet their eyes. We were driven back to Tildonk and sent to bed. Next morning breakfast was brought to us and we were told to pack. Mère Elizabeth saw us in her study. She had an envelope with train and boat tickets to London where Oonagh's sister Danielle would meet us and send us on to Dublin. She took me aside and put me in charge of our passports and documents. She thought I had some vestige of sense, enough to avoid further trouble. We were a disgrace to our families, our school and our country, and we were lucky to escape so lightly with our crime.

At Victoria Station we were met by an unsmiling Danielle, who swooped upon Oonagh and turned a glacial eye on Anne and me, informing us that she knew who to blame for leading Oonagh astray. She bestowed yet another envelope upon us with money for a bed for the night and tickets home if that was our choice – we could find our own way to a doubtless shady future either in London or Dublin. In the meantime, she was taking Oonagh out of our sphere of malevolent influence. Anne and I did not see or hear from Oonagh for another twenty years.

We decided to stay in London and never be a burden on our families again. We found a cheap guesthouse near the station and set out to find jobs. When we met later, Anne had been more successful than I – she was to start as shopgirl in Tottenham Court Road the following day. We agreed to phone Pearse Street, as Leeson Park had no phone, in case anyone should worry about us. Poor Anne, I think it was the hardest call she ever had to make, dropping the shillings one by one into the coin box in the hall. Ten minutes later we were both crying down the phone, first Margaret, then Phil telling us to go straight to Euston Station and get the evening boat train to Holyhead. Mr Leahy had met with Mr and Mrs O'Mara; it was all right, no one was going to be angry with us, just come home, they all loved us. A huge weight lifted. As I left Euston that December evening, it never occurred to me that I would return to that same station three short months later with a lighter heart and fresh prospects, snakes beaten back and new ladders to climb.

II. *London Calling*

I was eighteen in January 1959 and went to London to work the following March. I was just twenty-one when I came back to live in Ireland again, three eventful, mind- and eye-opening years later. It was almost inevitable I should leave home – sackcloth and ashes as penitential garb soon faded, and jobs were scarce. The summer I left school I had worked in the Tourist Office in O'Connell Street, courtesy of Joe Groome's contacts, but there were no tourists around that winter, and a few weeks serving in Switzers during the Christmas rush and the January sales petered out. My dear friend Anne had been subtly distanced from me at this time by parental mutual agreement and had started work with her sister Margaret in the Irish Sweepstakes, although we met every chance we had to plot our escape. Then Mary came to the rescue. She was working in the Piccadilly Hotel in London, and wrote home saying London hotels were crying out for nice Irish girls as trainees and she could find me a job. Joan and Power were dubious but surrendered on the strict understanding that I would be living under supervision and that Mary, then a mature twenty-six-year-old, would look after me. And so began my hotel career as chambermaid in the Grosvenor House Hotel, Park Lane.

Twenty-five years later when I was appointed Chair of Great Southern Hotels in Ireland a friend gently chided me for saying in a media interview that my hotel career started as a chambermaid – would it not have been more diplomatic to say receptionist or management trainee? But I had no hesitation in expounding on the fascinating life backstage in another kind of theatre, a kind of upstairs-downstairs peek at hotel life in mid-twentieth century London. It was hard work and I wasn't much good at it but I loved it. Grosvenor House was, and still is, an extremely posh hotel. We never entered through the front doors but through a side entrance round the corner. Indeed I never actually walked through the lobby or lounge areas, my duties being confined to the upper floors. We wore uniforms straight out of *Downton Abbey*, pale grey print dresses with long sleeves and small white collars buttoned up to the chin over which we put huge starched white aprons, fresh every day. Hair was pinned up at the back and covered by a shapeless grey cap, which on me always sat askew. I shared a bedroom with another girl, which wasn't too bad as we worked different shifts and literally only slept there, our time off spent either out, or in the staff room, which was equipped with a black and white telly, a treat indeed for a TV-innocent Irish emigrant. We did out all the bedrooms every morning, working in pairs. I was teamed with one of the older staff who flew around, scolding my clumsiness in getting my side of the bed straight. We swept and hoovered and washed out bathrooms, pushing the big trolleys before us as we went. Then we had a few hours off and went back on duty in the evening to turn down the beds and put in fresh towels where necessary. On one occasion when I was turning down the beds, the guest came in. He was an American, small, thin and balding and nervously pressed a five-pound note into my hand as I was leaving, muttering something about 'coming back later'. In my naivety I asked if he wanted anything – I'm not sure which of us was the more embarrassed when the penny eventually dropped and we both slunk away. My fellow workers screamed with laughter when I told them about it in the staff canteen. The housekeeper was a red-haired Cork woman who had emigrated to London after the war. She kept a beady eye on me and quickly forecast by my accent and general demeanour that I wasn't going to make a long career in service and advised me to look for something better in a smaller hotel where I might get a trainee receptionist job. She was right, and by summer I had moved to the Whitehall Hotel in Bloomsbury Square where I was to remain for almost a year.

Mr Tredwell, the manager of the Whitehall Hotel, used to stand behind me at the reception desk as I desperately tried to complete the evening tot, pressing his fingerless fist into my shoulder for extra emphasis. He was in his sixties so probably had lost his fingers in World War I. Unconscious of any discomfiture on my part, he was a good, fair boss. I learned a lot, such as the intricacies of operating a switchboard with long twin snakes of red plastic, which had to be plugged into the correct guest bedroom slot for every incoming and outgoing call. It soon became a nest of entangled cords, which required a gimlet eye coupled with unerring aim to attach and detach the connections with speed and accuracy. I also mastered the daily accommodation sheets whose columns of guest charges had to be balanced at the end of each day, both down and across. It was also part of a receptionist's job to cash in the restaurant and bar accounts as well as nipping behind the bar in the lounge to serve drinks in the pre-dinner rush. No demarcations, no union rules, no computers or even adding machines – starting my own business some fifteen years later was a doddle by comparison.

Bloomsbury Square – in the heart of the London my mother aspired to in the 1920s, when she worked on a comptometer machine in Clapham – was a dingy but still elegant haven, tucked away from the hustle of Tottenham Court Road and Oxford Street. The small streets linking square to square were reminiscent of my own Georgian Dublin and I settled down happily in a little room, my own at last, on the top floor at the back of the hotel. My co-receptionist on alternate shifts was Jane Clews who had the room adjacent to mine. We became great friends. I admired her cool English beauty: although we rarely had the same days off, she introduced me to the coffee-house culture around Soho, already hinting at the swinging sixties to come.

Another parallel world opening for me, that of the British left-wing movement, was epitomized the day I listened to a venerable Bertrand Russell, now champion of the cause of nuclear disarmament, speak to the crowds at the CND rally in Trafalgar Square. What would his reaction have been, I wondered, if I had approached him with greetings from the young Salisbury girl, my mother, whom he had pursued so ardently thirty years earlier? I didn't have the nerve to try. I was now meeting regularly with a group of Mary's friends who had adopted me on behalf of Mary when she returned to Ireland for a fairly brief career as one of the first, much-touted CIÉ rail hostesses until she came back to London to work for *The Economist* in mid 1960. The meeting ground was Elsa Sobel's flat in Highgate. Elsa was Jewish, about thirty, small, dark and intensely devoted to left-wing causes, at that time centred around the struggle for independence by Britain's African colonies. Through Elsa I too became enthused with the ideal of 'Free Africa'. To that point, to my knowledge, I had never met either a Jew or a black person – in point of fact Ruth's friend Sydney Lazarus was obviously Jewish but whether it was a tribute to my mother's upbringing or not, I had never conceived of Jewish people as a distinct race of people but had simply assumed it was a religious faith such as Protestantism or Catholicism, members otherwise being Irish, English or whatever. Elsa disabused me – she was not only a left-wing intellectual but a fervent Zionist, so my political education made serious if somewhat patchwork strides in a short space of time.

Harold Wilson's 'winds of change' were blowing strongly through Africa from the South African veldt to the deserts of Arabia. The British government had learned hard lessons from the Mau Mau guerrilla war in Kenya and was reluctantly working towards finding a peaceful path to independence for its former dominions. The Lancaster House talks were in session on the subject of Kenya while African nationalists in the white minority who ruled Southern and Northern Rhodesia were also struggling for self rule. It was in support of these territories that our protest activities were concentrated. Back to leaflet-stuffing envelopes again and placard-carrying marches in front of Lancaster House where talks were in never-ending sitting. There was a house in Golders Green where many of the nationalist delegates stayed and it was here that I met a number of the negotiators and their supporters. One night we held a fund-raising dance in a nearby hall and I spent a lot of the evening dancing with a slim, handsome Kenyan, who, when he heard I was Irish, led me off the floor to find a quiet corner and talk about Irish nationalism, which he had studied in depth. I was totally shamed and barely managed to make intelligent responses to his queries on the current political scene in Ireland. Thank God for my mother and Noël Browne – at least I had some inkling of the ill-fated Mother and Child scheme. Fortunately he was happy to lecture me on the important contribution Douglas Hyde, James Connolly and Arthur Griffith had made to his own political education and conversion to socialist republicanism. I would have loved to have seen him again – but perhaps fortunately didn't, as he was much too fascinating and was returning to Kenya the following week. His name was Tom Mboya. He subsequently served as Minister for Economic Planning in Jomo Kenyatta's first government until he was assassinated in 1969. In recent years I have been proud to walk down Tom Mboya Boulevard in Nairobi and to reminisce about my encounter with the charismatic Kenyan patriot with my friends Jean and John Duffy, shrewd Irish observers of modern Kenyan society.

My sister Mary was far more involved in African affairs than I was. She became a close friend and supporter of Kenneth Kaunda, then leading the nationalist movement in Nyasaland and later to become the first president of Zambia. It was through her that I met another revolutionary hero, Joshua Nkomo, a genial giant of a man from the Ndebele tribe of Southern Rhodesia, known as the father of black nationalism. He and his colleagues were at that time banned from participation in Edgar Whitehead's white minority government and were in temporary exile in London. Money seemed in plentiful supply. I later learned Joshua's ZAPU party was funded by the Soviet Union whereas his one-time ally and later rival for ultimate control of Zimbabwe, Robert Mugabe and his ZANU party, were financially supported by the Republic of China. Joshua took a kind, and I thought avuncular, interest in me and my affairs – that is until the evening I was invited to a party in his flat. I found it was in fact an evening *tête-à-tête* alone with the great man. After a certain amount of huffing and puffing on his part and some Irish *plámás* and quick footwork on mine, I managed to leave, my virtue and his male pride intact.

To tell the truth my virtue was becoming a bit of a burden. On the one hand I was eager to get rid of it, on the other I was an inhibited Irish virgin who had not yet met anyone who either attracted me enough or was sexually proficient enough to get me over that particular stile into the Elysian fields beyond. Two men featured in my life at this time who would have liked the job. First there was Chef – French of course – who reigned supreme in the kitchens of the Whitehall Hotel. I used to slip out to his kitchen empire in the evenings when the night porter came on duty. Chef would be fairly mellow at that stage, clearing up after evening dinner or preparing the next day's vegetables or desserts. I would sit up on the big scrubbed table and listen as he railed against the vicissitudes of his day and the romantic complications of his domestic life. Then he would take on the role of mentor and guide to a young woman on the brink of life and love. He was my 'Mr Gentleman' although I never saw him outside the hotel, or wearing anything other than his chef's white-and-checked uniform. He warned me against English men, whom he said never understood women, especially Latins or Celts who needed passion and persuasion to unfold and flourish. He told me I had depths of passion hidden away and that I would enjoy sex enormously once I had found the right lover: an older man would be best, more patient, more tolerant of my Irish Catholic scruples. If only he had more liberty from his other duties in the amatory field he would take me on himself – all this in a somewhat interrogatory, wistful tone. I always felt more attractive and light hearted after these sessions as compared to the self doubt and frustrations that usually followed my dates with Ray.

I had met Ray Shapiro through Elsa. A teacher and volunteer ambulance driver, he too was Jewish and active in left-wing politics, but his real vocation was as a member of the Communist Party. Much against his better judgment as he informed me regularly he fell seriously in love with me. He lived with his elderly father who was blind and for his sake had avoided any serious relationships. At first I was overwhelmed by his pursuit and flattered by his attentions. He was an ardent proponent of workers' rights and filled me with a strong desire to join the cause. Unfortunately he was less exciting romantically, where his intellectual verve and dynamism became diffident and tentative.

I went home for Christmas and returned restless and moody. Some weeks later we went to stay the weekend with his friends Elias and Catherine, a mature, serious pair who were more shocked by Ray's discreet request for separate sleeping quarters than if he had suddenly demanded group sex. Much of the evening was spent with me in the dock defending Catholicism in general and my own extraordinary repressions in particular. Catherine took me aside next morning and lectured me about the psychological damage I was inflicting on Ray with my foolish behaviour and superstitious beliefs and urged me to enter into a more rational and normal relationship forthwith. Sadly it didn't work and our friendship became more and more fraught with tension and silences.

Other matters took precedence that spring and I gradually lost contact with Ray, Elsa and even Jane, who had left Bloomsbury for faraway Bayswater.

Mary was back in Ireland busily flitting from Dublin to Cork and back or she might have taken a hand in what happened next. I was soon to leave the safe nest that the Whitehall Hotel and Mr Tredwell had provided for nearly a year to move in with a more recent friend, Emma, and face with her a test of her courage and my friendship.

Emma Kingsley (not her real name) was tall, leggy and graceful with shoulder-length blonde hair that always fell just right. Although I had met her in the circle frequenting the *Partisan* left-wing coffee bar in Soho, she had never joined my circle of serious-minded – in her eyes pontificating – friends. She worked in a trendy boutique in Knightsbridge and liked dining out, going to the theatre and occasional jazz clubs. Her family lived in Yorkshire and were of the hunting, shooting and fishing kind. Emma would talk about the shows she had seen, the restaurants she had dined in, but never revealed much about her friends, or indeed boyfriends. I knew she was serious about one in particular. His name was John, he was a good deal older than her and rich as he sometimes used to send a car to pick her up and took her away on weekends, once to Paris to stay in a hotel near the Champs Élyseés, to me the height of luxury and romance.

One day not long after I came back from Christmas holidays she told me she was pregnant. She admitted she hadn't told John yet and confided that he was Irish, a businessman who lived only part of the year in London. A month later she still hadn't told him and kept putting it off, perhaps instinctively knowing his reaction. She was right. She came to my room one night in March. It was the first and almost the last time I saw Emma cry. He had been so cold, so distant and told her that getting married was out of the question; she was a lovely girl but he had never intended or promised marriage. However, she was not to worry, she would be well taken care of and he would be in touch soon. It was the last time she ever saw him.

Her next contact was with John's solicitor who took the situation well in hand. Emma would be provided with a flat and an income of £10 a week for six months and all her maternity costs would be covered in a private nursing home. The deal was that Emma would sign an agreement stating the child would be given up immediately for adoption and she would not seek any further contact with John. Emma agreed, with one proviso – that she should be allowed to have a friend live with her until the baby was born.

Thus it was that I came in live in Eaton Place, among what my almost favourite author of the time, Georgette Heyer, would have called 'the ton'. The house, whose first-floor flat we adorned for the spring and summer of 1960, belonged to an actual lady of the realm. Even entering through the pillared portico sent frissons of delight to the soul of this recent habituée of bedsitterland. We had a bedroom each and a comfortably chintzy lounge with delicate watercolours depicting rustic landscapes on the walls. A small kitchenette and mirrored bathroom with brass taps, where you could not avoid seeing yourself naked top to toe, completed our domain.

To celebrate the move I found myself a new job as telephonist (at which I was now expert) cum typist in a nearby Knightsbridge office while Emma dreamed and jigsawed her days away. I would come home in the evenings to see her absorbed in the intricate picture emerging on the table top out of the myriad of tiny pieces that had been just a jumble of colour when I had left for work that morning. She also made her maternity clothes: elegant pinafores in dusty pinks or beige that gradually got more voluminous as the months passed. Whatever emotions, fears or regrets Emma was coping with, she kept them to herself. All she would say was that she never wanted to hear John's name again. She never told her family about her situation, receiving and writing occasional chatty notes to Yorkshire. We developed a cosy domestic life together, quite solitary as Emma cut herself off from her friends and acquaintances and I never invited anyone home. Everyone knew I'd changed my job and that I was sharing a flat with Emma somewhere in Chelsea but as I had broken off with Ray at last and Elsa and her gang were all living in remote Highgate, I saw less and less of them and shamefully became less and less interested in African Freedom. After all I was but nineteen, Emma was twenty and it was the warmest, sunniest spring and summer London had experienced in years. I was going out sporadically with a pimpled youth who worked in the office, a trainee for something important in the City. He brought me to dinner in Simpson's on the Strand and also to see Judy Garland perform in Top of the Town in Leicester Square, both experiences I recall with gratitude even if I have forgotten his name.

If one had to be pregnant and unmarried in 1960, Emma's situation was privileged indeed and mine was feckless and highly enjoyable. My only concern was that Emma would keep healthy and that no early onset of labour would put me to the test of an emergency delivery. The baby was due in early July so for the months of April, May and June Emma and I lived life as if we had not a care in the world. Weekends were spent wandering around Sloane Square and Chelsea. Emma loved Peter Jones but I yearned after the trendier boutiques on the King's Road. It was not yet the era of the mini but I acquired a couple of knee-length sack dresses and some pencil-slim skirts, which I wore with a cardigan worn backwards, complete with chiffon scarf tied nonchalantly around the neck, very *outré*. We became avid theatre- and cinema-goers. The Royal Court Theatre was on our doorstep in Sloane Square. We were spellbound by Joan Plowright in Arnold Wesker's *Roots*, my first taste of 'working-class' drama after my Dublin diet of modern classic and Irish theatre. Another theatrical shock in London was Brendan's Behan's *The Hostage* at the Wyndham's Theatre. I loved the anarchic direction of Joan Littlewood and I was proud of its Irishness and anti-war message. Ruth was also on one of her professional outings in London around this time and we used to meet in the Salisbury pub in St Martin's Lane, where I looked hopefully for theatre idols. It was our favourite meeting place with Power when he came to London, and even in later years when she and John Brown were living in North Ealing.

But like time and tide, the advent of babies awaits no man, or woman either so, as politely and gracefully as she had carried through her pregnancy, Emma duly checked into her extremely discreet nursing home and I stayed somewhat anxiously at home to wait. When I phoned next day I was told that my friend was resting comfortably having been delivered of a baby boy in the early hours. Yes I could visit her but only for a short time, and no, she didn't need me to bring anything with me.

It was a tall house in Kensington with a small garden front and rear. I was shown upstairs by a smiling nurse in crisp uniform. Emma had a private room and when I went in she seemed to be asleep but quickly woke and sat up. She was very pale, her normally bright hair dull and lank. Suddenly the composed girl I knew so well was transformed into a distraught woman who wept and clutched my hands: 'Have you seen him, have you seen him? Please make them let me see him!' The baby had been taken away immediately after the birth and she had not been allowed to hold him once. They told her it was for her own good, she could not become attached, it was best for the baby and for her too in the long run.

She begged me to go to the matron and ask to see the baby for her, just to check if he was all right, that he was healthy and not deformed. What colour eyes did he have, had he much hair, did he look like her? I did as I was told and was brought into a nursery where there were four small cots in a row. One tiny figure was wrapped in a blue blanket, a minuscule fist in its mouth, the other waving helplessly in the air. He was awake, but, try as I might, I couldn't make out the colour of his eyes, other than they seemed an indeterminate hazel and he had a faint fuzz of beige hair. In fact he looked much like the other three babies except they all had pink blankets so I assumed I was looking at the right one. I didn't want to pick him up, but I put my finger out and touched his face and he wrinkled up his mouth as if to cry. Then I went back to Emma and told her he was the most beautiful baby I had ever seen, with bright blue eyes and blond hair. I visited her daily and every time she asked me to go and check his progress. On the eighth day she came home. We didn't talk about it after that.

We were to leave the flat at the end of July. The summer and London had lost some of their sheen and I decided to leave my job. Emma and I talked desultorily about emigrating to America. She was going home at last to Yorkshire and I to Dublin. We promised to keep in touch and went our separate ways.

12. Paris, L'Education Sentimentale

My aunt Eileen O'Mara Carton, my father's elder sister, was a pillar of the Catholic Church. Word had it she acted as Archbishop Charles McQuaid's advisor on all matters connected with women and family life in the Dublin archdiocese. She was a large, genial woman with untidy brown hair always escaping from her hairnet. She and Uncle Fonso lived in Ailesbury Road, the most valuable street on the Dublin Monopoly board, with their six children and their maid Mollie. I spent several childhood holidays in Ailesbury Road, and once at the seaside house in Greystones, where I contracted whooping cough and where Joan descended to carry me away in high dudgeon at my declared neglect at the hands of her sister-in-law; their relationship, never warm, grew colder as the years passed.

Number 18 Ailesbury Road was an enormous rambling house, far bigger and grander than Moyola Terrace. My cousins were all much older than me. Even the two youngest, Garret and Mary, who were about Mary and Ruth's age, seemed quite grown up. But they were great fun and the house was always noisy and crowded, that is until the appearance of Uncle Fonso, who was severe and frightening with his bald head and mirthless smile. They had a vast room downstairs known as 'the den' where the young people gathered; it had a Pianola with pedals that produced loud tinny music for everyone to dance to. Aunt Eileen held court upstairs where she served tea from a large silver teapot through a strainer and handed out thin slices of fruitcake she baked herself.

An unlikely introduction to a life in Paris it may seem, but it was through my Aunt Eileen and her ecclesiastical connections that I came to live in Paris for the first time in September 1960. Eileen Carton was President of the Irish Catholic Women's Federation, which was in turn affiliated to the World Union of Catholic Women's Organizations headquartered in Paris. My aunt, be she forever blessed, thought of me when asked at a collegiate meeting in Rome if she could recommend an Irish girl who might like to assist in secretarial work in the Paris office. Not having anything to lose – even my virginity had been technically erased by then during a late-night scuffle with a charming Indian medical student named Iqbal Grewal, a Sikh from Kashmir – I took the job.

This was quite a different venture to my London beginnings eighteen months earlier. I knew no one in Paris and my French was of Leaving Cert standard with a little Belgian polish added. I was to live in a girls' hostel situated at the same address as the UMOFC offices (short for l'Union Mondiale des Organizations Féminines Catholiques). My 'salary' was enough to cover accommodation and living expenses and would be increased after six months if I turned out to be satisfactory. I found some of my letters home amongst my mother's bundles after her death (a sharp needle of regret at my own loss of her so-precious letters to me). Let them speak in my nineteen-year-old voice on UMOFC notepaper:

> September 21 … about my room, suffice to say it's small but pleasant, with big windows looking out on the courtyard. No 91 rue de Sèvres actually backs on to a large courtyard with the hostel facing the entrance along one side and the other side are all offices, I think, including ours which is very handy My working day begins at 9 am, lunch from 12 to 2 pm and off again at 6.30. The work itself looks like being quite interesting as they are tied up with all sorts of United Nations and Unesco goings on as well as purely Catholic things.

In November:

> On Thursday I had dinner with the Farringtons [the writer Brian Farrington and his then wife Constance] again and talked politics. I get quite hungry for that, as here either the French talk nonsense or I can't express myself properly, it's infuriating! Brian talks quite casually about civil war, but not in the immediate future, some small crumb of comfort – I'm ashamed to say I don't get the French papers regularly, I get the *Observer* every week though which keeps me well up. Southern Rhodesia does seem about to blow up, I bet there's great excitement in London…'
>
> I saw De Gaulle on TV last Friday. Claude [my office colleague] had invited me home for dinner and he was on for about twenty minutes, being very French and dramatic. I turned round at the end expecting everybody to be rather amused or to say 'what a chancer!' but not at all, they almost had tears in their eyes and obviously look on him as some kind of deity. On Saturday I had lunch with Danaë and saw the same programme with the same reaction.

I was not yet sufficiently aware of the Algerian crisis or of current French concerns about De Gaulle's ability to survive the attempts to overthrow the new Fifth Republic.

These letters keep up a brave front behind which lay a lonely and less confident daughter. I was in fact a poor typist, and I remain now a four-finger practitioner on the keyboard. How I disliked those upright unforgiving pre-Tippex machines where an error meant an attempt at correction but usually ended up in a total retyping of the offending document. Then there were the dreaded stencils, attached to monster inky rollers, forerunner of the photocopier, for printing off newsletters and circulars. My chief usefulness to the organization was in my surprisingly adept translations of French documentation into English for distribution to the important English-speaking affiliates all over the world. UMOFC's international reach was quite impressive, numbering over forty countries as far flung as Chile and Cuba and as diverse as Vietnam and Senegal.

My godmother Aunt Nora, married to country doctor Billy Cussen, had put me in touch with her ex au-pair Danaë Moreau, who lived nearby in the 14th *arrondissement* and became a firm friend and mentor. She and her husband, Jean-Pierre, were 'charming with an adorable little daughter, they had some people in who were very nice too and very complimentary about my French … I've offered to baby-sit as they hardly ever get a chance to go out … they've issued a permanent Sunday lunch invitation.' The same Danaë sat me down one day and told me there were two pieces of advice she would give about life in Paris: '*Il faut se défendre et se méfier*' – the strong reflexive verbs, both negative in a uniquely gallic way, warned me to look out for myself and to trust no one. I took neither of them seriously and only had one occasion to regret my decision when I narrowly escaped being raped by the Farid mentioned in an earlier letter. It was one of the few times I have ever been physically terrified by male physical strength or aggression.

Another introduction brought me to the studio flat of Dorothy Henzel Willis, an eccentric Canadian ex-pat painter of indeterminate age who looked a little like a plumper version of Katherine Hepburn. She lived on the third floor of 119 Boulevard St Germain and brought me for the first time to Les Deux Magots, although she preferred The Old Navy, farther towards Boulevard St Michel, smaller and less expensive and situated right opposite the front door of her building where she introduced me to a fellow Canadian Joe Pleskett, whom I learned later was a distinguished painter with a studio in the Marais district. I once accompanied her to a party there but much to my disappointment she insisted on leaving early saying the guests, mainly attractive young men, were unsuitable acquaintances for one of my youthful innocence. A more valuable introduction was to the American Library then on the Place de l'Odéon, which proved a real boon for one starved of English books. It opened up a whole new literature for one who had read little other than Louisa May Alcott, Joan's odd collection of the *Elsie* books, a bit of Hemingway and some Nero Wolf thrillers. During the following months I trawled through Scott Fitzgerald – oh the bliss of *Tender Is the Night* – Steinbeck and Faulkner, the Dust Bowl and Deep South inextricably mixed, Sinclair Lewis and Nathanael West; Schulburg and even Miller (Henry) all disappeared down my insatiable craw, although it is Edith Wharton who jostles with her friend Henry James for most lasting pleasure.

As the nameless heroine of *Rebecca* used to dream of Manderley, I some-times dream of my first Paris winter, very different to my second winter there in 1967: grey skies, chill air, the walk from Rue de Sèvres to Boulevard St Germain, hurrying along past Le Bon Marché with its outside stalls selling vegetables and fruit, sometimes stopping if funds allowed at Le Sip Babylon, a trendy café outside the Sèvres Babylon métro station, then crossing busy Boulevard Raspail, up Rue Dufour, turning left at Rue de Rennes if going to Les Deux Magots, otherwise continuing straight on to the junction with Boulevard St Germain and right until I reached Dorothy's building just before the corner of Rue de Seine. Or if I was going to the American Library, continue on to the Place Danton and turn right up the narrow rue Monsieur Le Prince, past Le Polidor with its crabbed handwritten menus displayed daily. If I was going to the cinema I would have continued as far as Boulevard St Michel to push through the crowds of students, avoiding the letching voices and hands of the despised Algerian and Morrocan immigrants, to the Rue des Écoles and the choice of three tiny cinemas on the Rue Champollion, where there was a continuous diet of black-and-white movies, if you were lucky in V.O. (version originale), if not you struggled with Wayne and Bogart both sounding like Jean Gabin, or sometimes Jean Gabin himself playing Maigret or a French gangster in a trenchcoat. There I saw and screamed at Simone Signoret in *Les Diaboliques* and squeezed my eyes shut in horror at the eyeball slicing in Buñuel's *Un Chien Andalou*.

On pay day we might go to Le Polidor, push through the heavy door curtains to the inside hubbub, where we slid along the benches at the big communal tables trying to decipher the closely written list of edibles, my favourites being *rognons au vin rouge* or maybe *poulet au riz* with *mousse au chocolat*, topped with *crème chantilly* to follow, or *tarte tatin* – an almost impos-sible choice. That restaurant with its coarse paper-covered placings, scooped up and replaced for each sitting, taught me everything I ever needed to know about French food and good service. Although it never quite stretched to *oursins* or *steak tartare*, I learned to gobble down *escargots* and *cuisses de grenouilles* with gusto, as well as *fricassée de lapin* and even *blanquette de veau* providing it was well buried in *crème champignons*. We always had a pichet of red or white wine but I was learning French ways and alcohol came far behind

74

the food if budgetary constraints dictated. Then, replete, walking home alone, on a different route through the Rue St Sulpice, past its wide Place and église to join the Rue de Rennes again at the end of Rue Madame.

Writing home about travel plans for Christmas 1960: 'I'll be arriving in Collinstown at about 4 pm on Christmas Eve, it's disappointing about Daddy but I quite see it would be silly for him to come for such a short time in the Christmas rush ... yes, do invite people round.' It was thus casually I dismissed the lonely spectre of Power's first Christmas in London albeit with his favourite daughter Mary and her left-wing friends

Like all holidays at home during these three years, I return to Paris after Christmas, restless and dissatisfied with my lot, yearning after Dublin's gaiety and gregariousness, the façade she puts on so well for every generation of emigrants before and since: 'I really do wish I was back there, pubbing, arguing and all the other typically Irish things no one here understands...' A stop off in London included the theatre, *A Midsummer's Night Dream* at the Old Vic, lunches with Power; outings with Mary and her Kenyan boyfriend, Nathan, and linking up with Emma, who travelled back to Paris with me, both full of plans for flat-sharing once she got a job. In the meantime I worried about money and reaching my twentieth birthday. However, according to the diary I kept for most of that year, life perked up considerably a few days later at Danaë's soiree: 'Felt so young and inarticulate, it's exasperating to have some-thing to say and not be able to express it ... Pierre? is going to ring me, wonderfully graceful movements, though 40ish...' Pierre did phone me and so began my éducation sentimentale and beginnings of genuine integration into *la vie parisienne*.

Pierre Catzeflis was an artist, at that time living by his art, although later forced to take up a job. Incurious as ever about other people's personal finances, I was content enough to know he was divorced with a teenage daughter. Within two weeks we were lovers. He was exactly what I needed, taking all decision-making from me. Far from a Ray wooing me with cerebral persuasion, far from Irish swains or even my lovely dusky Iqbal fumbling in the dark, hoping drink would overcome my qualms, Pierre calmly and gently took me to bed: no soul-searching, no alcohol required, just a modicum of passion, plenty of laughter and supreme gallic conviction that we were right for each other and good for each other. Of course I tumbled head over heels in love with him – I amused him, I charmed him, I even intrigued him. How young and gauche I was – he had to teach me everything. I knew nothing about contraception, he instructed me like a small child to use the bidet – the old joke, 'Darling, is that to wash the baby in? No dear, it's to wash the baby out.' He taught me not to be prudish, not to worry if my breasts were too small or my bum was too big, I was young, straight-limbed and beautiful and soon I was walking around the studio stark naked without a thought. He had that wonderful French all-over olive skin that never loses its annual tan – even his head was tanned under its close-cropped receding hairline. Clear grey Steve McQueen eyes, full-lipped and square-jawed, he gazes straight at me from the tiny passport photo I found in the diary, side by side with my own taken the same day. I have a limpid look, serene and pleased with myself, and why not? Paris, Pierre and spring were on the way.

From now on I led two parallel lives, one working hard at l'UMOFC preparing for the upcoming International Congress to be held in Rome in May, the other drawn more and more closely into Pierre's orbit: his views on life, on art, on politics, dominated every waking moment outside the office, even when he was away on one of his *congés* with an unknown and jealously regarded circle of friends in the provinces. He brought me several times to the Musée d'Art Moderne. My own devotion to the Impressionists he dismissed or rather expanded to his favourite Fauve period: Vlaminck, Matisse, Dérain. I was drowning in colour.

> Jan 26 Depressed again today. I think it comes from reading Henry Miller. If there is nothing in human relationship except a good f--- I'll go drown myself. I want more than that – much more

> Jan 28 Pierre started on my portrait 'Girl reading in slip' or something on those lines. I felt really pleased as it's much the kind of painting I prefer, nice and thick and colourful.

> Feb 2 Enjoyed dinner. Pierre is really very sweet and has nice friends. Invited for weekend in Normandy, something to do with frescoes. Stayed the night.

> Feb 3 Crept out like a mouse in the morning. Emma and I spent evening at Danaë's place messing about with tape-recorder. I do hate my voice. I believe Pierre was at party Danaë went to.

> Feb 10 After lunch set out with Pierre, Jean and Cecile for our mammoth weekend. Fantastic place at the back of beyond, built by their own hands. May as well be living in the year 1561 as 1961.

> Feb 11 Pottered around all day, everything cooked over the open fire, see by candlelight. Toilet a polite word for a hole in the ground. Played hopscotch with Pierre – he won. We all sat round the fire in the evening and played French card games. My education is progressing.

> Feb 12 Actually did in a little bit of Pierre's fresco, it's great fun. Explored the underground quarry, BATS … Came back to Paris at night looking like 2 tramps. Had a wonderful shower and went to bed while Pierre went out to a soirée. Fast asleep when he came back, had my period.

> Feb 14 Got somewhat tired and depressed as the day wore on. Reaction I suppose, what if Pierre is tired of me? I must be rather boring after a while,

really I'm so inexperienced and stupid. No word from P and he's going away at the end of the week. I'm sure I seem terribly childish to a man of 40.

Feb 17 A very happy evening with Pierre playing gin rummy. I felt very close to him. I wonder what his real feelings for me are. I know of course he likes me but do I make any deep impression. Sometimes I think I'm 'so sweet and gentle' (quote) I don't make any mark in people. Crept out without waking P. Saw Danaë at night and went to 'Streetcar' again. Marlon B is almost enough to put P. out of my head. Danaë warned me against the dangers of older men, I expect she's quite right really but I don't care.

Mar 5 Day in Versailles. Met friend of P's, Bernard. Picked up Emma and spent evening dancing at the studio. B & E hit it off very well.

Mar 11/12 Spent day with Renee, dispensed tea and sympathy in generous measures. Why do people always pour their hearts out to me? Emma & I (she's started an affair with B. but hasn't admitted it) went to Rodin's Museum. Beautiful.

Mar 13 I always feel frightful on Mondays, I don't know why. Lunched with Colette. Brightened up somewhat. Saw 'On the Waterfront', terribly impressed. Emma quite got the wind up me about dangers of conception etc. The thought terrifies me.

Mar 17/18 St Patrick's Day Aer Lingus, Embassy, the latter boring. Arrived late and tired at Pierre's but cheered up later in studio, spending 2 solid hours sitting motionless on a very hard stool with nothing on. Oh well it's all for the sake of art! Pierre seemed pleased with the finished product. I wasn't so sure..

As the spring wore on I saw more and more of Pierre and he included me increasingly in his life. Meeting his friends was both good and bad: good as it vastly improved my French and understanding of French society, bad because I often felt unable to keep up with the twists and turns of the conversation especially when it turned to politics and was left feeling like a young and gauche outsider, which of course I was. There were strong differences of opinion expressed at the occasional dinner parties I attended. We once or twice visited friends who had a house at La Frette on the Seine on the outskirts of Paris: 'Lizianne has a lovely climbing garden full of lilac.' I suspected she was an ex-girlfriend of Pierre's and regarded me askance. As far as I could gather, De Gaulle was seen by some as the saviour of France yet again, and by others as a traitor to the last vestiges of the French Empire in Africa. Scenes reminiscent of Joyce's Christmas dinner in A *Portrait of the Artist* were enacted with great French eloquence and passion. Pierre, I thought, championed De Gaulle and Algerian independence though sometimes I was not so sure, as he was much more ambivalent about the Indo-China war and the battle of Dien Bien Phu. He gave me a book to read, the bestseller by Jean Larteguy, *The Centurions* later filmed as *Lost Command*. I struggled through it and found it jingoistic and macho in the extreme. That and a slim inscribed volume of Rimbaud's poetry remain on my bookshelves today as contrasting mementos of those heady times.

My Paris now extended to the 16th *arrondissement* where Pierre lived, though not in its most elegant quartier. His comfortable, old-fashioned flat was made up of large studio cum living area, bedroom, bathroom and tiny kitchen on the fourth floor of 40 rue Lauriston, off the Avenue Kleber. I now embraced the *métro* with enthusiasm; it brought me to him quickly, though never quickly enough. I would leave the office at 6.30 and squeeze with the rush-hour *foule* into the steamy carriages heaving with people, where even the seats reserved for *femmes enceintes et mutilés de guerre* were taken and dare any one-legged ancient or nine-month pregnant lady challenge its occupant! At Solferino I change lines to the Étoile, race across its star spokes of suicide-seeking drivers, down dignified Kleber till I reach Lauriston. The electric bell clicks open the door, I take the right-hand entrance past the concierge's *loge* and climb the wide shallow wooden stairs to the *4ème étage*. There I pause, heart fluttering and panting, to dig into the handbag for compact and comb. I ring the bell and try to appear calm and unflustered when Pierre opens the door with a '*Bon soir, ma belle*' and a quick peck on both cheeks.

My parallel existence included continuing to search for a flat with Emma – it was becoming more and more difficult to disguise my increasingly frequent nights staying over with 'friends'. Mlle Swagemakers, innocent Dutch lady that she was, suspected nothing, but Claude made some saccharine comments about my busy social life. Emma was living from hand to mouth, working afternoons picking up children from school for a French family and speaking English to them in exchange for a *chambre de bonne* at the top of a house near La Motte-Piquet. Our finances were always in a hopeless state: Not a sou between us til I change 10/- to last til Wednesday ... Changed books at Irish Club and stayed for free tea. Got paid thank heaven and Renee and Emma have paid me back almost in full. I'm looking forward to getting something new ...

Numerous complaints are made of 'work piling up', a reference to the approaching major event for l'UMOFC, The World Congress, the Paris Secretariat being responsible for its complex organization of meetings, plenary sessions, speakers and delegate accommodation. I was torn between the excitement of visiting Rome and the despair at parting from Pierre. Elsa Sobel also arrived in Paris and stayed a week en route to a Pan-African Conference in Cairo. She and Pierre took an intense dislike to each other, like two cats with their fur erect. They circled warily, barely keeping claws in and hisses muted:

> April 5 Back to work. Remember feeling my usual Monday depression even though it's Wednesday. Elsa didn't help any, she obviously thinks P is not serious ...

April 6 A wonderful evening with P. I've never felt so happy. He became quite serious, talked about my life and him etc.

April 7 Of course Elsa depressed me again even when I told her about yesterday but I know I'm right about him. You can't be mistaken about sincerity in cases like this.

April 10 A beautiful day. Went driving with P, Bernard, Emma and Elsa. A horrific storm blew up in the evening, great yellow clouds, thunder lightning – the lot. Elsa, P and I sat round in the dusk and talked. P accused Elsa of homo tendencies towards me! I think we managed to persuade him otherwise. Stayed in all evening and played cards.

April 18 Bought new dress at very last minute for dinner at Maurice's, felt lousy but surprisingly enough was success of the evening. P was quite astonished but pleasantly so.

April 19/20 Have found flat – will have to move by Sunday. Renee came to lunch, her 'crise de nerfs' seems to be over. I'm so tired and had to go out to Farringtons, hence slept in the office. Brian was in good form, but I couldn't keep it up.

April 21 Went to Exhibition at the Grand Palais. Pierre had 3 pictures …

On 23 April we left for Rome on the 8.58 night train, 'another 3 weeks till I see him again'. Rome was strange and exciting, not that I saw much of it for the first week as we were cloistered in the Domus Aurelia working flat out to prepare all the necessary documentation for the 250-odd delegates from all over the world, including my Aunt Eileen bringing family news, which I hurried to pass on to Joan: 'Hugh has left the business and is travelling to Spain with an elderly invalid Mr Fred Barber.'

What struck me most on that first visit to Rome was not its churches or fountains, but the warm yellows and ochres of its distinctly dilapidated streetscapes. It seemed so gallantly down at heel in comparison with the dignity and splendour of Paris, like coming across a once beautiful courtesan parading her fading glory, after knowing her sister, the proud married lady. With the passage of time she has become quite respectable herself these days and tidied away most of her dishevelled locks and refurbished her make-up considerably but I preferred her before her EU makeover.

A week after our arrival, a Father Kavanagh took me under his wing and showed me around:

Council meeting … Still haven't seen Rome … Bishop Fulton Sheen!!! Father K kidnapped me for the morning, drove around, brought me to the Embassy, beautiful house and surroundings, saw Red Hugh O'Donnell's tomb … At last, spent afternoon sightseeing, Palatine, Senate etc … cocktail party at Irish Embassy with other Irish delegates, then visited Trevi Fountain and Spanish Steps with Father K and had a meal, very pleasant. Father K only bright spot, how tired one gets of women ...

However, there was one woman I glimpsed by accident on that afternoon outing who was not to be dismissed. I was walking somewhere near the Forum and I noticed a growing crowd lining the roadway looking expectantly towards a motorcade travelling slowly towards us. After a couple of uniformed outriders on motorbike and some black gleaming limousines came an open horse-drawn carriage, and in it sat a young couple. He was in a smart uniform with gold braided hat but all eyes were on her. I had a vivid, fleeting impression of dark hair, blue eyes and a translucent complexion and they were gone. It was Queen Elizabeth II on a state visit to Rome.

We heard Mass in St Peter's and had an audience with Pope John XXIII. It was a private audience for the Congress delegates and workers, and we were ushered into a vast ornate chamber somewhere in the fastnesses of the Vatican to await His Holiness. Vatican II was still only on the horizon, and possibly our delegates were in the vanguard – or the rearguard – of liberation theology, judging by the issues I was addressing daily in my humble secretarial duties. I recall nothing of the ceremony itself, only my shock and horrified amazement when the door opened and a retinue of Swiss Guards carried in the Pope, seated on a silken litter, bedecked in a gold-and-white jewelled chasuble and, I swear, tiny jewelled slippers on his little fat feet. They processed up the long room, delegates craning their mantillaed heads and pushing genteelly to get a better view of the obese object of their adoration who genially waved his plump be-ringed fingers at us, saying something like '*Bene, bene*' as he passed. My mother's Saxon ancestors rose within me and I did not bow my head.

A couple of undated letters from Pierre arrived before I left Rome. Like all the half-dozen letters I still have, they were short, laconic and practically illegible:

> *Chère petite Eileen*
>> *Ne crains pas que je t'oublis ou t'abandonne, mais je n'arrive plus à trouver ta lettre. Tu sais que je prends mon courrier en descendant de chéz moi – ta lettre a du glisser de mon imperméable. J'ai téléphoné à Emma pour qu'elle me donne ton adresse à Rome, mais elle m'a dit qu'elle ne l'avait point. J'envois ce mot à la rue de Sèvres, espérant qu'ils te le feraient suivre.*
>> *A Paris, rien de spécial, je travaille beaucoup.*
>>> *Mille baisers et à bientôt*
>>> *Pierre*

Chère Eileen

Cette fois ci, de peur de perdre ta lettre, je réponds à la minute. Comme toutes les intellectuelles, tu écris très mal, même ton adresse, aussi l'ai-je noté au hasard sur l'enveloppe. Je ne sais si on t'a fait suivre la lettre que j'ai envoyé rue de Sèvres? Les derniers temps j'ai beaucoup travaillé, mais tres peu peint, car j'avais besoin d'argent.

Téléphone-moi en arrivant samedi matin.

Je t'embrasse bien fort. Pierre

Not perhaps the kind of love letters that young girls dream of, but they were enough for me to read between the lines that I was in his thoughts and perhaps even missed a little. For Pierre there were a few worrying clouds on the horizon, his references to 'working hard and painting little because he needed money' signified a mounting and unwelcome change in his circumstances, leading to his moving from Paris in the autumn and our eventual breakup. But he never dwelt on his problems and I remained largely unaware of them.

Back in Paris I settled down with Emma in our new flat in St Cloud. We realized however that the reason it was cheap enough for us to afford was because it was much too close to the owners' flat in the same house, which was unusually small and left little room for privacy. The Flachs were an unpleasant couple with all the French *petit bourgeois* characteristics of parsimony and propriety, who led lives of unfailing routine and barely concealed curiosity about their neighbours, in particular their upstairs tenants. Emma simply ignored them and disdained my more conciliatory efforts to placate them when we disturbed their repose by late-night entries and frequent calls from strange males on our shared telephone line.

For a few weeks life went on peaceably enough. I spent my days waiting for Pierre to call and my time with him wondering if he did really love me or was it all just about 'sex'. Pierre, anything but sentimental, petted me, teased me and got on with life, including me increasingly in his hitherto private concerns. I even met his daughter, Michelle, a voluptuous sixteen-year-old, which I found most disconcerting.

His true worth as a rock of strength and French pragmatism manifested itself quite suddenly. It was early June, Emma had been complaining of feeling ill and stayed in bed. On the second day she looked really bad and I wanted to ask Madame Flach about a doctor but Emma dispatched me off to work saying all she needed was peace and quiet. I walked in that evening to a scene of carnage.

She was lying in what seemed like a sea of blood. There was blood everywhere, in a basin by the bed, on the bathroom floor, in the toilet, shockingly red against the white tiles. She was almost unconscious, her face bloodless, her eyes pleaded with me, 'don't tell…' My instinct was to rush downstairs and hammer at the Flach's door but my good angel murmured 'Pierre' and instead I ran to the phone. I don't know what I said or what language I said it in but it seemed in no time at all Pierre was there, cool and collected, though he must have broken every traffic light getting to St Cloud on his motorbike. Asking no questions, he sent me out to hail a taxi, then he wrapped Emma in a blanket and carried her down with me trailing after, past the speechless Flachs at their doorway and into the waiting taxi. He carried her into the hospital emergency department where people in white coats took over and wheeled her away. We sat there for hours until a nurse, speaking mainly to Pierre, told us she would be alright but it was a close thing: she had had a severe haemorrhage after a botched abortion and would not have survived another twelve hours. Between shock and exhaustion I could hardly take it in. Pierre brought me home with him and put me to bed.

The next morning I called the office and said my friend had been taken ill and was in hospital. I never discovered anything further about the abortion. Emma, true to nature, clammed up and, though grateful for our intervention, refused to give any details either to us or the police whom the hospital had been obliged by to inform by law. Bernard was left out of the story although it must have been through him that Emma found the services she needed. Whether it was because she was a foreigner on a temporary *carte de séjour* or the offence was not considered worth pursuing, the police left Emma alone after that. I however found myself embroiled in a deeper and deeper web of deceit. Firstly my airy explanation of Emma's appendicitis did not cut the mustard in the office. Mlle Swagemakers called me in to inform me that the Hôpital Bouçicaut was a hospital specializing only in maternity and gynaecology cases and what was my friend's real condition? I bluffed as manfully as I could and swore blind that I had no idea of any sinister reason for Emma's illness and duly confessed my horror of discovery after interrogation of Emma's 'miscarriage'. I was forgiven and warned yet again about consorting with non-believers. At home I had to face the wrath of the Flachs, a mixture of prurience about Emma's emergency illness – they too knew the Hôpital Bouçicaut – and rage about the damage done to their property as they had naturally explored the sanguinary scene as soon as we had left the house. Again I used every ounce of my native cunning and *plámás* to soothe them, even confiding my fear that Emma would soon be quitting Paris and I would be left alone. They too forgave me on the clear understanding that our deposit would be forfeit and that all damaged bed linen and accoutrements would be replaced forthwith.

> June 12 1961: Am so tired and bored of working and worrying and rushing here and there and everywhere and having about 6 different selves to change about, it gets quite a strain sometimes, I don't really know which is the

honest one, I suppose there is one? Finally Emma was released. After nearly two weeks and three blood transfusions she came home

Emma and I had a slap up lunch to celebrate her return, chicken, raspberries and cream and even a bottle of Muscadet.

Emma left Paris for good shortly afterwards. She later moved back to Yorkshire and about two years later I received an invitation to her wedding to her childhood sweetheart, now a country doctor. We kept up a sporadic correspondence through the births in rapid succession of three daughters but gradually lost touch as our paths through life became ever more divergent.

How I missed her in Paris that hot summer. I moved temporarily into Danaë's and Jean-Pierre's apartment, kindly offered as they were going to the Midi for two months. Everyone, it seems, was going away. Pierre too was off to the legendary Midi, which it appeared lay anywhere between Nice and St Tropez. How was I to survive on my own without him for a whole three weeks?

> June 29 My last evening with Pierre. Oh I love him so, we went to see 'Shadows' beautifully done. Why do I love him and if so, why can't I tell him! Half the time I don't even agree with what he's saying – is it just the lovemaking – I don't think so.

There were bright spots amidst the agonizing: 'Saw Micheál MacLiammóir in 'The Importance of being Oscar' at Le Vieux Colombier. What a magnificent old ham he is! The whole Irish colony seemed to be there.' And I was renewing friendships with Dorothy and the Farringtons, which had somewhat lapsed over the past busy months, but nothing could make up for Pierre's absence, not even the colourful postcard, 'une petite pensée tendre', which arrived in time for Bastille Day, spent in the deepest depression: 'I think this was one of the most lonely unhappy days I have ever spent.'

> July 21 Alleluia Pierre back. How stupid I am to worry all the time. Why can't I remember how sweet and sincere (I do believe he is) when he's not there. Lizianne brought us round to see 2 friends of hers, pleasant evening. I'm so happy to see him again and I know that I mean something to him.

> July 23 Went down to La Frette on scooter. Very nice day, sunbathed in garden and played cards at night. P. very affectionate.

But the days of wine and roses were coming to an end. This time it was my turn to leave Pierre and go home to Dublin for the month of August: 'July 28 He rang me to say goodbye. Suddenly I felt I didn't want to go at all – I love him, I love him, I love him.'

13. Paris: Rue de Vaugirard, 1961

Once again Dublin cast its spell. As I ruefully noted on my return to Paris in September, 'I was a large frog in a very small pond.' The diary-scattered notes contain none of the heart-searching or musings of earlier entries, just a monotonous litany of pubs, people, drink and dancing. The folk music revival was in full swing, or what we more commonly called 'ballad sessions'.

O'Donoghue's pub in Merrion Row was the centre of the revival and there I spent most of that summer with occasional sorties as far as Neary's – all of 250 yards away – to meet my mother or Ruth. Anne Leahy, still my ideal friend and soulmate, was my passport to this new set. For good or ill, Anne had recently met her own soulmate, a young poet, Joe Hackett, whom she was to marry six months later. I was not surprised at her choice. Joe was not only gifted, blond, blue-eyed and stockily handsome but hugely warm and funny, with a great gift for storytelling. He and his coterie had invented a kind of Dublinese all their own: someone or something would be described as 'mighty' and their jocular expressions soon melted into the vernacular. Artists Michael Kane, John Kelly and sculptor James McKenna were part of this inner circle as was Ronnie Drew and John Molloy. Joe and Ronnie had recently returned from Spain where Ronnie had acquired a modicum of Spanish, an abiding love for the Spanish guitar and a beautiful New Yorker of Greek heritage named Anita, who accompanied him back to Dublin. Leahy's upstairs parlour was often our gathering place before heading out on the town. A snapshot memento remains of one such occasion: all the Leahy sisters, Joe, a couple of aunts, young Tommy and Aeneas, and in the corner the sultry Anita with a slim unbearded Ronnie Drew, he of the unmistakable, globular blue gaze, leaning protectively over her. Anita, however, never took to our male and pub-dominated Irish culture and took up residence in Paris, opting instead for café culture and debonair Albert Cesbron, whom she married. Over the years their cosy ménage near Pigalle provided many an overnight haven for weary Irish travellers en route to, or from, more southern climes.

But there was a modicum of interest in an existence outside the magic circle of O'Donogue's that summer. I saw John Molloy's one-man show with Ronnie Drew backing on guitar in The Gate Theatre, the Lane pictures and *The Seven Year Itch*, followed by a session in Neary's ending up in Leeson Park with a mixed bunch of followers including Bob Bradshaw, he of the shock of white hair and piercing blue eyes. Legend had it that Bob had spent years on the run, refusing to accept Dev's capitulation to mainstream politics, and had a price on his head. By the mid fifties he was a bitter ex Republican who made a precarious living as builder/decorator. He had a fine mind and had a particular interest in American history and literature. He liked the company of women, particularly young women, and developed a special *grá* for me that summer. He wrote regularly when I went back to Paris, newsy letters full of malicious gossip about some of the better-known personalities of that era in the life and times of Dublin at the tail end of the Catacombs era:

> I owe something to Donleavy [J.P. Donleavy, author of *The Ginger Man*] and his bad book it would appear – I was with him half the night before the morning we were to meet in the Bailey – one of the many occasions the field telephone broke down or was sabotaged. I looked around for you thinking you might like to meet him. He bought a half-bottle and took me back with him. We had a violent row about the American Civil War and almost came to blows. Apparently he had never heard of the Rappahannock or the Susquahanagh – that I took this as a personal insult is an index of the amount of drink taken. Imagine what might have happened if we had got as far as Chattanooga! Anyway he's a megalomaniac, always talking about the people he killed with his bare hands! Incidently a friend of mine had a letter yesterday from Gaynor [the real-life *Ginger Man*], he's still living in Spain with Pam O'Malley – a Limerick O'Malley, belonging to your father's family. She is quite a nice girl, doesn't belong to this set-up. Did I tell you that story ? Probably. Gaynor has had an offer from some firm to publish his memoirs – what is happening in the world that messing, drunkenness, irresponsibility and escapism are suddenly considered proper subjects for literature? The Catacombs [basement haunt in Fitzwilliam Street of artists and writers in the 1950s] era was remarkable only because it brought its way of life to a logical end, and many of the people who went there were very intelligent and sometimes the women were good looking.
>
> Behan's new play was about the Catacombs also. A few nights ago walking through Stephens Green in a state of savage despondency, I met the Behans

coming out of Sean O'Sullivan's studio. Brendan had arranged a dinner party and asked me to come along. I at once refused. He had the 'Gouger' Mackey [Des Mackey, man-about-town, brother of well-known barrister Ray Mackey] with him, a social fixer who hangs around the film world and lives on women. He and I don't get on, and looming behind, O'Sullivan doing his party piece, mumbling, bumbling, shuffling and shambling. In my speechless gloom it looked like a lovely party myself contributing least of all to the gaiety of nations. However, Behan insisted, took us all to a restaurant of the intimate, candlelit kind and gave me a most enjoyable evening. Good food, good wine, good brandy with Brendan in good story-telling form – international chat about Camus and Tennessee Williams and how he nearly got Norman Mailer out of his present wife-stabbing charge. This sort of chat is very interesting, when it is first hand, well told, and there are plenty of funny details. I was taxied to the door at 3.30 am in such good form that I was totally unable to go to bed or sleep and went off next morning to work without sleep at all. At least in Dublin the unexpected does happen.

Brendan offered to get me stuck into the film of the 'Quare Fella' which they are starting to make now. I summoned up enough strength to refuse. Any money would be a godsend at the moment but I couldn't make much on the low level open to me. Did I tell you I worked in films here and in Pinewood, also in a Theatre? It was appalling from my point of view and I would not go into it again. Film work of any sort comes next to a quick shot in the temple.

When collecting your letter today I met O'Sullivan and O'Flaherty [Liam O'Flaherty, the writer]. Normally I only row with O'Flaherty but today was a curious session. They have met nearly everybody between them, including about half of the French painters of about 20 to 30 years ago. The chat was very funny and interesting – O'Sullivan did a drawing of Siegfried Sassoon and has much conversation with him that re-told well. O'Flaherty had an affair with one of the Sassoon women. For once he was interesting about it. Both knew Joyce and had good stories. Joyce had a passion for Opera and tried to get a boxer called O'Sullivan billed in Covent Garden. Apparently the boxer also sang opera. When Joyce met O'Sullivan, he thought he was the boxer and insisted that he sing a song ... The pubs are very lively at the moment, it's probably something to do with the Theatre Festival which has everybody drinking for the last two weeks ... I saw one play. I ran into a critic in McDaids who dragged me there. Somebody gave me a hatful of press cards so I went to the Festival Club. The latter was very dull though I met my bank manager and was able to patronize him and offer to introduce him 'to a few people'. The bastard has taken it out on me since.

This letter arrived soon after my return to Paris in September, more unsettled than ever, but this time determined to go back to Ireland for good at the end of the year. Reunion with Pierre, although affectionate, had lost its first, fine careless rapture and I was less distraught than I should have been when he announced he was taking a job in Alsace but would try and get back to Paris most weekends. I had moved into a charming 'pavilion' at the rear of 188 rue de Vaugirard. This was a little like a mews, but an internal one, built as a separate small residence in the rear courtyard of a large apartment building. It belonged to the *marraine* of Claude Faroux, my UMOFC colleague (godmothers were hugely important in French family life), and was lying empty for a few months pending refurbishment. I jumped at the chance and moved in straight away, much to the envy of my friends. Now at last I had a place of my own and I could invite people to stay. My London friend Jane Clews came, as did Anne Leahy, glad to get some breathing space from family rows, which had erupted on her announcement that she was going to marry Joe Hackett. Mr Leahy saw no reason why any of his daughters would want to leave a good home to get married, and certainly not his youngest, and to a poet of no fixed abode or income.

Two new friends emerged around this time, both Irish, who were to remain influential in my life for many decades, and so, almost unnoticed, my internal compass veered more and more away from Parisian life as lived by the French and more and more towards Parisian life as lived by its expat citizens. I had known of David O'Doherty for some time, but had never made contact until I moved to rue de Vaugirard in the 14th *arrondissement* not far from Montparnasse. David lived in the rue Bargue just a couple of streets farther along Vaugirard, so in an effort to entertain my friend Jane on her trip from London, I decided we should call on him one evening.

David was the youngest sibling in a family of six elder and domineering sisters, which perhaps accounted for his conflicting and sometimes infantile attitude towards women, in his mind either angels or whores – which category I fell into he couldn't decide. Like all Irish people we had more in common than our youth and galloping hormones – the sepia photograph of the gathering of the First Dáil in the Mansion House in 1919 features not only cousin James O'Mara but David's father, elected Sinn Féin TD for Donegal.

No one could be blamed for falling in love with David – he was tall, over six foot, with a long bony frame, white, white skin and glossy black hair. Not only was he a talented painter but also a gifted musician. His American neighbours in rue Bargue, Ed and Shirley, had a piano and David would sit down and play Chopin, Lizst or Brahms on demand and without sheet music. Even then he always carried his tin whistle and metamorphed into the Pied Piper of Montparnasse to entertain the bemused late night tipplers in the local bars. In later years his passion for Irish music became his abiding interest: whenever he travelled back home to Ireland he would listen to and collect tunes from musicians he met in small towns, fleadhs, and sessions all over the country.

A Donegal friend of his mother's, Daisy McMackin, called one day to the studio when I was there, accompanied by her daughter Mairead. These were impressive women indeed. Daisy was a Gaelic scholar who also happened to lecture in Russian in Trinity College where Mairead had just completed an MA in French and Irish. I was prepared to feel inadequate and therefore inimical towards these newcomers but once Daisy's rather alarmingly grim exterior relaxed, she showed a wry Donegal wit and shy charm. I fell into friendship with Mairead immediately, a *coup de foudre* of the soul. She was the kind of friend I'd never had in Paris, loved the same books and films, and was living similar emotional upheavals and ill-fated affairs. When my other visitors left she joined me in the Pavilion, and shared those last precious, bittersweet times when I struggled, not very successfully, to cope with David's temperament, Pierre's periodic demands and my increasingly dyslexic relations with my Catholic Women employers. As if to counteract my weakening links with French friends I began keeping the diary in French; my attendance at Claude's long-awaited wedding, in provincial La Roche-sur-Yon, unintentionally funny: 'I think I would literally expire from boredom if I had to stand much longer of this *milieu*, or at least go raving mad within a week. *Le mariage est tres bien passé; malgré moi je sentais un peu sentimentale: la rêve de toutes les jeunes filles, même les emancipées comme moi – la vièrge en robe blanche* – ah well …'

The civilized evenings having dinner with Pierre's friends or staying in playing cards were a thing of the past. Now Montparnasse became our playground, sometimes David and I on our own, more often with Mairead, Anne while she was there, André Camboulas, a fiery French Communist friend of Daisy's, or Robbie, a sweet Irish fellow who often slept on the floor of David's studio and was between jobs, working as a round-the-world sailor on tramp steamers (or maybe they were just tankers). We simply transferred our Dublin pub-crawling culture to the cafés of Montparnasse. The adjacent trio of Le Dôme, La Coupole (scene or Marlon Brando's drunken tea-dance in *Last Tango in Paris*) and Le Select, were preferred, as they were by previous generations of expatriate writers and artists.

Occasionally when David and I wanted to be on our own we went to a small bar hidden away in a narrow street behind La Coupole. It was called Le Rosebud, presumably in deference to *Citizen Kane*, already a legend amongst French cineophiles but whose significance was a little too abstruse then for David and me to grasp. Once or twice we saw an interesting-looking man there, who David said he'd like to paint. He was usually on his own, but one evening he was with an Irish Professor from Trinity, Con Levanthal, whom David had met through Daisy and as we were leaving he introduced us to Mr Beckett, the writer.

Sometimes we went to the more downmarket Le Chien Qui Fume, near the station. It was there that a dramatic row with David erupted. He was rather morosely drinking Pernod while Robbie and I chatted harmlessly. Suddenly he rose to his full six foot two and glared at the assembled patrons. 'Mice', he shouted, 'Ye're all mice!' Waving his arms about for emphasis he turned to me and purposely or inadvertently drove his fist into my eye and stormed out into the night. I collapsed sobbing into Robbie's lap surrounded by compassionate onlookers. *'Ah la pauvre petite … quel salaud … donne-lui à boire.'* I recovered fairly quickly and was seen home by the faithful Robbie, swearing vengeance. A minor incident all told, until next morning I awoke with a classic shiner, which was to turn all colours of the rainbow over the next twenty-four hours when I finally had to face the office. My story of 'bumping into doors' did nothing to alter poor Mlle Swagemaker's rapidly growing disillusion and we reached a mutual agreement that I would not return to l'UMOFC after Christmas.

I spent a weekend with Pierre in late November saying goodbye. I wasn't sure to be relieved or upset when he took my departure in his usual pragmatic way, saying he knew he had neglected me over the past few months. I was still his *chère petite amie*; he hoped that I would come back to Paris when his fortunes were on a more even keel. In the meantime Dublin might be good for me. As I wrote in a letter home, 'Everyone says I'll never stand Dublin after London and Paris but Pierre says "why not, after all people are much the same everywhere and by all accounts a little more varied in Dublin".' Even so I wavered about going back to Ireland permanently, looking for a job and adapting to living with Joan in Leeson Park, a dutiful daughter once more.

And so came the day of departure: 'Dec 16 *Le grand départ – Paris n'avais jamais semblait plus belle.*' I stopped off in London to pay tribute to Mary's new small son and duly made a safe landing in Dublin.

The year ended with an underwhelming comment in the diary, still in bad French: *'Dec 31: Le fin de 1961. Une année assez heureuse, je me demande si jamais je reverrai Paris?'*

I did see Paris again. In summer 1965 I stopped off with Margaret and Nora Leahy en route by train to Oviedo in northern Spain, where Anne and Joe Hackett were happily settled with young son Martin. It was at least two years since Pierre and I had exchanged even a postcard and I was doubtful about his reception of a call from his *petite amie irlandaise* out of the blue. At last over a bottle of white wine at Les Deux Magots I went downstairs, clutching my *jeton* and squeezed into the narrow telephone booth to dial the still familiar number, KLE 2476. The phone was answered by a woman's voice. I managed:*'Est-ce-que je peux parler à Pierre?' 'De la part de qui?'* Conflicting thoughts flitted through my mind: Who was she? … Had he married again? … Did she know about me?

'C'est Eileen, une amie irlandaise,' I trailed off. A small silence ensued, *'C'est Michelle içi, Eileen, je me souviens très bien de toi.'*

And then she told me Pierre had died of cancer eighteen months previously. I put the phone down and went back upstairs.

'Well, are we going to meet the famous Pierre?' I was asked. 'No, there was no answer,' I replied.

14. Baggot Street, 1962

It snowed on my twenty-first birthday on 15 January 1962. Mairead and I stood in the back garden of Leeson Park in the dark under a sliver of a moon and some wintry stars. 'I can see the T' I said, remembering Joan pointing the slanting T shape out to me under Limerick skies repeating the mantra of how the Little Flower used to tell her father that her name was written in heaven. We drank to both our futures and wandered back inside where Ronnie Drew was playing Spanish music on his guitar.

Anne Leahy and Joe Hackett were married in Westland Row Church at the end of that icy January with Ronnie Drew as best man and me as brides-maid. We all repaired to the Moira Hotel in Trinity Street for soup, sandwiches and pints. Black-and-white photographs of the occasion look like shots from a Nouvelle Vague film, with artists John Kelly, Michael Kane, Brian Bourke and James McKenna striking poses against grey walls at the rear of the hotel.

Quite unwittingly I had picked a pivotal time to come back to Ireland. The nation's first television station had been launched by a reluctant President de Valera just two weeks earlier: Irish society was soon to be pulled, kicking and screaming in some cases, hungrily and with both hands by others, into a brave new world of 'The Late Late Show', 'Radharc' and 'The Riordans'. I applied for jobs in RTÉ and Aer Lingus but neither seemed too impressed by my 'fluent French, secretarial skills and pleasant manner' as my applica-tion forms stated unenthusiastically. Although I cited Martin Sheridan and Justin Keating as referees, the only respectably employed people in our family circle, I got no further than a group interview with Aer Lingus, which failed to bring me to round two. On the social scene, however, I was meeting with a *succès fou*. A new face and figure with a semblance of Parisian chic, I soon gathered a group of admirers with whom I danced, flirted and drank within the territory bounded by, at one extreme, the Grand Canal bridges at Leeson Street and Baggot Street, and on the other, the front and back gates of Trinity College. O'Donoghue's in Merrion Row was our preferred venue for casual-on-purpose meetings where the clientele was a mix of musicians and artists, culchies and Dubs drawn together under the tolerant eye of Paddy O'Donoghue, who didn't mind the competing sounds of fiddle and flute, *bodhrán* and box, accompanying Ronnie Drew's velvet bass or Luke Kelly's raucous tones as they belted out 'Fine Girl y'Are' or 'Up in the Zoological Gardens' in the back lounge, far enough away not to disturb the regular pint drinkers at the counter in the front bar.

I was receiving a more eclectic education from three young men I met at the time in the more genteel surroundings of Robert Roberts Café at the top of Grafton Street. Brian Fallon was a budding journalist, Louis Marcus a young film-maker and Brendan Ó hEither an Irish-speaking writer from Inishmore, nephew of Liam O'Flaherty. Their common passion was classical music and I listened enthralled as they la-la-ed, hummed, played arpeggios on combs or drummed on any available surfaces a repertoire ranging from Mozart to Ó Riada. From each I soaked up new knowledge, espied new horizons. Louis left me with an abiding if mystified admiration for a strange Cork phenonomen with a hurley, Christy Ring. Brian, whose tortured expression and lustrous black curls I fell briefly in unrequited love with, talked a lot about art and Irish artists of whom I was woefully ignorant. Brendan Ó hEither seemed older than the others, grave but with a great belly laugh and mellifluous Irish, which I tried hard to follow. They discussed issues of the day with intensity and depth, such as ecumenism and its champion, Pope John XXIII. Louis, the Jewish Corkonian, said Bishop Lucey would soon put paid to all that communist stuff. President Kennedy and his anti-Castro machinations was lambasted, much to my surprise, as, although not as yet flanking the Sacred Heart on many an Irish parlour wall, he was our own man in the White House and as such could do no wrong. Contemporary poetry and poets were discussed with familiarity and affection. I had not yet come across Patrick Kavanagh in person, but he at least I had heard spoken of as 'Mr Kavanagh' in reverent tones by my mother, who had by then joined the fluid and often fluid-filled literary coterie of McDaid's public house in Harry Street, off Grafton Street. My inclusion within this cerebral circle was to be short lived as was my membership of the 'Dubliners' set in O'Donoghues. I moved on or, more truthfully, was transported, subsumed into a new orbit, that held me in helpless, often hopeless, thrall for the next dozen years.

On a not especially enchanted evening in February 1962, across a crowded pub, Neary's of Chatham Street, I first became aware of Owen Walsh. He was a striking figure then, slim, blond and blue eyed. He had the look of a Greek Pan, full lipped, eyes slanted, high cheekbones, hair long, thick and often unkempt, a cross between Peter O'Toole and Rudolf Nureyev. In fact this was a Mayo man from Westport with all the conservative traditions of a male rural culture in perennial battle with the artist within. 'I'm going to get you into my bed' was his opening gambit. I was not impressed, but Dublin was a small place and our paths crossed again and again. I was then finding my way into a more permanent group of friends moving betwixt and between the writers, poets, actors and musicians who characterized our milieu. The Broes formed one such sub group: Des Broe, a professional stonemason and sometime sculptor, his wife Pat, trying to write poetry at her kitchen table and railing against her fate as wife and mother; Des's sister Irene, a recognized sculptor in her own right, her husband Jimmy McDonald, a UCD professor; Norman Stewart, one of the few businessmen who ventured into our circle, rotund, bearded and bald, his companion and later wife, Silvia Boyd Barrett was one of the few of my age and we became firm friends. But it was Pat Broe who initially took me under her capacious wing and became as much mentor as friend.

It was with Pat that I first glimpsed the man behind the motley of wild Irish bowsie that Owen assumed on most public occasions. We had been to the Theatre De Luxe in Camden Street to see a reissue of *For Whom the Bell Tolls*: emotionally exhausted from weeping throughout the last harrowing half hour of Ingrid Bergman being torn forcibly from the side of mortally wounded Gary Cooper, we found our way to a corner chipper, when Owen unexpectedly walked in and joined us. An hour later, Pat reluctantly took her number 14 bus to Rathmines, and Owen quietly escorted me home through Stephen's Green and Baggot Street.

According to my 1968 attempt to write a rational account of these months:

> He asked me in for a cup of tea and said 'And I mean a cup of tea.' I think we both actually thought he did. It was cold and he had a big fire lighting. We had tea and talked and then he said 'I'm going to make love to you' and for a first time, it seemed to happen so naturally and sweetly I knew I was lost once and for all. I also knew from the start he was married. He was very careful to tell me so and also to tell me what a silly little person I was and how soon he would get rid of me. Mind you, these hurtful remarks were interspersed with glimmers of gold. He told me after the first time that he had gone to bed with a pretty girl and woke up with a woman; although he never seemed unduly impressed by my physical charms 'no breasts, a nice arse and eyes like a whore'. The next time we met was in Sean O'Sullivan's studio, a labyrinth of rooms at the top of 6 St Stephens Green. Sean was drinking

a lot at that time and getting little or no work done. He had a deadline to meet on a religious painting commissioned by the Medical Missionaries of Mary in Drogheda and had hauled Owen off to 'help'. It must have been about midnight when I got there: Owen, naked to the waist, paint spattered and slightly jarred, was up on a ladder vigorously working on a couple of saccharine angels, part of an equally saccharine composition of the Virgin appearing to some natives. Sean weaved in and out insisting that only he must paint the face of Mary. Another Mary was there too that night, Mary O'Donnell, the talented couturiere in Irish lace and crochet from Donegal. Sean called her 'his Gaelic Lolita'. Owen suddenly stopped painting, looked at me and said: 'My God, Eileen, but you're a beautiful woman!' Mary left soon after and there was an ecstatic interlude that has happened occasionally since when our whole skins seemed to feel like mouths and eyes, intermingling till I could not tell which was my body or which his. And yet it was sexless, we didn't make love, just talked and hardly touched. He said he had been seeing me in every bog pool and sky in Mayo and much more in the same vein until Sean came in regarding me resentfully for interrupting the work. I went home in a daze.

Thereafter we seldom met by appointment other than his request that I should sit for him. That first painting required many more sittings than any since. I soon came to love that big draughty studio looking out on the early blooming cherry trees that lined Baggot Street central median. 108 Lower Baggot Street then was a near-tenement house, with a mixed bunch of residents whom I soon got to know quite well. At the top were an elderly couple, Mr and Mrs Mallon. Mr Mallon died soon after but Mrs Mallon stationed herself most days on the front step, garbed in black, smoking Woodbine, and noting all the comings and goings, not only of the house but also of the street. 'Mr Welch' was a real gentleman, who often stood her a glass of stout in Phil Ryan's snug opposite. His abode was 'the front drawing room' whither she would direct callers, except of course the landlord or his agent who were persona non grata to all residents. The Underwoods were notorious landlords who practised Rachmanism long before the term was invented. They carried out a long-lived battle with the 'bloody artist', their last and most immovable tenant, who clung stubbornly to his eyrie on the first floor long after all other residents had fled, been rehoused or simply died. For well over forty years, he paid his rent, sometimes a month in arrears, which brought rapid notices to quit but was always paid in full before the bailiffs could be summoned.

After his death in 2002, amidst the effects hastily rescued in the face of security men with crowbars sent to 'dump all this stuff' into the waiting skip, was a case full of documents. Among carelessly scattered remnants of exhibition notices, reviews and love letters were meticulously kept bundles, in elastic bands, of rent receipts and copies of payment slips dating back to 1960. Owen, at least, enjoyed the battle to the end. In latter years he found an unexpected ally in Dublin Corporation who, for their own reasons, were glad to pursue the Underwoods on his behalf for damage done to the roof (a common ploy to have old Georgian houses declared derelict), mysterious break-ins, basement infestations and plumbing repairs – even finally in the 1990s, to having a hot-water geyser installed on the upstairs landing.

No such luxurious appliance existed in 1962. Mr and Mrs Mallon, Peggy Mahon and her ancient mother who lived directly above Owen, Miss Caffrey, the single lady who was unfortunate enough to live in the adjoining room to his studio at the time, and Owen himself, all shared the single cold-water tap on the landing as well as the lavatory on the same level. The downstairs tenants, the Molloys and their three children in the return flat, the two maiden Brennan sisters in the back hall and the single middle-aged gent in the front hall, all shared similar conveniences at the top of the basement stairs. There were also two brothers who lived like moles in the basement and had an outside lav, but they decamped quite soon after I became familiar with the house and it was never lived in thereafter.

The studio was a fine high-ceilinged room, spacious with two large sashed windows looking directly onto Baggot Street and Phil Ryan's Pub on the opposite corner of Fitzwilliam Lane, where the ESB had its offices. Furniture was spare but adequate and hardly changed in the forty years I knew it. The large double bed travelled a bit during those years, moving from the window alcove to its final position backing on to the never-opened double doors between the studio and the back room. The move was occasioned by the gift of a piano in the 1970s, the property of Mrs Mulvany, my sister Mary's mother-in-law. A large open hearth with iron grate and discoloured but beautiful marble mantelpiece dominated one wall. In the left-hand alcove, opposite the window, was the classic black gas stove with powerful hob and oven jets that did an excellent job as auxiliary heater as long as the shillings for the gas meter lasted. Beside the stove was a neat wooden cabinet flanked by two shelves, efficiently put together by Owen, and its sister piece, an upturned butter box with larger timber top, which served very adequately as combined dining and bedside table. There was also a much larger, longer trestle-type table strictly reserved for drawing materials, sketch pads, drawing paper and work in progress. Underneath the table were stashed portfolios of different sizes, rolled-up canvases and an assortment of boxes. On the back of the door hung the wardrobe: Owen was a natty dresser –his painting trousers were always changed before sortieing into the outside world, a shirt and tie de rigueur. Easel and large palette, a paint-encrusted pane of glass on a waist-height stand, stood back from the right-hand window. Along the back wall were bookshelves, an old record player that transmogrified into a hi-fi at some stage, precious collections of LPs, 78s and even 45s, and growing stacks of art books bought on some kind of continuous never-never deal from May O'Flaherty in her legendary Baggot Street Bridge bookshop, Parsons. Leaning against all surfaces and hung on all walls were canvases in every stage of composition, from newly stretched and primed to half finished, never-to-be-finished and completed work – all of which became almost unnoticeable and unremarkable, just part of the ever-changing wallpaper, as the smell of linseed oil and turps was part of the air around us.

One elegant mahogany chair with curved slatted back and armrests doubled as the sitter's chair or his own armchair, plumped up with pillows, in front of the fire. Guests had to make do with a couple of straight-backed kitchen chairs and a single stool. To be fair, more often than not guests were given the comfortable chair while Owen dispensed hospitality. He was a great host: in good times, there might be a beer or a naggin of whiskey, always a cup of scalding tea to accompany brown bread and honey or coarse-cut marmalade. He was a healthy eater before healthy eating became fashionable. He loved fish from Molloy's in Chatham Street, or Buckley's Butcher for a good steak, his favourite provision merchants. Other than these, everything came from Woods' vegetable shop next door to Tom Cowley, the chemist in the little row of shops next to Lad Lane, two doors away. Mr Woods was a taciturn old man who sat in splendour behind the counter, but his much younger and buxom wife was really in charge – she loved Owen and he her, scolded him, laughed at him, managed him if he arrived drunk and tended him if he had 'the horrors'. The courtesies were always adhered to – she was always Mrs Woods to his Mr Walsh. The Woods had two sons, who as they grew up came into the shop and became lifelong friends. It must have been because Woods' was primarily a vegetable shop that Owen acquired the habit of eating fresh vegetables and salads daily even if funds didn't stretch to meat or fish, the Woods could always be depended on to provide staples of potatoes and vegetables.

Owen's culinary habits were fussy and precise. First the plastic basin was carried upstairs for a supply of fresh water, then potatoes and carrots, peeled and washed, were put to boil, in the same saucepan for economy's sake. Then the fish, covered with pepper and butter, was either put in the Pyrex dish into the oven or the pan was put on the hob to fry the steaks. Lastly the small table was cleared and laid with a fresh double sheet of *The Irish Times* or *Evening Herald*, mugs, knives and forks, sugar bag and milk bottle, and the repast was served, piping hot and delicious. In summer vegetables were replaced by salads which involved a lot of chopping scallions, tomatoes, lettuce and cucumber on the old newspaper before the virgin sheets were laid again.

However, breakfast was my favourite meal. I was allowed or strictly speaking exhorted to stay in bed 'out of my way', while Owen bustled around, getting fresh water, putting the big saucepan on to boil for his ablutions, which were a daily ritual, winter or summer. The remainder of yesterday's newspaper was spread on the floor, the basin, soap and shaving gear on the small table. When the water boiled it was added to the cold water in the basin, Owen stripped, soaped himself all over then doused himself with the warm water, tied a towel round his waist and proceeded to shave with the help of a small cracked mirror on the mantelpiece. Then, a Christian once more, the basin was carried upstairs to be flushed down the toilet, the newspaper rolled up in a sodden ball and breakfast preparations could begin. I speak here about weekend or gala breakfasts, when both mood and money were in good fettle. One could almost always depend on the brown bread, marmalade and hot tea, but the best breakfasts took time and leisure to be fully savoured. The big fry was mouth-watering. A speciality of the house was pork kidney (not smelling of urine), which was procured weekly in the pork butcher in Camden Street, along with the sausages, rashers and black pudding. But best of all were the days when the whiff of buttered kippers, sizzling in the oven, battled and often won supremacy over the linseed oil and turps. A large oil painting featuring a dark-haired girl, face somewhat shaded, sitting up in a bed covered by a red and orange rug and reading the Sunday newspaper, dated 1964, pays testimony to those days. The rug, one of the last items rescued in the studio clear-out, lies at the bottom of my wardrobe. It still smells of linseed oil but not thankfully of kippers.

Sean O'Sullivan was Owen's great mentor and friend during the early sixties. He was a bear of a man who lumbered through the pubs, bellowing genially in several languages at a time – sometimes it was Irish, sometimes French and occasionally English. As he was often drunk and incoherent it didn't really matter which language he conversed in. I was in awe of him; he was after all a famous artist with pictures in the National Gallery so when one evening he gazed at me fixedly and said, 'I want you to sit for me tomorrow', I was truly impressed. I worried over what to wear and how to do my hair and whether he would be there when I turned up or have forgotten all about it, but he answered the brass bell on 6 St Stephen's Green at midday the following day, quite sober, attired in a splendid dressing gown. He brought me upstairs to share his breakfast of boiled egg and toast and then ushered me into the studio and pointed me towards a large throne-like chair mounted on a dais. 'Put this on,' he said, and busied himself behind the easel while I modestly disrobed and donned an off-the-shoulder shapeless garment in black taffeta. He gave me precise instructions as to how to sit and where to put my hands and then set to work with little of no small talk. I was used to sitting at this stage but got cold, stiff and bored before he allowed me get down. 'May I look?' I enquired, only to see a large, plain, middle-aged woman who more than filled the black dress, gazing back at me. Sean had the grace to look a little apologetic: 'Did I not mention it? I noticed you have rather beautiful hands and thought I could get this bloody thing finished in time.

Never mind, I'll do a drawing of you another day, come and have a drink.' He never did and some bank manager's wife in Cavan, or her descendents, are still admiring my mother's bony Plantagenet fingers.

I was still living in Leeson Park with a worried if tolerant Joan. She was a little smitten with Owen herself. Surprisingly gentle, he showed her his best side, matching her musical enthusiasms for BBC 3 with his own knowledgeable ardours. She used to quote 'L'après-midi d'un faune' on his arrival and on one famous occasion in the family annals, cried 'Traitor!' when he inadvertently opened her bedroom door on the way back from a woozy nocturnal visit to the bathroom, on one of the nights when he had come tapping at my window at midnight. Not many Irish mothers then would have had the wit or innate self-esteem to face a midnight prowler with such a greeting. But Joan's patience soon wore thin and I decided to move away from home. I was gainfully employed at last, working as bilingual clerk in the French Embassy and so could afford my independence. Proximity to Baggot Street was a priority, also the number 10 bus route, which would take me daily to Donnybrook and the Ailesbury Road embassy belt.

No. 15 Herbert Street had a history of bohemian life before I moved in. Brendan Behan had lived there before his marriage to Beatrice Salkeld, daughter of the painter Cecil Salkeld, whose paintings are still to be seen in the front bar of Davy Byrne's on Duke Street. My bedsitter on the hall floor front was a sublet from its permanent tenant, the painter Patrick Pye, who lived in the rear room on the same floor. Patrick and I were to share the same kitchen and bathroom and his genial bearded personality was reassuring. He must have been about thirty-five at this time but appeared older; he was single and had lived with his elderly mother for many years. He was a devout Christian and his artistic output was almost entirely concentrated on beautifully executed biblical scenes. Our timetables rarely clashed and as I was an intermittent resident and never cooked if I could help it, we lived peaceably together for some time. He took a kindly if pained interest in my welfare and tried to warn me against associations with dubious characters, particularly Owen Walsh, whom he disliked and dismissed as a serious artist.

Life took on a pattern. My growing absorption with Owen was threaded through with the 'normal' daily and weekly round of relationships with family and friends. Mary had started a new job with the BBC in Alexandra Palace, coping with the challenge of single motherhood of a black son but with the loving support of Power who shared her flat and life and became David's much loved Grandpa; Ruth, on the surface, was forging ahead in the Dublin theatre world, but her drinking and destructive relationship with Marie Conmee were beginning to take their toll.

Two friends came back into my life during the summer of 1962 and I participated from the sidelines in their choice of future partners. Mairead

Breslin returned from Paris and occasionally drew me away from Baggot Street to more pastoral environs. We sometimes took the number 44 bus to Enniskerry and walked the surrounding hills, empty of anything but sheep. An unlikely companion on one such outing was James McKenna whose uncompromising devotion to hewing Egyptian like figures out of rough wood or stone was matched only by his talent for making working-class youth spring to life on the Dublin stage. His angry, black-humoured musical *The Scattering*, directed by Alan Simpson of *Rose Tattoo* fame, had opened at the Dagg Hall in Abbey Street while I was home on holiday from Paris, and launched many a new career, some to flare brightly and briefly, some to go on to become well-loved names in Irish theatre such as Charlie Roberts, Eileen Colgan and Noel Sheridan. Audrey Corr became a particular friend: a gifted dancer and mime artist, she went on to partner John Molloy in his Revue shows. A generation and four children later, she has written two riotously comic books and grows flower gardens in a Mayo wilderness. That day in Wicklow, as Mairead, James and I panted our weary way towards Ray and Mary Carroll's Pine Forest Studio, two artists, Michael Kane and John Kelly, were sitting outside. 'Here comes James,' said one, 'with two fine motts.' 'I'll have the little one,' said the other, he of large spirit but slight stature. So John Kelly met his Mairead and I was bridesmaid yet again at their wedding the following November.

My London friend, Jane Clews, wrote to say she was bored with London and hotel life and had decided to emigrate to the United States but would love to come to Dublin for a holiday before she left. I was delighted to see her again and introduce her to Dublin life. One evening I brought her down to York Street to renew her acquantence with another Parisian refugee, David O'Doherty, who was living and painting in a building that almost bettered 108 Baggot Street as an O'Casey stage set. They didn't seem to hit it off. For once, David was very quiet and I was disappointed he hadn't come up to my descriptions of his charm and sense of fun. But he did call round to see us next day and, forty-eight hours later, I quote rather bitterly from my diary: 'Jane and I went to see David, I didn't stay long, quite obvious I wasn't wanted.' Jane never did emigrate – she and David went to London and married there. They had a flat and two children in Torrington Place off the Tottenham Court Road and were eventually joined by James McKenna who took the basement flat in the same building. When he moved out he left life-sized figures in granite behind as a memento. He and David both worked in the night telephone exchange, a popular workplace for artists and writers at the time, in Dublin as well as London. David and Jane's marriage did not last – the mix of Donegal and Staffordshire, fireworks and fastidiousness was just too unbridgeable. But they became good friends: friendship is easier than love any day and lasts longer.

The 1968 notebook gives a bald account of the first heartbreak:

It must have been about six months after we met in the autumn of 1962 that I was brought brutally to face reality – Owen was in love with another woman. Genuinely, passionately in love. Her name was Maura, aged about thirty, married to a wild, west of Ireland vet with four children. We were in bed together one night, we had made love and I was half asleep. Someone was at the door, an insistent tapping. Owen got up to open it. I looked at his naked, graceful back as he whispered in the doorway. Then he came and sat on the bed and spoke very gently, stroking my hand. I would have to get up and leave; he was sorry, he would phone me tomorrow. I don't think I said anything, just dressed and left. We never referred to that night again, or to Maura.

I remember being ill about this time and having to come home from work. Owen called that afternoon and sat in my room talking. It must have been immediately after this incident. It was so largely between us but never mentioned. Owen asked me could he get into bed with me, he just lay there, holding me, a kind of comfort I suppose. Maura left Ireland shortly afterwards to join her husband in Canada, Connemara having been made too hot to hold him. I was drinking with friends the night she left, some people drove me home and a man, with a female feeling for malice, entertained us with an account of the leave-taking he had witnessed at the airport and how Owen Walsh had been so affected. I felt sick with anguish.

She was gone and I couldn't forget her and have never forgotten her. She wrote him several touching letters, which I made it my business to read. He never answered them I am quite sure. I don't think he ever trusted a woman sufficiently to write. He told me once, and I always connected it with this woman, that he had written once or twice to a woman he cared for and had burned the letters before posting them. Can the fact that he does write to me, sometimes very tenderly, be an indication of some progress or unfolding of the sealed chambers of his trust?

By now I had learned a good deal about Owen's background. One of six children, his father owned a thriving grocer's shop and bottling plant in Westport. His mother was one of the Hughes clan from small farming stock, soon to become the leading business family of the town. He showed early and unexpected talent as an artist. His doting mother, head of the family following his father's early death, did not stand in his way when he begged to go to the National College of Art in Dublin. He quickly became the most spoken-about young artist of his era and was awarded the prestigious McCauley Scholarship. Fate or fatality stepped in when at twenty-one he fell in love with Beryl Lyons, swept her off her feet, married her in the face of both families' disapproval and carried her off to live first in Spain, and then in Italy, on the proceeds of his bursary. Five years and two children later, the young couple separated and Owen, after an abortive period of working in an advertising agency, moved away from his young family to take up permanent residence in his Baggot Street studio. His guilt and remorse scarred him for life, as it did those, like myself, who tried, failed and failed better at forming a lasting relationship with him.

15. 'So True a Fool is Love'

In 1963 I changed jobs. I was now working for a joint quango, the Irish Council of the European Movement, sharing Merrion Square offices and secretary (me) with the US Chamber of Commerce. I was interviewed by three business-suited gentlemen, an ordeal I managed not only to get through, but get the job. It could not have been due either to my knowledge of European affairs or to Irish trading links with the United States, which were rudimentary to say the least. Flagging interest in my responses was rekindled when one of the interviewers, Denis Corboy, later a European Commissioner, asked a question, which determined that I was one of *the* Limerick O'Maras. He, too, hailed from the Shannonside capital – the job was mine from that moment.

I had at last put a name to Owen's recurring 'fits', which I had witnessed on a number of occasions and found incomprehensible and terrifying. At first he clammed up and would tell me nothing, but gradually, as we became more intimate, he confessed, as if to a shameful secret vice, that he suffered from epilepsy. An episode could range in intensity from a slight twitch, which he would instantly cover up by some gesture or grimace, to a full-body jerk causing him to stumble or drop anything he was holding in his hand – cups and glasses never lasted long in the studio though fortunately the tin teapot was made of sterner stuff. If he was lucky it would pass off but his self-taught defence mechanism was to grab 'a bunch of pills', strip off and curl into a tight ball on the bed or floor, covering his head with his arms, trying to enter a hypnotic state of stillness until the tremors stopped. But sometimes the tremors would last for hours, pinning him to the bed, forcing him to pee into milk bottles when he couldn't make the stairs. It was at times like this if I was around that he would beg me to get him some whiskey, which proved again and again to settle some trip switch in the brain that set off the attack in the first place, a pyrrhic victory usually, but hard to deny. It was almost preferable when the tremors increased in frequency and intensity to become a full-blown *grand mal*. Though painful to witness and taking a couple of hours to sleep off, he recovered well after a *grand mal* attack and showed no ill effects. I became accustomed to it, making sure he was lying down and couldn't hurt himself, and would try and carry on with whatever I was doing until the seizure reached its crisis.

For what seemed an endless interval, but only lasted for a minute or two, his face would contort into a silent rictus and his breathing stop to the point of his turning blue, then the air would force itself back into his lungs and with a huge gusty cry he would fall back; I would re-enter from where I had been hiding, holding my own breath behind the door. An hour later he would wake up quite naturally but vague and listless, not querying what had happened until much later, when he might say, 'I must have bitten my tongue again, it's damn sore,' or rub a bruised shin if the attack had come without warning and he had knocked himself falling. He never had a serious accident; he fell like a piece of jelly or a sack of flour with no resistance. How he never broke a limb or fell under a bus was incredible, but he had learned to live and cope with his condition, so I learned to live and cope with it too, and life went on.

Over the next number of months my sporadic diary entries, in tiny bound notebooks, give a sense of the goldfish-bowl existence in those early sixties Dublin years, where the daily round of pubs formed the glue of friendships, casual encounters, and family life, perceived through the prism of my all-consuming obsession with Owen. Here and there sparse references are made to the boring necessity of earning a living, or casually reported events such as Brendan Behan's death, Kennedy's visit to Dublin and his assassination a few months later.

> April 2 Neary's again with Mummy, Justin Keating and Jim Gilbert. Long political discussion about rights of private ownership. Visited Dolly Fossetts (reputedly a brothel on Capel Street) with Owen and Darkie O'Dwyer, very unexciting
>
> April 2 Old Mrs Mahon died this morning and Owen was asked to help lay her out, but by afternoon he was so tight he just collapsed
>
> April 30 O. arrived at midnight tight of course, but very sweet, frighteningly so. I know he'll regret it. He said he never felt anything like this with anyone else, he'd been waiting for it to die out but it was getting worse then ever. 'I've been married once, I don't want to be married again.'

May 30 Determined not to see O. today and have an early night. Went to 'Look Back in Anger' to keep out of trouble, enjoyed it thoroughly. Then Patrick [Pye]'s exhibition opening. Was home about 10 in time to do some washing and tidy the place. Patrick came in a bit tight and affectionate. Mercifully the Carrolls and Michael Kane arrived to be followed by Norman and Silvia and Owen, all jarred. A row between the rival factions was barely avoided.

June 26 The highlight of the week is Kennedy's arrival of course. John Kelly's news beat that in my eyes. Mairead has had twin girls! [Niamh and Fiona] I had to battle my way through the crowds in O'Connell Street to the Rotunda. Caught a glimpse of Kennedy standing up in the limo – very tanned – never thought he had red, certainly reddish, hair. Mairead looking terrific but nervy, heard the whole history of the labour. Met Anne and Joe in the Metropole and told them the news.

July 21 I was alone when Norman S arrived with some tale about Owen. I found him hanging out of some railings in Baggot Street refusing to go home, f...ing and blinding all round him. A squad car drew up twice but wouldn't take him. Eventually I managed it followed by a trail of young boys, ladies with dogs and general Sunday afternoon people who enjoyed the diversion.

July 31 Stayed in the Bailey until about 10 then repaired to McDaid's where a hectic night was in full swing. Owen, I don't know how, seemed to organize a party in my place which was very successful in spite of Patrick's [Pye] disapproval. Garech Browne and girlfriend, the Cronins, Broes, Kevin M., Norman, Deirdre and a few oddbods.

August 2 Met Daddy in O'Neills about 8, Mary coming home tomorrow. Chatted with Eithne Dunne [the actress] who tells me Brian Fallon is engaged as is Iqbal – so two of my erstwhile boyfriends have found consolation elsewhere. Ah well, I wouldn't swap even the half of Owen I have, for either of them. Mc Daids, Owen joined us, plastered. Daddy left early. A long involved night looking for a restaurant, refused in Bernardo's, too late for Gaj's. Went to bed hungry in the end.

August 4 Mary came home today. Baby looks wonderful. Spent afternoon in the Green. Then met O. who brought us and baby to Phil Ryan's for a drink. God knows what the barman made of David. Mary, Daddy, Ruth and I met for drinks later, a surplus of O'Mara's.

August 24 Watched TV in the Majestic, lucky enough to catch a programme featuring Irish writers, including Tony Cronin and Brian O Nuallain, who was drunk. Went down to McDaids about 9, very lively. Stan told me Owen had been drinking all day; everyone asked me was he alright. I presumed he'd got home as he made no appearance. Joe Conneely drove me home, I didn't ask him in which was fortunate as O. was tucked up in my bed fast asleep.

September 13 Had a drink with Mummy at lunch time. Brian O'Donovan Shiels [man about town] took us off to Jammets for the Holy Hour. Working in the morning Brian rang about my scarf. Met in the Majestic, all well until O. refused to go out to Enniskerry to Frank Morris [sculptor, married to Camille Souter] if I came along. I decided to stay behind. Brian was upset about it. Owen came around about midnight and in attempt to climb in the window fell into the basement. It's a wonder he didn't break his neck. A sprained wrist is all he had to show for it.

September 16 Met Michael Jessel in the afternoon, sat for him for a couple of hours and what's more was paid for it. Tea at Leahys, then baby-sat for Mairead and John. Got home at 1 am dog tired. An undisturbed night.

November 22 Owen arrived unexpectedly for lunch. We lay down together for a while and made love. Met Mummy, saw 'The Birds'. Brief announcement that Kennedy had been assassinated. Weird end to weird film. Went to McDaid's for company. John Jordan drunk in tears. O. arrived about 2am.

November 23 O. still in bed at 1 pm. Feel tense and depressed, don't know whether it's Kennedy or what. Went to Independents Opening.

December 1 Owen hanging the pictures today.

December 2 Opening went off very well though Owen arrived late, a bit jarred but not overmuch. [Owen's Exhibition at the Dublin Painter's Gallery, St Stephen's Green]. Siobhan McKenna opened it beautifully by buying a picture. A good crowd though mostly friends. I didn't notice many buyers. Retired to McDaids, had the bright idea of raffling a picture, 15 names in a hat, £15.

January 15 1964 My birthday, 23! Had lunch with Mummy, got £1 from Aunt Nora which paid for some drinks. Was disappointed when O. didn't call but met him with Norman about 9 pm and things went well from there. McDaids, Davy Byrnes, the Majestric. Then we had a spaghetti in the Baggot Mews and actually danced! I enjoyed it very much.

January 20 Period. On time fortunately. Went to 'The Manchurian Candidate', complicated but fantastic. Bought hat of all things – nice but for me? Leahy's for tea, they approve of hat but not with coat, may change it. Home early. O. did not arrive.

January 27 Norman rang. Met him in McDaids at lunchtime, he brought me to the Bailey for lunch. Behan clan all there. Brendan in awful condition. Spent evening with Sheridans. Nice to see them again, must go out more often.

March 1 Moved to Ruth's flat, 101 St Stephens Green.

March 20 Behan died. Worked all day. Vaguely intended going to the concert again but met Pat and changed my mind. Wish she wouldn't get so intense when she's jarred. Norman rescued me and I had a pleasant few drinks with him. Sylvia's coming home next week.

Saturday March 21 Film Society day 'Viridiana', enjoyed it very much. Went back to McDaids. Lunia and Kathleen Ryan [actress, sister of John Ryan, starred in *Odd Man Out*] were there, both are always very charming to me which is flattering, being older women and sophisticated ones at that. ...

Sunday March 22 The hour was put forward today. Mummy called in at lunchtime and stayed till about 4. So did O which surprised me as he's not usually so interested in my mother's company. I met him again about 9 in Davy Byrnes. Also a rather strange man, Aidan Higgins, who seemed very interested indeed in our company. Went quietly home at 10.

Monday March 23 Brendan Behan was buried today. I met Mummy in McDaids at 6.30 and found a wake going on, got a bit jarred and a bit bored. Went to Davys and the Majestic in search of O. No luck so came home to bed by myself and fell asleep very quickly. O said he called but I never heard the bell.

Friday March 27 (Good Friday) What a day – Owen says I'll be talking about it for years but really I didn't enjoy it. We were still in bed when Brian Shiels came with a bottle of whiskey that disappeared in no time; then we left amidst scandalised faces of the landladies. Got more drink and then Brian drove like a madman out to Frank [Morris]and Camille [Souter]. Never will I get in a car with him again. Owen wandered out in the rain and fell into a bog. We got back to town eventually.

March 31 O was in a bad way today, couldn't get up without falling all over the place. He was still in bed when I got home at 6. Bought him a naggin of whiskey. We went out about 9 to meet Norman and Silvia. Went back to my mother's place but left early ... one of those nights in a thousand. O kept me awake until dawn ...I wish I could believe all he said ... I wish he'd go on feeling it and saying it and wanting me. I wish we lived together openly – I'd like to have a child – that's not romantic ramblings, I've known him more than 2 years. In the last six months I've felt I'd like to get pregnant.

April 13 Back to the office, what a job getting there in the morning. Home to lunch. Quiet night in McDaids, I was tired. Marie Conmee, Kavanagh, John Jordan etc. O also quiet, was glad to get home to bed. Understand these 'Woman's Own' articles now, I'm really so tired I hardly notice when O makes love to me – what a waste!

April 26 Walked through the Green with O this morning, lovely day, the trees are out at last. Dickie Riordan brought Mummy and me out to Dun Laoghaire for afternoon. Called on Deirdre, we met O in Baggot Street slightly jarred ... went home for a meal, then another drink and danced in the Green Lounge. My hat was pinched.

April 30 O down for a meal as usual at 8, then to McDaids, very good company. I had a 'succès fou', that man Aidan Higgins bit tight and more voluble that when we last met. Wandering home rather disconsolately when O bent down and picked up a £5 note!!!! Needless to say we didn't save any for a rainy day. Got a taxi to Baggot Mews, lovely night joined by Brian Shiels and wife, Celese. Home 3.30.

Thursday May 14 Daddy is due home this evening. Have written to a few places in Achill [planning August holiday with Mary and baby] only hope it's not too late. Aidan Higgins rang me just before 8. I met him for a drink. He lent me a book by some obscure French modern.

Friday May 15 Not a very successful day, Daddy is home in good form. Spent afternoon shopping with Mummy then met N & S in Bailey and on to Nearys. Big party organized to go to Gaiety, bad start with Daddy getting really angry with Pat B (on mine and O's account). Then the theatre [Roses are Real] with Micheál MacLiammóir, Owen's portrait best thing in it. N stuck it for 10 minutes and walked out followed by S. The rest of us more or less stayed. Awful play. O waiting for me when I got home.

May 16 Trying to plan economic meals for weekend, money getting short again. Called to O, was in bed, had a bad day. Got him some whiskey, he recovered but I hate him taking it. We had a meal and wandered through several pubs. O suddenly got terribly affectionate, could hardly wait to get home, how I love him like this, walking hand in hand is more of a thrill to me than going to bed.

May 30 Lunch in Jammets, wore new hat. Mairead asked me to babysit for a few hours. Met Aidan Higgins, Davy Byrnes, half promised to go to cinema with him tomorrow. John Kelly, Sean O'Brien turned up.

May 31 Awful night, bad asthma again. Breakfast in Majestic. Called to see Sylvia and baby [Paul] again. Spent afternoon in bed and left note in Davys for AH saying I couldn't meet him.

July 31 Owen rang me at the office today and asked me to sit for him. It's a long time since he's done anything. This is a full length figure, quite large, so far I like it.

September 11 Went to see McLaimmoir 'I Must Be TalkingTo My Friends'. Owen walked out midway …

September 18 Aidan Higgins brought me out to Celbridge, used to live there. Writing a book about Castletown estate. Gave me a book by Italian jewish author *I am a Man*.

October 5 O. was in bed when I got home at 9, in fact he stayed here all day. I realize now how right he was about this place [101 St Stephen's Green] – it's like a trap, dark – we seem to be on top of one another all the time.

October 16 Moved to 30 Elgin Road.

One factor that helped maintain a sense of stability among surrounding chaos was another change of job. In the autumn of 1963 I moved to the French Cultural Centre, also known as the Alliance Française, conveniently located in 18 Herbert Street. I was to work on a shift basis of either 10 to 3 or 3 to 8 on a generous salary of £11 per week. Much happier in this more relaxed and cultural ambiance and with working hours better suited to my lifestyle, I settled down for the next four years. The director was a French official loosely attached to the Embassy but it was May McKenna who ran the show with superb, understated efficiency and French of a standard I groped to achieve. May, married to the actor T.P. McKenna, was the main breadwinner for their growing boisterous family of boys; the late arrival of a girl, some years after I joined the Alliance, gave her great joy. May replaced Patsy Sheridan as an earth-mother figure and someone to emulate; Patsy, having spoken out too frankly, once too often, about my throwing my life away on married wastrels, was no longer my confidante. A true forerunner of the feminist superwoman, May, in the years I knew her, was de facto a single parent as T.P. was carving out a career on the London stage and British TV and made sporadic trips home to May and the boys. I saw him first in Jim Fitzgerald's production of *Stephen D* (Hugh Leonard's adaptation of James Joyce's *Portrait of the Artist as a Young Man*) at the Gate Theatre. It was this production that shot him to fame and mainstream London theatre when it transferred with much acclaim to the West End and thence to Broadway. Although undeniably handsome in a thin-lipped way, I reserved my judgment, seeing in him once again the facile charm of the actor's mask I had grown to distrust. Later when his name was linked frequently with that Celtic temptress Edna O'Brien, who May described loyally as 'being so good to T.P.' in his lonely London sojourn, I boiled with possibly misplaced rage and could barely be civil when he dropped into the office on his trips home. When May finally left the Alliance to set up home with T.P. in London, she became that rare bird, a simultaneous translator in English and French, commuting weekly to the European Parliament in Strasbourg.

The Alliance, as it was known, ran afternoon and evening French language classes from September to June and operated a lending library of French literature. Duties were not onerous but could be hectic at the beginning of each term. I invigilated in the library, while registering students, keeping the books and dealing with general bilingual correspondence.

One summer when there was very little to do I typed up a new drama for James McKenna, *At Bantry*, and was rewarded by a graceful three-foot-high nymph in pear wood, which is my second-most-prized possession and will be saved, along with the Sunday morning painting *Girl Reading*, whenever that mythical blaze consumes my home. James would lope into the room, smiling shyly, his hair flopping over one eye, and stay for hours, giving forth on socialism, the role of the artist and the pusillanimity of the establishment. He had the most extraordinary soft skin. Impossible to imagine him bearded, he was big chested and had huge, oddly graceful hands. I sat for him too at about this time, perched on a hard stool in the tiny cottage he was renting in the Coombe. Thirty years later he appeared one day in the O'Mara Travel offices in Donnybrook, staggering in with a huge canvas-wrapped bundle. 'I found that head of yours while I was clearing out the studio, I never got round to casting it. It's a bit rough but I painted it to brighten it up, would you like to have it?' Unwrapped, it revealed a swan-necked (would it were so) Nefertiti-like head with high headdress, fired in clay, the whole a strange ochre colour with the exception of the whites of the eyes and the blueish headdress. The headdress puzzled me for some time until I realized it was a perfect interpretation of the high, fiercely back-combed bouffant style that was my pride and joy in 1965. After repeated protests from staff and callers alike bemoaning ochre stains adhering to any garment that brushed by it, the head was removed to a safe unfrequented corner of my bedroom. I would miss her unblinking gaze when I awake each morning if ever she and I are banished to separate sleeping quarters.

James's feminine counterpart in my eyes was my friend of Dartmouth Square days, Deirdre Kelly or McMahon as she then was, her blonde ponytail and rosebud lips that belied her inner toughness, stubborn adherence to principle and commitment to unrewarding causes. If James's hands seemed large, Deirdre's hands were tiny. Her childlike fingers and fine calligraphy were employed during those years by the National Museum's Fine Art Department. I still have her meticulously etched copy of the eighth-century manuscript poem *Pangur Bán*. Outside the dungeons of Kildare Street she developed her love of Dublin's Georgian heritage, inherited from her bus-driver father. She was an early militant in the battle against the Fianna Fáil backed developers of the 1960s, protesting against the destruction of the ESB offices, a stone's throw from her basement flat in 4 Lower Fitzwilliam Street. That battle was lost but she was later to hone her skills in the battle for Hume Street in 1970 and we both wheeled our push-chaired toddlers in the Wood Quay mass protests of the late seventies. We had many a conversation about love, sex and marriage in Deirdre's basement flat, handily enough right opposite the Majestic Hotel and beside the Arts Club, either of which were good for after-hours drinking. On one such occasion, in deep debate about moral values, Silvia wistfully queried,'But sure, what sins could you commit if you were married?' for which pithy comment on all our conundrums we had no answer.

My friends were deserting me, swept, if not always into Church-blessed marriages, at least into fecund motherhood. Mairead, Anne and Jane were already into seconds when Audrey and Silvia started on the same ripening roundabout. Even Deirdre was to give in to the same inexorable process when she fell victim to Aidan Kelly of Ballaghdereen, Co. Roscommon. The Dub and the culchie came together over their love of Georgian Dublin. I remained pregnancy proof. Owen practised the infamous *coitus interruptus* method of birth control and I experimented with a newfangled diaphragm that an undercover liberal doctor fitted me with. I was scared, not of pregnancy, but of Owen leaving me, which he convinced me he would. He had made a mess of marriage and fatherhood and would never go down that road again. In any case other than Ethel M. Dell fantasies about 'bearing a son for the man I loved', I didn't overly relish the thought. My friends' babies seemed full of orifices that either yelled or leaked, both activities that seemed to be in full swing whenever I babysat, a job for which I was in much demand. This also coincided with a change of attitude in my friends whom I suspected of casting increasingly pitying glances towards me as Owen and I pursued our erratic courtship, defined by my wise mother as one where: '*Entre deux amants il y a un qui aime et un qui se laisse aimer.*' (De La Rochefoucauld)

As I grew more alienated from my girlfriends I became closer to Joan. We came to depend on each other, allies who soldiered together and supported each other's quirks and vicissitudes. She was lonely with Power away in London and Ruth, whose drinking was of growing concern to her, an intermittent lodger in Leeson Park. My own drinking she tolerated as being connected solely with my social life, as I never drank at home or appeared dependent on it, or at least only in the same way as she was herself, as a passport to membership of the Dublin pub culture. In Joan's company I had a temporary visa to the McDaid's literary circle, ironically greeted 'Oh here comes my beautiful Eileen', as Joan was wont to call me. Full-time members were never listed but they knew who they were; it was like a secret code passed on only by word of mouth. 'Mr' Kavanagh, a title that Joan, always respectful of genius, gave him in the presence of third parties, was the undoubted monarch, a grumpy Aslan, yet to attain sainthood in post-mortem adulation. He usually sat up at the bar, with Dinny Dwyer or Tony Cronin talking horses. Phyllis Dwyer was tough and well able to join them pint for pint, or not at all if family duties called. Therese Cronin was a frailer vessel, a beautiful, petite blonde, who it was said had been an Aer Lingus hostess in the glamorous early fifties. She had more than a little of Zelda Fitzgerald in her, competing for Tony's attention, pitching herself into the maelstrom of male poetic egos. They had wildly dramatic rows, much enjoyed by all except tender-hearted Joan.

Once I was sitting with a diverse group around one of the small tables when Therese got tired of trying to get Tony to leave. It must have been lunchtime, when a modest supply of ham or cheese sandwiches were available: she picked up a bottle of tomato ketchup and upended it over the nearest head. Some time later Tony got a post of Writer in Residence at the University of Montana and they disappeared off the scene for two years. Occasional missives came through, one memorably included a newspaper cutting with the immortal heading: 'Ireland's Bonnie and Clyde strike again!' I realized that the women who survived in this society had to be Amazonian by force of circumstances if not by nature. Another woman I admired but was rather afraid of was the poet Leland Bardwell, who lived in a dreary basement in Leeson Street with lots of children and a sinister man named Finton, who always seemed to be watching but rarely spoke. A younger subset of poets and writers who inhabited the top end of McDaid's also intrigued me, but from a distance. With my coterie of friends, like cats we sniffed the surrounding air and passed by each other in mutual disdain. We thought they were 'snobs', all UCD or TCD-scarved and superior: Nuala Ó Faoláin was gorgeous, her curly hair an ever-enviable contrast to my own MacDara Woods, impossibly Byronic; Eiléan Ní Chuileanáin's brooding Sitwellian gaze; Harden Rodgers, daughter of the Belfast poet. They seemed on a higher par intellectually than us mere mortals and consorted with legal Olympians like John Jay and Paddy MacEntee. If they thought of us at all, it would be as hangers on, mere wage-slave amateurs of the arts.

Mr Kavanagh once sat down next to me on the seat beside the telephone just inside McDaid's back door. He huffed, puffed and coughed for a few moments before uttering the immortal words, 'Are ye a good hoult, are ye?', as if to say what good was I otherwise. But he was kind enough in general, saluting gruffly if encountered in Baggot or Leeson Street. On another occasion he climbed on the same number 11 bus with me at the top of Dawson Street, sat beside me all the way muttering in a fearsomely genial way and insisted on paying my fare, an unusual gesture from one whose poverty was an indictment of Irish society. Around this time he was sharing a flat in Upper Leeson Street with the Scottish painter Robert MacBryde (later killed in a traffic accident on Leeson Street Bridge in 1966) and ever-devoted Dr 'Dickie' Riordan. His rare geniality may well have been because he would have then been a regular late-night visitor to nearby Leeson Park. Much more common was the time when he yelled across the superior expanse of The Bailey: 'Welsh, have ye the lend of a fiver?' and got short shrift from an equally impoverished artist.

However, I had my allies in McDaid's: Bob Bradshaw ever watchful, ever hopeful, would draw me in if I ventured in alone, as would Kevin Monaghan, an American artist and ex GI, who had somehow settled in a damp base-ment in Dawson Street, which doubled as an 'antique' shop full of dusty curios and flybitten old masters, from whence he sallied forth impeccably arrayed, to while away his evenings in adjacent public houses, Davy Byrnes,

The Bailey, McDaids or nearest and smallest, The Dawson Lounge. If I joined one I was ignored by the other as they carried a strong mutual antipathy to their graves. Two more different personalities would be hard to find in the same milieu and yet they shared certain qualities that each would have firmly denied in the other. They were of an age: Bob, the unreconstructed IRA man, with his white quiff, labourer's hands, and yen for young women; Kevin, ex Omaha Beach GI, whose carefully oiled Mephistophelean goatee, velvet waistcoats, and drawling witticisms lent credence to his 'queer' reputation. Both hid a fine sensitivity, one with gruff cynicism, the other with outrageous camp. Both had faced and dispensed death, both were deeply disillusioned with militarism, of either the regular army or guerrilla brand, and both lived proudly and independently on 'the clippings of tin', refuting the honours of their separate wars.

In a surviving diary entry from 1965 I admitted: 'The only thing I remember clearly is Owen's part in my life which often only comes at the end of the day – the rest of what I do seems vague and uninteresting.' Weeks merge into months of routine attendance at the job, nightly rounds of the pubs. Encounters with Owen swing violently from passion to rejection, ecstasy to despair, with large amounts of alcohol the only defining common factor. It was a schizophrenic existence, illustrated by an unsent letter, perhaps never intended to be actually posted, found in yet another notebook, *a propos* that strange man I had first encountered in Davy Byrnes in March 1964, Aidan Higgins:

> You sat at the bar alone, dark, pale faced, taciturn. I noticed you watching me. Next day, like the man who wasn't there, you appeared silently again, propping up the counter, dregs of a pint, brooding gaze roving sightlessly over me. Going up to order a drink you spoke to me, unsmiling. I can't recall you smiling ever, or what your teeth were like. You became a familiar figure, usually solitary. I heard you were a writer, a friend of the Cronins. Bob Bradshaw, always curious, sniffed out your interest. You pursued me in a non-threatening, mournful fashion. We met occasionally. You asked questions, which I squirmed to avoid answering because of my shyness, not for what you wanted to know. I was painfully in love, sometimes rejected, sometimes on pinnacles of hope renewed, spending my periods of exile on the margins of the literary/arty world in Neary's or McDaid's. My sister Ruth provided me a haven among the theatre people in the back bar of Neary's. My mother gave me the excuse to launch, her too ladylike to venture into a public house on her own, into the literary circle in McDaid's. I was part of neither but accepted without comment in both; sufficient cover to explain my presence on the off chance my lover might put in an appearance. You became a sort of spiky crutch in my frequent bouts of despair. I took on the role of naive but nubile listener to your work in progress. Never likely to impinge on your real life but possibly to provide a sexual encounter either in fact or in fantasy.

You talked about the vicissitudes of writing for a living and warmly about the support of Samuel Beckett who had introduced you to the publisher Calder. In your turn you introduced me to European writers beyond my small radius, Italo Svevo's *Confessions of Zeno*, Primo Levi's *If this Is a Man*, Beckett himself. You brought me walking in Wicklow and once we caught a bus to Celbridge and the Castletown House Estate. You had been brought up there; I had friends who lived in one of the Lodges on the Estate. You were writing a book about a family of women who lived there too. You told me you used me in one of the characters, a needy kind-hearted creature; 'my nature is my fool', you quoted me. When we returned, walking up Grafton Street to McDaid's, we bumped into the Cronins. Your reaction was to walk a little away from me, the guilty reaction of a happily married man. I babysat for you once in Ranelagh. I think you found it titillating; certainly when you both came home and your wife went up to the children, you kissed me passionately for the first time. I thought your wife very beautiful, dark eyed and dark haired like me but with a Junoesque figure. We did finally make love but only once. It was in one of my many bedsitters, this one in Elgin Road; none were ever far from the magnet of Lower Baggot Street. Not a great success squeezed into my single divan. I fell asleep, you held me spoon fashion and made awkward love, which I pretended to sleep through. You said afterwards it was the only way; you could not look me in the eyes, I was only a fantasy after all.

16. The Plateau

The roller-coaster eventually slowed to a more even pace and by the end of 1965 Owen and I had settled down to an almost domestic existence. I had moved to a pleasant top-floor flat in 46 Upper Mount Street and Owen gradually moved in with me, retreating to his Baggot Street bed only when I risked becoming too obviously proprietorial. It was a happy time.

Easter 1966 was the fiftieth anniversary of the Easter Rising – not a great event in my blinkered life at the time, but it left me one surreal image, and a small piece of striated granite on my mantelpiece. A slight detour, brought about by the previous summer's sojourn in Achill with Mary and three-year-old son David had brought me into the world of traditional music. Not of the ballad-singing O'Donoghue's variety, but the more serious precursor of the Chieftains and the *seanchaí*-keening type, taking place then in places like the Pipers Club in Church Street or in the many bedsitters scattered throughout the near-city suburbs of Rathmines on the south side and Drumcondra on the north side, occupied by Kerry men or Connemara men or Donegal men, who loved their native music. There, devotees would sit on floors, back to the wall, nursing a bottle of stout or beer while the Noble Call went round, when murmurs of '*maith an cailín*' '*Guth Amhain, le do thoil*' '*ciúnas anois*' and such terms of fluent Irish and musical appreciation accompanied the singer/musician's performance. It was at one such gathering that I spent the night of Easter Monday with my Achill conquest, the golden-voiced and lazy-eyed Rory, whom I quite fancied but seldom met. He gave me hope of someday, sometime, finding another male of the species sexually attractive. He also had a motor car, which meant on this particular occasion I was in foreign territory on the north side of Dublin. Too far to walk home, I sat through hours of solemn intoning of endless verses of 'The Lament for Art Ó Laoghaire' until Rory's VW Beetle set off through Mountjoy Square, down Gardiner Street towards the Liffey in the early hours. Stopped at the lights at the Talbot Street-Earl Street intersection, I glanced sleepily right towards O'Connell Street, and then jerked wide awake. Etched against the paling night sky was a jagged outline where Nelson's Pillar should have been. We tumbled out of the car: the mighty and much-loved landmark lay in shattered boulders all over the surrounding streetscape, passers-by congregating to stare and a few gardaí hastily assembled to keep order. We had the wit to grab a couple of bits of rock and fled back to the car, home and sleep. Next day Owen didn't believe my night-time ramblings till the newspapers screamed their headlines 'Explosion wrecks the Pillar' and I was vindicated if not forgiven for waking him up at 3 am.

It was a sun-filled summer. It was the summer I became a prostitute for a week, acquired a niece, and also an island. I blame Ruth for the first, Mary for the second, the third was entirely Owen's doing. Ruth, from her snug corner in Neary's, had entered a new field, a rare one in Ireland then, that of film making. That is to say, she became a shareholder in a new film production, to be shot entirely in Dublin. The film was *Ulysses,* the director Joseph Strick, the star Milo O'Shea. Ruth was appointed props manager, salary extremely low, but greatly to be enhanced by a share of the profits, a deal applied to all permanent crew members. For years afterwards, a brown envelope would arrive at irregular intervals in Leeson Park enclosing a cheque for £2/10/6 or some equally tiny sum. The film was never a box office hit but it is now a screen classic and although the cheques have dried up, close scrutiny of the black-and-white images mark our family presence in the enterprise.

It was in Neary's pub that Ruth whispered to me there was a chance of signing on as extras. Some young Dublin girls were to be recruited for a few days' shooting in the film's Sandymount location. The word spread like wild-fire. Ruth put myself and Silvia on the list and we turned up at Sandymount Green the following morning. A large rambling house on one side of the Green was the location for shooting interior scenes. Neither Silvia nor I had ever read *Ulysses*, and when told it was for the night-town episode that our services were required, we had no idea of what to expect – even at the end of our session we were little the wiser. I felt myself to be an old hand at the game, as I had already had experience as a film extra; not quite as a 'singing' nun, more of a 'running' nun; fleeing from the aerial bombardment of George Peppard in *The Blue Max,* also filmed in Ireland. On that occasion we had problems coping with running very fast in the full garb of a nun's habit. This time it was the opposite. We were to dance like dervishes on one spot, wearing

as little as possible. Wardrobe budgets being as tight as in all other depart-
ments of the making of *Ulysses*, we were instructed to provide our own under-
clothes, fancy if possible. Some of the better off among us sneakily purchased
brand new, lacy garments, I had to make do with an ancient pink affair, at
least edged with a black frill, a souvenir from my Paris days with Pierre, who
liked a bit of style in the bedroom. We duly paraded in front of the director
who checked us out before the day's filming began. I passed muster but he
picked on one or two particularly fetching models and barked 'Take it off',
much to the discomfiture of the wearers. For the best part of a week we sat
around, walked around, enduring hour after endless hour of meaningless but
energetic gyrations around a dimly lit room while Anna Manahan, in top hat
and tails, wielded a whip over Milo O'Shea on all fours. One of us, not me
unfortunately, was given a speaking part. She had to stand in a doorway and
leer: 'Hey mister, how's your middle leg?' to Milo as he shambled by. We never
saw the rushes of our performances, and as the film was banned in Ireland
until the dawn of the new millennium, hardly anybody else ever saw what
is now described as 'Joseph Strick's masterpiece'. Owen and I made a grand
excursion to see it in an Art Cinema when it was released in Paris in 1967.
How mortified, yet pleased I was, in the split second when my form appeared
on screen, when he yelled 'Jaysus, O'Mara, there's your arse!' Thus ended my
show-business career.

In late July 1966 my niece Nancy was born in London. I travelled over to
see her and help out if I could. It had been a home birth, innovative at the
time, but for practical Mary with her partner Reg New, a six-year-old son and
his grandfather to look after, it was the preferred option. I missed the event
itself but all went well. Grandpa Power and David shared a boiled-egg breakfast while the birth took place in the next door bedroom. It was six months
since I'd seen Power. He had visibly aged, become shaky and, uniquely for
him, complained of pain in his hip. Walking with him to Wood Green for an
evening pint, he joked about his three speeds – slow, very slow and stop. It
was early intimations of what was to come but it was a happy time nonetheless. Mary was up and about in no time and I had plenty of leisure to enjoy
London again and link up with old friends, although Owen was ever present:

Sunday night

Eileen L – - -

  *Waiting all week to hear from you I finally conclude you are similarly
engaged in London or too occupied with your niece. You must write if
you have not already. This loneliness is now getting too familiar and the
hunter instinct is beginning to sniff the air very closely (especially with
some of the micro skirts skittering around).*

The week here has been lovely and the beginning taken up with Sean and Noreen [Thomas] and putting their stall in order [at the Antiques Fair in the RDS]. Mad absolutely mad the first day putting up shelves, collecting the antiques, displaying them and eventually covered in sweat and dust, just ready when the doors were open and all Dublin society started appearing until the place was so packed that your elbows were a great help for moving the swarming women. I think I would have been thanked by Sean with a handshake and the one or two meals he bought subsequently if I had not 'borrowed' £2 for a drink from him after it became possible to get out of the place. They have invited us both to their big house in November. It's an invitation I'm now not too interested in.

There is no sign yet of Anne's baby. I called to Leahy's this evening and had the news from Mr Leahy who confronted me square across the door as if I intended breaking and entering and had to have every word drawn out of him like trying to get a cork out of an empty bottle with a loop of twine. Obviously I'm not trusted.

No one calling here or at my own place all week so it's been a completely lone week. Sorry, the gas man called and found your meter 16 shillings short and on Friday there was a final notice (7 days) to produce £2/10 or thereabouts so I'm going down to them tomorrow and doing some talking. There must be something wrong so I'll try and get them to test the meter before cutting off the gas.

There seems to be a lot of sad news this week but of interest to you might be that Brian Shiels' father died during the week. ... My sister Mary who was to have arrived last night has had to postpone her trip as her father-in-law died during the week and Stephen's mother-in-law also. But as you know oysters have nothing on Walsh's for tightmouthedness and I only heard this news when ringing Westport yesterday to find on what plane Mary was arriving: even though Stephen's in-law is dead about a week and Mary's the same.

Enough of that, the only ones I've met have been Silvia and Norman who have invited me up to eat on Tuesday evening, and I'm writing no more as I must have taken 1 1/2 hours to get this much on paper so Good Night.
Owen

It was soon after this London trip that I visited Mayo with Owen for the first time. By now I knew and liked his brother Cathal, now married to Kay and practising as a country vet in Carnew, Co. Wicklow. I had met one or two of his other brothers briefly on one of their Dublin rugby jaunts when they would meet up in Larry Murphys pub, across the road from the Baggot Street studio. One Good Friday when all pubs were closed for the day, Owen painted a mural on one wall of the bar celebrating a famous Leinster rugby final and depicting some of the local personalities crouched in the scrum. Recently rescued from layers of covering emulsion paint, its colourful vigour is on show once more.

Owen made infrequent trips to Westport, both drawn and repelled by his multitudinous family. Drawn, because he passionately loved his home place and yearned for family acceptance; repelled, because of his self-imposed exile, the scandal of his runaway marriage and its subsequent failure, and most of all by the trauma of his mother's death. I only knew his version of the story. He was the apple of his widowed mother's eye. She supported his artistic talent in the face of family scepticism and agonized over the onset of his epilepsy as a teenager and his sudden marriage at twenty-one. His disappearance to Europe for more than a year on an art scholarship caused her yet more pain and anxiety. As Owen recounted it to me, he returned from Spain and sent a telegram to his mother announcing his arrival on the afternoon train – by the time he arrived, she had suffered a heart attack and died in his arms. Whether apocryphal or half-true, it led to almost irredeemable damage to family relationships thereafter only finally healed in the months before his own death forty-odd years later.

His casual suggestion that we might take a few days in Mayo in late summer 1966 was accepted with alacrity. Although, according to the mores of the time in rural Ireland, no respectable girl could be seen to consort with a married man in an open liaison, I longed to be known as Owen's acknowledged 'mistress' and was eager to meet his family on home ground. I was brought formally to meet the family Don, Owen Hughes, a beloved uncle and Owen's mother's favourite brother. He was a large man with a tiny wife. Both teachers, they gave me a warm welcome. My Limerick roots were soon winkled out and my stock rose accordingly. Oweny, as he was known, was a big Fianna Fáil man, although he had earlier dabbled with Clann na Poblachta, being a loyal admirer of Sean MacBride. He was an influential figure in the local county council and a thorn in the side of the Earl of Sligo, residing amongst his acres at Westport House. A running battle was carried on for years between them. Owen Hughes won a major victory when the council placed a compulsory purchase order on part of the demesne for local housing and the walls of the 'big house' were breached at last.

Perhaps because of our ambivalent status or more likely the strain of spending too long in close proximity of the family, our stay in Westport itself was brief and we headed even farther west. I had never been to a smaller island than the one I was born on and I had never been on a small boat on the open sea. The crossing between Roonagh Pier and Clare Island takes about twenty minutes on a good day – ours was a good day, sun shimmering, sea shining. *The Pirate Queen*, captained by doughty Chris O'Grady, chugged on its twice-daily run to the island. The squat stone tower beside the pier, the walk round the edge of the horseshoe beach to the hotel where Chris O'Grady reappeared as host, sitting outside quaffing beer, and looking out and back at the strangely unreal coast we had just left, I realized we were in looking-glass land at last. I had found the tiny key into the garden of talking roses where you could do at least four impossible things before breakfast. We stayed for three days and three nights. Owen painted, I swam and walked and got lost, finding myself back at the harbour when I had supposed myself to be on the other side of the island, a very Alice-like occurrence. The snaps retain some of the magic: a radiant sea-soaked me clinging to the gunwhale en route back to the mainland; a less radiant but equally soaked Owen, proving we were there together. Today Grainne Mhaol's grey castle, the sunlit sea and softly curved shore hangs on the wall of my Louisburgh home, the canvas and paint gift of his island to me.

It was certainly a happy time, two pieces of music and an abandoned bird ended the year. Owen was the music man who kept the collection of worthwhile listening jealously in the studio. I had Ruth's old record-player from the Stephen's Green flat that played one record at a time, two of which evoke those rosy-hued days. I dreamed away winter afternoons to Elgar's 'Chanson du Matin' until Owen burst in to dance me round the room roaring 'What's New Pussy-Cat?' as Tom Jones belted out that winter's hit tune. I wonder about the feasibility of having them played at my funeral service. A witness in oils of that time hangs on someone's wall somewhere, a reclining nude with black cat, cheekily entitled *Girl playing with her Pussy.*

I cooked my first Christmas dinner in that Mount Street flat. My parents' friends Jack and Gertie Boland always presented my mother with a turkey, Jack being in the grocery business. On Christmas morning, having consulted Margaret Leahy who provided the sage and onion stuffing, I duly stuffed the bird and placed it in a shiny new baking tin in the oven. Owen and I sauntered off for traditional drinks with Norman and Silvia in Clyde Road. Joined by Joe and Anne Hackett, we got back in good time to add potatoes to the roasting bird. As I proudly lifted out the sizzling tin, I realized something didn't look quite right: the unfortunate creature lay before us, tip-tilted legs splayed wide in a gooey sea of sausage meat and stuffing. 'Like all the world' Owen cruelly remarked, 'an abandoned poor hoor.' Why had no one mentioned sewing up the orifices and tying the legs together? I wondered plaintively.

Joan had moved to London before Christmas. Power's health was deteriorating and he had been hospitalized for 'tests'. She did not, however, stay with Mary, but took up residence in a boarding house in Crouch End from where she looked after Power while Mary was at work and also began her latter-day career as childminder to small David in school holidays. Her letter to John Jordan in January 1967 puts up a brave front but more than hints at a lonely exile from the warm circle of McDaid's:

Dear John

32 Coolhurst is a boarding-house and I am a woman of slender means. It is funny after 30 years to be living in a bed-sitter again, though it is very like the nun's cell I have sometimes sighed for. The gas fire burns merrily but is voracious of half-crowns.

Nothing could be further from my former existence. Last night I brought my little grandson to the local pantomime. It was so appalling that there wasn't any comfort anywhere – every bit of local talent had been obviously utilized, until even David was heard to moan: 'Not singing again!' It was during these three interminable hours that the Genius of Jimmy O'Dea burst upon me and the memories of a box at the Gaiety – Dickie and yourself and the Cronins and various infants – and you and I ostentatiously leaving for a drink when the performing dogs came on. It seems to me, in comparison with my present life, that we were a highly sophisticated lot.

I will now describe my day. I get up much earlier than I had ever dreamed of. I descend from an enormous height (I am near Alexandra Palace) and walk about a mile to Mary's flat, where during the Christmas holidays two people are awaiting me – an old man and a young child. Power is not really old, but he is terribly enfeebled. He has Parkinson's Disease – a form of paralysis – he rages against his physical weakness, but thank God, his mind is not affected. David (mark the name) is my last love and makes up to me for much that I miss in my old life – where will I begin the litany? Ruth and Eileen (of course) and Solomon, who is 10 years old and used to share my siesta, curling up with me in my big armchair. Then yourself, and Dickie and Robert [MacBryde] (for whom I pray every night). Gail Price (that was) wrote me a long affectionate letter at Christmas, addressing me, very properly, as Mrs O'Mara.

I meet with scant civility here and I begin to think that Tony Carroll was wrong when he said 'The Irish have no virtues, only vices'. Generosity, hospitality, and good manners. We will ignore the other side of the balance sheet. I think of you very often. Your Christmas card 'cheered me up' in Therese Cronin's phrase. Please write to me. I have worn out several horrible biros and reams of paper since coming here. Letters, mostly to Ruth and Eileen, but also to Daisy McMackin and to my other friend Gertie, whom I don't think you ever met. Daisy writes: 'Come back and bring Power with you.' I have thought of this but I doubt would he be able for the journey. Also he has love here, it would seem cruel to transplant him.

Mid June you say – All being well – yes.

Much love, Joan

In Joan's absence Ruth had taken over Leeson Park, and supposedly paid the rent. I was plotting a move of my own and had applied for a job with the Irish Tourist Board in Paris. Then came the news from London that cancer, rather than Parkinsons, was the cause of Power's pain with major surgery a possibility.

During this period of flux Owen was in Drogheda, painting a mural of 'The Marriage Feast of Cana' in the refectory of the Medical Missionaries of Mary's Convent, being treated like a lord by the founder of the order, Mother Mary Martin herself. She used to visit him in the evening to share a cigar, her personal indulgence: he in turn was allowed a whiskey until the medics began treating his epilepsy and the whiskey was replaced by tea and biscuits. A spate of letters followed after he was taken into Garda custody during a weekend break in Dublin and badly roughed up by over zealous members of the notorious 'Lugs Brannigan' squad.

(Written in black ink on greaseproof paper):

February 1967

Dear Eileen

I am writing to try and keep some control of myself in the selfish masculine way of wailing my woes on some female's breast. But since coming back here this thing, whatever it is that hit me in Dublin, has got twice as bad and I seem to be existing in a state of approaching hysterics or else running to some nurse or doctor for knock out sleeping pills or injections, or else talking, talking to patients, nurses, sisters or anything that offers itself in a wild attempt not to lose my reason and keep my mind occupied otherwise than thinking all the time as my brain seems to have started going like a dynamo, and even working or reading does not occupy it anyway fully; even talking to people seems only to occupy a small portion while the rest is approaching a condition that I can only describe as the horrors and doing things like talking etc has a slight effect of making me control this, and occasionally forget myself and what's going on inside me. Everything seems to have acquired a new and deeper significance and meaning, and sometimes I am positively approaching a state of terror. Terrified of what I don't know but it is terror to the extent of sweating all over my body frequently and having the novelist's favourite 'cold fingers' running up and down my spine regularly. It's a fearful but at the same time fascinating experience but if I am able to stand up to this pressure I'm certain I'm going to start producing good pictures.

My apologies for such a long winded egocentric wail when I ought to be enquiring after you and how you are feeling, but you are in my thoughts and the memory of the night with Nora and yourself and Aeneas (is my spelling wrong) is a golden gate to some escape from these knots. If you see either of them please give them my best wishes, also Norman and

Silvie as without Norman I have no doubt as to where I would be now and as to the sort of treatment I would be getting for behaving in such a highly excitable fashion as I am here.

For yourself there are no words at my disposal to convey my feelings except to reassure you of the comfort and pleasure of having had you near me on Monday.

Love

Owen

I've had a bunch of pills and must go to bed … and beginning an attack …

In March I was appointed travel adviser to the Irish Tourist Board's new Paris office, a dream job, a new venture for Ireland's neophyte tourism industry and a chance to return to my beloved Paris. Owen's proposal to accompany me to Paris to paint for six months was greeted with delight. For us both it represented a real, if unspoken, commitment to our relationship, now five years in its often precarious existence.

Happiness was mixed with dread, the news from London increasingly ominous. In a last and fruitless attempt to halt the spread of cancer, Power's left leg was amputated at the hip on 22 February. He lingered on for several weeks, I visited him and told him my news. He was proud and pleased, gently cheerful, tended by big Jamaican nurses who called him 'love' and 'deary', joking with them when they gave him his nightly Guinness through a straw … would he get a baby 'Power' if he allowed them cut off the other leg? They never got the joke. On 5 April my diary entry reads 'Call from Mary. Daddy sinking.' April 8th '12 noon Daddy died'. Mary and I were with him. Joan was minding the grandchildren. Ruth had not yet arrived in London. It was the day of the Grand National. The day before he had whispered instructions to put five bob each way on the favourite. Every year in the forty-odd years since, each of us, his grandchildren, and now great-grandchildren, carry out the tradition of placing a bet in our local bookies in his memory.

But there was no family harmony that day. Joan raged against Mary who had 'purposely' kept her away from her husband's death bed. Mary kept silent counsel with gritted teeth. I uselessly moved from one to the other trying to broker a ceasefire if not a truce in their long-running battle for Power's love. That night Joan came to my bed and begged to sleep with me. We had never been a demonstrative family, I was rigid with disgust and pity as she lay sobbing beside me. The funeral was a farce of family solidarity, joined briefly by Power's two sisters Eileen and Nora. His brother Joe, who would have brought the warmth of his likeness to Power, was not there, neither was Ruth. The vastness of Highgate Cemetery, the cold anonymity of the unfamiliar burial service left grey images of a bleak day, although it was spring. There was no mourning for Power, none of the comforting Irish reminiscences of the dead man. Tea with the aunts at a nearby hotel, they to return to Dublin, we to Crouch End, each wrapped in our own silent misery. I never grieved for my father. Going straight back to Ireland to the relief of a new life to plan, time and thoughts were filled with the bric-a-brac of practicalities, sadness gladly replaced by joy.

The grief came upon me suddenly, twenty-five years later. I was at the Gate Theatre with a friend, enjoying a unique production of *Three Sisters*, with the three Cusack sisters playing and their father Cyril in the role of the Doctor. He was frail, but a scene stealer as ever, and received the inevitable standing ovation. As we rose to leave with the hubbub of the audience around us, I was overcome with an extraordinary sense of loss – tears streamed down my cheeks and I found myself sobbing violently. I could only sit there and wave my thunderstruck friend away. I, who never cried, often envying friends who can call on easy tears in every emotional emergency, sat there crying my eyes out. Cusack, shuffling around the stage for the previous couple of hours, had forcibly pulled back the shutters of my memory. Power was seared on my inner eye as he was in those last few forlorn years. I pulled myself together and joined my friend in the bar.

'What will you have to drink?' he asked. 'You seem to need one.'

'I'll have a large Power's Gold Label,' I said, 'with a squirt of soda water.'

But the siphons had all gone, along with the black and white china dogs of Scots Bar, Kilkee, Co. Clare, where Power and his 'little Princess' shared those halcyon summer afternoons.

17. La Maison d'Irlande 1967

I made an initial journey to Paris in March 1967 for training but my real schooling was back in Ireland when I underwent what was known then as a familiarization trip. Not being able to drive, I was passed like a parcel from region to region, beginning in Wexford and proceeding round the whole coast of Ireland to Donegal, in and out of hotels, castles and stately homes, up and down historic hillsides, climbing over ancient monuments, and risking life and limb on such far-flung mystic mounts as the Skellig Rock and Knocknarea. These three weeks of exploration provided the key to my lifelong passion for the country that is Ireland and the essential tools of my new job. The major move to Paris with Owen in tow was to take place at the end of April. It was the nearest thing to planning my wedding, without the ceremony but with the going-away outfit, cheering friends and even a honeymoon cruise. After my father's death I threw myself into this new venture. Diary entries consisted of lists: passports, clothes, books, money, bank accounts, travel, hotels, pheno-barbitone for Owen. Owen was equally enthusiastic and highly organized. If passports, money and logistics were my concern, he meticulously put together his painting gear, from travelling easel to rolls of canvas, from basic supply of colours to a tool kit fit for a master carpenter.

Owen was never a traditional present giver – Christmas or birthdays would often come and go without acknowledgment, but he possessed an instinct, as gift-giver, unconnected with the seasons, of choosing something that initially appeared odd or eccentric, but would become increasingly more thoughtful or appealing as time went by. Thus it was with the Mary O'Donnell ensemble, a dress and jacket made entirely of white hand-woven crocheted lace, with which he came home one day soon after Power died. My taste in clothes leaned towards the trendy Mary Quant mini rather than the classic Mary O'Donnell knee-length, and I never wore white, but I accepted with good grace if inner reservations. It was my 'going away' outfit and he insisted I wear it at our farewell party, although I would greatly have preferred my newly acquired dashing purple kilt and matching tight sweater worn with white plastic boots to the knee.

Predictably the Mary O'Donnell outfit was greatly admired in Paris and worn to every embassy and official function I had to attend over the next several years. It was eventually worn by a real bride, my sister Ruth, when she married John Brown in London five years later, fashionably midi-length on her diminutive frame. Like the George Campbell painting, it too has been lost in the wilds of North Ealing. Another going-away gift was an emerald green Foxford mohair rug intended to grace our bed in our new Paris home but I found a far better use for it. Nora Leahy, that most skilful needlewoman, cleverly cut it in two, added a zip and it became my winter cape, again much admired on the Place de l'Opéra and surrounding quartier. Not to be outdone by Owen's generosity, I had bought him a fine bawneen jacket in Millers Tweeds of Clifden on the Connemara part of my Ireland odyssey. Two photographs attest to our patriotic elegance, each taken by the other with Notre Dame as backdrop: we looked carefree, debonair, two Truffaut-style *flâneurs*.

'Le grand départ' started with a flourish of trumpets and ended with a mocking toot. Burdened with being greatly over the baggage weight limits, even in those generous pre-Ryanair times, I had decided to travel by sea; not the normal arduous landbridge Holyhead-London-Dover-Calais route for us but in the legendary *Queen Mary* which was to call at the port of Cobh, Co. Cork on her regal transatlantic route from Southampton via Calais. So on a windy, misty day looking out to sea, like stout Cortez on his peak, Owen and I, with only two or three fellow passengers, boarded a small tender at Cobh harbour and set out, on the disquietingly rolling waves of inside the harbour walls, to reach the mother ship, pulling at her anchor, on the much rougher open sea off the Cork coast. We battled along against a strong head wind for about fifteen minutes when to our despair the pilot announced he was turning back. A signal had come from the *Queen Mary* that the seas were too high, she was weighing anchor, all passengers would be reimbursed or found alternative travel arrangements. Bedraggled and dismayed we were decanted once more in Cobh. An overnight in Cork, several panic telephone calls to Paris and an investment in one-way flights and baggage surcharges landed us in Paris twenty-four hours later, sadder if not wiser from the experience.

We spent the first few weeks in Paris at the Hotel Henri IV on the Pont

Neuf. At 13 francs (just over £1) a night for a double room on the fourth floor, no lift, we could just about afford it, although it meant eating all meals out. After a week of this, even in such cheap bistros as Le Polidor, we began to learn a few tricks from fellow residents, whose rooms often exuded unmistakable culinary odours in the early evenings Subsequent investment in a minuscule spirit lamp, saucepan, two bowls and plates together with a couple of purloined knives and forks enabled us to enjoy café au lait with fresh baguettes in the mornings, while soup and frankfurters with cold tomatoes and salad provided a sustaining evening meal. It was early summer so hot meals were not a necessity and soon replaced by the delicious and cheap array of cold meats, cheeses and quiches to be found in any of the épiceries in the side streets off the nearby rue de Rivoli. As the overworked chambermaid cleaned the rooms and changed the sheets only once a week, we had ample notice of her visitations and removed not only evidence of our illicit cooking but also Owen's painting gear, which gradually took over every corner of the not very spacious room. Luckily there was a tiny balcony, more like a large shelf surrounded by waist high railing, but the floor-to-ceiling double windows opened inwards, and Owen would sit on the single chair with a canvas tacked to a board perched on his knee and work away impervious to everything else until my return from work.

My working life was very different to my first experience in 1960 when I was treated as an inexperienced young girl by kind, caring employers. This time I was a grown-up, employed on contract by a state agency. I was paid a salary and left to my own devices as to how to survive until the end of my first month's employment. I was too proud or shy to ask for help. Accustomed to the mores of the Irish system I kept my domestic arrangements strictly to myself. Perhaps there were rules about non-marital cohabitation in the civil service manual: I remembered that John McGahern whom I used to see sometimes in McDaid's looking like a conventional buttoned-up teacher had been sacked for cohabiting with his Finnish girlfriend. In later years I envied the newer batch of overseas appointees with their generous removal and relocation expenses but as I felt extremely fortunate to have got this great job I never expected any such transitional facilities. Therefore at the outset I led a kind of double life, from nine to six, a smiling saffron-uniformed hostess in the spacious, well-appointed and upholstered (also saffron) *Maison d'Irlande* with floor-to-ceiling glass windows looking directly onto the side of the Palais Garnier, otherwise known as the Paris Opéra. At six I hopped on the number 27 bus down the Avenue de l'Opéra, through the Jardins des Tuileries, along the Seine to the Pont Neuf, in the middle of which lay the tip of Ile de Cité, the Place Dauphine and the picturesque, ancient and cockroach-ridden Hotel Henri IV. We would fall into each other's arms, Owen exhausted and exhilarated pounding the streets of a strange city, me fighting fear of failure at the challenges of the new job: was my French good enough, did I really tell that family the right route from Rosslare to Killarney, could a horse-drawn caravan travel round the Ring of Kerry in a week?

When *L'Office Nationale du Tourisme Irlandais* was officially launched in May, Joe O'Reilly, a Corkonian entrepreneur and pioneer tourism operator, drove a horse-drawn caravan down the Champs Elysées, much to the bemusement of natives and tourists alike. That evening a magnificent party was held in a chateau on the outskirts of Paris. Swirling uileann pipes greeted the guests as they entered, Bunratty Castle singers and a harpist strove to be heard above the noise of the feasting throng, and our own in-house boy minstrel, Justin O'Mahony, played the penny whistle from the musicians' gallery. With little or no idea as to what my role was and with everyone far too busy to instruct me, I took it on myself to act as unofficial barmaid, urging an Irish whiskey or glass of Guinness on the dubious French but with approbation of the myriad Irish expats who had wangled an invitation or just tagged along with friends. It was a night to salute hiberno-gallic friendship in style. But next morning, party over, hangovers on hold, it was business as usual in La Maison d'Irlande with prompt arrival expected at 8.45 am.

A new venture in international marketing, La Maison d'Irlande was the flagship in those uncharted territories 'where no *Irish*man had gone before' and testifies to the post-De Valera, pragmatic Lemass era of 1960s Irish government policy, now discovering tourism as its newest and least tested means of foreign revenue. In another imaginative stroke, an Australian had been appointed to head up this Gallic initiative, though more likely due to the difficulty of finding an Irish businessman who spoke French fluently, or to the self-preservation among the permanent upper echelons of Bórd Fáilte. After all, an unsuccessful foreign national could be safely dumped, should the experiment prove, as many wise heads predicted, a catastrophic mistake.

Barry Maybury was anything but a typical Australian. No blond teak-skinned surfer was he but a spare beautifully dressed adman who had acclimatized completely to France and the French. In 1967 only his booming voice with its strange Aussie twang gave any clue to his antecedents. His French, though fluent had that same twang and often made his staff wince, as when he attempted with heavyhanded jocularity to make literal translations of some Anglo-Saxon phrase; 'That fellow has some guts!' became *Ce type, il a des boyaux, n'est-ce-pas?* (*boyaux* being a literal translation of intestines) followed by shouts of laughter. His junior staff regarded him with some trepidation. We were expected at all times to be pretty, docile and behave like clockwork dolls who were switched on at nine and off at six. Personal problems, period pains, homesickness or broken limbs were all the one to him, inconveniences to be frowned upon and got over without recourse to time off or extra holidays. Woe to the youngest and newest intake from Cork who begged to be allowed go home for Christmas. 'By all means, my dear, we close at midday on Christmas Eve and re-open at ten on Boxing Day, that should give you plenty of time!'

Australian though he was, with as much knowledge of Ireland as he had gleaned from a force-fed induction into its history and culture and a rapid tour of its physical beauties, he had the marketing man's gift of picking the essence of the product to be sold and matching it to the dreams of the consumer to be wooed. The encapsulation of that match made in heaven was a poster that soon adorned the windows of La Maison d'Irlande: a flock of extremely woolly sheep blocking a road in a suspiciously sunny Connemara landscape, a French-registered Citroen and its beaming passengers in their midst.

L'Homme Tranquille had always been a favourite with French cinema-goers; it was almost always to be found in one or other of the art cinemas that abounded on the Left Bank. Now that same cultural French middle class found that they could actually spend *les grandes vacances* exploring those iconic green fields and blue mountains, Ireland became both fashionable and accessible and La Maison d'Irlande was swamped with callers. It took some persuasion to convince the cautious French wife and mother that tourist accommodation, even hotels, existed in Ireland, and that sustenance other than potatoes could be obtained. Staying *chez l'habitant* seemed to appeal most, and the emergence of the innovative farmhouse holiday met with great success, as did anything connected with the equine, hence the horse-drawn caravan phenomenon. So visitors to Ireland morphed, almost overnight, from busloads of Americans whose sole aim was to kiss the Blarney Stone and see the Lakes of Killarney, to the individualistic French who eschewed the touring coach for a horse and carriage and preferred sleeping in rustic homesteads to castle hotels. It was all grist to the rapidly growing business of tourism.

Owen and I, after a full month enduring the malodorous if picturesque eccentricities of Hotel Henri IV, moved to a sixth-floor apartment (*sans ascenseur*) at 51 rue des Ecoles, just off the Boulevard St Michel and, oh bliss, next door to the beloved Le Champo cinema. It was a sublet apartment at an affordable 400 francs monthly from a Sorbonne professor leaving Paris for three months, the longest period we were to live at one address over the next eight months. Anything more permanent was beyond our means, given the necessity of having three months' rent to put down when signing a contract: one month's rent in advance, one month as deposit and one month security guarantee. But as we climbed innumerable stairs to our lofty eminence on the sixth floor we had no fears of the chills of autumn –like the grasshopper, we danced our way through that delightful summer. Long sunshiny days marred only by the inconvenience of my daily attendance at La Maison d'Irlande, the perennial shortage of money and those dreaded stairs.

Justin O'Mahony, first encountered playing his penny whistle at the opening ceremony of La Maison d'Irlande, was a waif, a sprite, a mischievous goblin of a boy-man who had been the first Irish tourism envoy on the Paris scene. He was a beautiful youth with a peaches-and-cream complexion and silky black hair flopping over his forehead. I knew nothing of his antecedents (he boasted a connection with Michael Collins); we were émigrés together, our past lives irrelevant in the excitement of the here and now. It was 1967, it was Paris and we lived in and for the moment. We recognized in each other kindred spirits of the new breed of Irish abroad, middle-class, educated youth out to experience the sixties cultural revolution under a foreign clime. Justin was there before us, spoke beautiful French and had the whole of Paris at his fingertips. He knew who were the movers and shakers of *le tout* Paris, he knew the in *boîtes* and the best bars, and he was an indefatigable imbiber of alcohol and that mysterious substance called 'pot'. I think he fell in love with Owen and was often to be found in 51 rue des Écoles where he would arrive at any hour of the day or night.

After the official opening of La Maison d'Irlande, his exact status became precarious. He had been on some sort of fluid contract to troubleshoot the setting up and launching of the new Irish enterprise. Had Justin had a little more business *nous* and a little less *insouciance* he might have survived the new administration, but as it was he stayed on with less and less to do with La Maison d'Irlande. After about three months he faded from the scene, supposedly guiding top journalists such as Guy Michaud around Ireland and I was not to meet him again after that summer until he re-emerged in McDaid's a few years later, more raffish, more down at heel and more obviously camp than I remembered. There was to be a tragic ending to that joyous, joyful and intrinsically innocent young life. Descending finally into alcoholism and homelessness, he was to die alone in a Merrion Square basement in the 1980s.

Among the images that stand out that summer of 1967 was sitting outside Les Deux Magots on 6 June while cavalcades of cars descended the Boulevard St Germain in a cacophony of three-syllable horn blasting *'IS-RA-EL! IS-RA-EL!'* their passengers waving the blue-and-white Star of David. Many passers-by cheered and waved their approval. Huge popular support for what was seen as a David-and-Goliath struggle between Israel and the Arab world overtook the country. Posters of one-eyed Moshe Dayan in full uniform were in every magazine from *Paris Match* to the left-wing *Nouvel Observateur.* Five days later the war was over and the good guys had won – or so it seemed. Another golden day was 14 July, anything but a repetition of my lonely vigil of 1961 when I wept in self pity and longing for the absent Pierre. This time, it was 'we', not 'I', and we were hosting a Bastille Day party in 51 rue des Écoles. Loads of people turned up: my new colleague Marianne Crowley, she of the fiery head and miniest of skirts, with her current beau, First Secretary of the Irish Embassy Eamonn Gallagher; a roving quasi-Irish journalist, Francis Evers; Mike McBride, the irrepressible son of a Dundalk greengrocer who had come to seek his fortune in

Paris and stayed for forty years; Dorothy Henzell Willis, as spry as ever. Justin played his penny whistle high up on the rooftops as we raised our glasses to the inhabitants across the street before sallying forth to join the festivities on the Ile St Louis, which had its own street party that year.

Owen turned out some great work that summer. He was in a fever of productivity, the heat seemed to suit him admirably. As soon as I left for work, or sometimes even beforehand, he would be at the easel in front of the two big windows, stripped to the waist and working furiously. He painted like one possessed: his canvases seemed to glow with new-found energy and colour, reflecting the hot blue skies and sweltering heat of those summer months. Colour, especially blues and pinks, leapt out of the growing number of canvases lining the walls. There was a marvellously rounded Molly Bloom or at least that was what she was christened, apparently floating mid air on the canvas; the large-limbed but delicate lovers in powerful embrace; the misty blue bridge joining the Ile de Cité to the Ile St Louis, each followed upon the other in a seemingly effortless sequence.

He had met another painter and hybrid Irishman (Sean O'Floinn by name, but little trace of Ireland in his strangled English or dark-hued visage) who spoke vaguely of an Irish father and Moroccan mother and an upbringing in many Mediterranean lands. Sean lived with his French wife Marie-Jo in the Cité des Arts, an elegant modern edifice of apartments and studios on the Right Bank, generously subsidized by the French government. He knew all the angles of the Parisian art scene, and it was he who persuaded Owen to enter a painting in a major International Art Show held that year in Juvisy, just outside Paris. Sean, Marie-Jo, myself and Owen duly attended the grand opening, taking a train from Montparnasse to join throngs of well-dressed invitees in a large exhibition centre in one of the many anonymous new towns springing up on the outskirts of the capital. We wandered through the rooms, helping ourselves to glasses of wine from passing waiters while we tried to find Sean's two and Owen's single entries. It was with a mixture of delight and disbelief that we finally came upon Owen's 'Blue Lovers' adorned with a white card with the magic words 'Médaille d'Or' inscribed thereon. Some time later, having lost Owen, I was standing outside sipping a glass of cool white wine when the loudspeaker crackled into life and the opening speeches began. As I weaved my way back into the main hall, I heard the words 'Prix de l'Or' and 'Irlande' spoken in the same breath ... then a slight pause and a further crackle on the sound system was followed by a stentorian and unmistakeable rendering of *'Anois teacht an Earraigh, Beidh an la dul chun shineadh'* ending interminable minutes later with *'go seasfaidgh me sios I lar Condae Maoigh Eo.'* The rest of the proceedings were painful, humiliating and ludicrous. Owen, shambling, muttering and bellowing 'Fuck the begrudgers', was finally ejected and took off at a crab-like run, still roaring as he headed he knew not where.

Sometime in August my mother made her much planned vist to Paris. She had by now moved to London and was living with Mary in less-than-perfect harmony. Each needed the other: Mary, someone she could depend on to take care of the children outside school and crèche hours, Joan for financial security and because she was loath to move back to the loneliness of Leeson Park. She arrived at the Gare du Nord in the early evening. It was a Friday and I had got off early to meet her. I was not so much shocked as moved to recognize the slight, shabby figure titubating towards me, smiling anxiously, as my mother. It was not to be a very successful visit. It struck me for the first time that Joan had become an old lady at sixty-two. Was it Power's death, her break from the shabby certainties of Dublin, her anomalous position in Mary's household? She had become timorous and touchy, carping and crotchety, and wouldn't venture into the Paris streets on her own. She, who had spoken with such nostalgia of the Paris she had visited as a young girl, was shocked and repelled to find her absinthe-tinged fantasies superceded by the technicolour reality of the 1960s *ville de lumière*, all bustle and brash, where franglais was the lingua franca of its youth, despite the efforts of Le Grand Charles to stop the rot.

My plans for showing Joan the great sights of Paris all evaporated in the presence of this new and unfamiliar Joan, who spent many sunlit hours lying down in the darkened bedroom. Her one expressed desire, to revisit the rue de Rome and seek out the hotel where she and Power had spent their brief honeymoon, was a sad anticlimax. The street was a dirty backwater behind the Gare St Lazare, the hotel, impossible to identify among the many anonymous doorways where girls plying their trade and their shady clientele looked suspiciously on the tourists encroaching on their pitch. The week passed somehow, a disappointing mix of my irritated guilt, Owen's wrung-out patience, Joan's plaintive moans about the heat, the stairs, the traffic, the crowds. Evenings were best, when we would walk away from the hubbub of the Boul Mich, keeping our excursions within a small radius of rue des Écoles, bounded in one direction by the Jardins du Luxembourg and the Cloiserie des Lilas, and the other Shakespeare and Company, where I think she would have been happy to spend the whole week. On her last day we took the number 63 bus to the Musée Rodin, where she regained some of her joie de vivre and became the Joan of old, wandering through the garden, quoting from *Les Fleurs du Mal* and eulogizing about 'The Kiss'. Her faith in romantic Paris was magically, if temporarily, restored.

Suddenly it was autumn. We had played all summer long and were ill-prepared for the chill winds of winter and finding somewhere to live. Sean O'Floinn held out hopes of getting a studio and apartment in the Cité des Arts a pipe dream that melted away the nearer we got to 15 September. We eventually found a *studiocoincuisine* (bedsitter/kitchenette) behind the offices of the left-wing *Le Point* on the rue Dumesnil near Denfert Rochereau in the 14th *arrondissement*. Neither the studio nor the area were at all agreeable: it was a long commute to work for me and, perhaps fortunately, also some distance from the *cinquième* and its social life. Owen began working again but this time very much with a view to returning to Dublin in the near future, enough work in hand for a one-man show.

But he was also drinking heavily, I was never sure where, or even, if, I would find him in the evenings. Sometimes Marie Jo would leave a message to collect him from the Cité des Arts; sometimes I would track him down to Le Petit Bar, beside Shakespeare and Company. Sometimes I went to bed alone, always on the *qui vive* for a noisy return. The morning after one such long night I had a call at work from the Gendarmerie of the 5th *arrondissment* to ascertain if I was indeed the *'compagne'* of a Monsieur 'Valch' who was currently enjoying their hospitality. A more alarming call came after thirty-six nail-biting hours from a social service department who again had a Monsieur Walsh in charge. This time I was summoned for an interview and found myself in an institution of forbidding aspect where I was met by officials in white coats. Owen had suffered an epileptic attack and been transferred to a mental hospital. My *carte de travail* was accepted as a pledge of official bona fides. I was allowed to see him but they would not release him until I returned with a letter from my employer confirming my ability to provide shelter for a foreign vagrant whose *carte de séjour* (note the distinction) would soon expire. I was led down a long corridor lined with locked doors, behind one of which lay Owen in a bulky white garment, arms strapped to his sides in what I took to be a straitjacket, although I had never seen one. There was no furniture in this tiny cell and he lay on a mattress on the floor. We were not allowed to touch – he was conscious but surprisingly passive. He told me afterwards he had been shot full of sedatives and had bruises on his backside to prove it. Twenty-four hours later he was released to my custody and we left subdued and shaken by the efficiency and impersonality of French medical bureaucracy.

Our landlord, however bohemian himself, had lost patience with Owen's drinking so it was back to a hotel room, this time on the rue de Beaune as it disgorged onto the frantic speeding traffic along the Seine's leftbank highway. The hotel was run by two elderly ladies, well inured to unconventional clientele from the nearby Ecole des Beaux Arts. We had a room just as high up, but far less peaceful than old Henri IV. The accumulation of finished canvases and collected bric-a-brac found unofficial storage space at La Maison d'Irlande. Out came the tiny alcohol stove and other accoutrements but the charm of attic existence had worn off, nerves began to shred and tensions throve amidst the rooftops, despite the pensively shadowed photograph of myself at a window, the classic Paris skyline forming a backdrop worthy of Chabrol.

Owen's move back to Dublin became inevitable. I veered between relief and trepidation, both for the same reason. I would be on my own again, free to enjoy my job and that circle of friends without the nagging worry of Owen continuously on my mind. Equally I knew I would miss him – quite how much I was scared to think. Still as we planned I began to look on the bright side. I had booked a week's holiday at Christmas and been assured of another week whenever the hoped-for exhibition would take place. In any event, my contract was up at the end of May the following year, when I could apply to stay on or transfer back to head office in Dublin. What's six months, we said? So in early December Owen returned to Dublin and our correspondence flourished:

108 Baggot Street
Tuesday morning [6 December 1967]

Dear Eileen

Just recovering from a few days non stop meeting people, shaking hands, smiling and of course drinking!! First stop the Dawson with Peter in his new role as proprietor. Then Davy's and the Bailey collecting Kevin, Norman Smythe, Denis (the butcher) so that by closing time there was a mob of about fifteen of us pushing and sweating in the Saturday night chaos at the Bailey; Jimmy McDonald was there and sends his regards, Irene had gone to Kavanagh's funeral in Monaghan. [Patrick Kavanagh died on November 30 1967] It seems a great mob left the city for this and were still arriving back.

Called into McDaids yesterday where all the regulars still operate. Topics of conversation 'Paddy Kavanagh', who knew him well etc and a TV programme that Paddy O'Brien, Dicky and various others of the mob talked about P.K. Met Ruth and Marie Conmee. Ruth is at home and working on the Operas, wondering were you coming for Christmas. The flat however seems to be there. My brother Cathal then called in the afternoon and took me out to the usual round. He's working in Wexford county and is owed £500 fees which he says he'll have to dig out of his employer. However he says he shall be able to get £50 for an exhibition and Mary O'Donnell also said she would supply cash. Also met Deirdre [Owen had sublet the studio to Deirdre Kelly] who had the room perfect and the bedclothes cleaned. Had a charming chat and then she was away down the country to draw some monument.

I am meeting John Behan this evening about the Project Gallery. John seems the chief mover in this group and from what I could gather is completely fed up with the fantasy weaving talk of Mick Kane and satellites, since he seems to run the gallery practically single handed with a wonderful background charm for help. I'll be trying the other galleries this afternoon and tomorrow and am keeping my fingers crossed. Kevin seems to have got the news of the gold medal around with trimmings. I think there was a bit in some paper here.

Thursday

It's grey and spilling rain outside. It has been bitter cold all week finishing with some snow and frost and I'm back now to square one facing the tea and dry bread. But at least I've a little fire going so maybe square one is tomorrow. The exhibition is arranged (I think) for the Project Gallery. They were to discuss this at a meeting yesterday so I'm waiting for news. The show is due at the end of January so I've got a hell of a lot to do in the meantime. This week I expect to go to Drogheda as M. Mary is continuing ill and depressed. Had a few drinks with Paddy Collins a night or two back who is talking of a London exhibition but seems in bad form. I have a feeling he hasn't got the stuff for a show or else that the gallery has got cold feet.

> *All my love and a little bit more*
> *Owen*

Monday
108 Baggot Street

Dear Eileen

I was delighted to hear from you on Saturday and to know you are well and 'facing the next ten days with fair equanimity'. I don't know how you manage that as I have just spent all last night wide awake and thinking about you and your arrival and by 8 am today I was in such a state of heat and apprehension, excitement at you coming, and terror you should not arrive that, had I not suddenly fallen asleep I swear I was on the point of going downstairs and raping old Miss Caffrey. I am now so nervous at feeling you warmly beside me and the thrill of going into you again and all the sensations of loving you of the touch of your hair, the warm body smell you bring and your legs holding me tightly inside you that Dublin seems to have lost its reality and become a shadow of something dark, fuzzy and delightful into which I am diving in like a pearl fisherman looking for the pearl – on your arrival.

PS
Just in case you won't accept the spoken word, I wish to say that I have never loved a woman as I now find I love you.

Christmas at home was a frenetic week of meeting, greeting and loving before my reluctant return to Paris. The much-anticipated exhibition was to take place in February in the newly founded Project Art Gallery, established by a group of artists in Lower Abbey Street.

The formal invitation reached La Maison d'Irlande in mid January and I booked my flight home, excited and terrified in turn as to its outcome.

The Project
31 Lower Abbey Street Dublin 1 Tel 40282
You are cordially invited to an Exhibition of Paintings
by Owen Walsh
to be opened on Tuesday 6th February at 4.30 pm
by the Minister for Finance, Mr Charles J Haughey

18. 'Since There's No Help ...'

Four weeks later, back at my desk at La Maison d'Irlande, the world as I knew it had changed utterly and a desert landscape lay ahead. I copied out, on French blue-squared paper, a sonnet by Michael Drayton and posted it to faithless Baggot Street:

> Since there's no help, come let us kiss and part.
> Nay, I have done, you get no more of me;
> And I am glad, yea glad with all my heart,
> That thus so cleanly I myself can free.
> Shake hands for ever, cancel all our vows,
> And when we meet at any time again,
> Be it not seen in either of our brows
> That we one jot of former love retain.
> Now at the last gasp of Love's latest breath,
> When, his pulse failing, Passion speechless lies;
> When Faith is kneeling by his bed of death,
> And Innocence is closing up his eyes-
> Now, if thou wouldst, when all have given him over,
> From death to life thou might'st him yet recover!

The three line reply came a week later:

To my one true love
And with relief comes loss –
Your untrue love

Although my brain battled to find a reason for the 'cold backside' that I had slept beside on the night of 6 February and the ensuing sleepless nights between the triumphant opening of his exhibition and my despairing return to Paris, my heart quailed and shrivelled at its harsh message. Desire had died and with it apparently all memory of affection, companionship and coupledom. Hints and veiled silences led inevitably to the friend over whose auburn curls I had slipped the Christmas gift necklace of green beads only a few weeks previously. My coded – and I felt dignified – missive positing a phoenix-like revival soon turned into undignified pleas for any signs of life, even abusive ones. All to no avail. Baggot Street was closed to me as if it had never been and the last six years a mirage.

The next few months passed in a muddle of depression and denial. On one level I enjoyed a much smoother existence. I found a small apartment in the Marais district, which I initially shared with Nora Leahy who joined me for a long visit between jobs. Ever dutiful and mindful of Nora's volatility I found myself acting as tour guide at weekends and chaperone at the occasional louche party given by the O'Floinns, or more sedate affairs within the Irish circle of La Maison d'Irlande. I still wrote to Owen, to no one else could I express my lonlieness and panic:

> I can't stay here very much longer. Maybury is coming back from holiday on Monday and I shall tell him I am leaving, where for I don't know. I feel so confused and frightened about the future, I can't bear to be with him and Ann, Marianne and Eamonn, their bright voices and enquiring eyes.

Without Owen as both obstacle to and protector from over-immersion in the official Irish fraternity, and with Nora in tow, I became perforce one of the 'gang' who lunched together, dined together and gossiped together all through that endless winter and spring. The newest recruit to La Maison d'Irlande shy, pretty dark-haired Ann O'Leary, was rapidly transmuting into an elegant Parisienne, sharing a spacious apartment in the rue du Chèrche-Midi with three British girls working at UNESCO. Her siren Cork accent, fey charm, flawless skin and navy-blue eyes, snared almost every male who came within her radius but although she flirted with them all, none broke through the tangle of her enchantment to kiss the sleeping princess awake until the advent of Mike George some three years after I had left Paris.

Would I have warned her, would she have listened if I had? Probably not. Mike was Ann's senior by twenty-odd years, an executive of Pan American Airways, based at that time in Istanbul. He was part of an international set, wealthy, divorced and from a distinguished New England family, raised in international diplomatic circles. Some of Anne's friends were convinced he saw in Ann the ideal girl-doll perfect for the role of consort. Inevitably he wooed her, won her and carried her off to Istanbul to the chagrin of her rejected suitors and widowed mother. For the next ten years, Anne O'Leary became Aine George – Mike preferred the chic Gaelic appellation – five years in Istanbul and five years in Buenos Aires, before Mike decided on early retirement and bought a home in Florida.

It was no accident that Mike George's overseas postings were in cities where he could command a luxurious lifestyle, within the society of a privileged ruling caste. In Istanbul the Georges lived in a spacious apartment in a traditional wooden Yali house in the Babek area overlooking the Bosphorous. Mike's passion was boats: his retirement to Bayou country in Florida fulfilled his dream to have his own marina in the backyard with boat attached. So the major treat planned for my stay in Turkey in 1972 was a trip on the Bosphorus. I was game for anything when, decked out with becoming black-and-white swimsuit beneath my white jeans and nautical striped top, we set out. Admittedly I found the bit between the pier and the boat itself daunting as we were rowed out in a leaky skiff by an ancient oarsman and then had to clamber aboard the boat, which rocked in an unpleasant way in the process. Mike however was soon at the wheel, started up the engine and edged us through the flotilla of small craft out into the open stretch of water. Ann posed gracefully at the tiller while I watched with great admiration as we headed out the bay. Knowing nothing of either the geography or maritime customs of the area I was happy to be wafted along the picturesque waterway, hazily aware that Europe lay on my right and Asia on my left, until we reached the open sea. It was the Sea of Marmara, a major shipping route where small boats ventured at their peril.

When Mike judged we had gone far enough he stopped the motor. Ann was instructed to wield the boat hook and, as we glided by, hook onto a nearby buoy so we could secure the tail rope and so drift at our ease, impervious of prevailing current or tides. Alas and alack, the neophyte sailor, although willing, was not exactly apt and the boat hook somehow caught the buoy at an awkward angle and was snatched from her grasp. With a strangled roar Mike dived overboard yelling to Ann to get the wheel. All went into slow motion before my horrified gaze: Mike in the water brandishing the boat hook, Ann clutching the wheel, the space between man and boat lengthening rapidly. 'Reverse, reverse for fuck's sake!' came his fading roar as the engine sputtered and stuttered, then master and commander swam for his life, still clinging to the boathook, as the boat came straight for him. Aeons later, dripping and white with rage, he regained the deck and snatched the wheel from his bride's beautifully manicured but useless fingers. In grim silence we began the return journey, all thoughts of picnic and lounging banished with our disgrace, as we were treated to a lecture on the vital role of the boat hook in seafaring etiquette and the hopelessness of women in general and Irish women in particular.

Worse was to come when some equally vital portion of the boat's inner mechanism sprang a leak: Ann and I spent the last hour of that endless voyage crouching on all fours 'down below' holding together two parts of a pipe spouting hot oil like a demented geyser, with my sodden T-shirt wound around its broken joint. Terrified by the rain of invective poured over our bowed heads we could only giggle hysterically and pray for the little old man in his leaky but seaworthy canoe to rescue us at last.

It was less of a giggling matter ten years later when I paid a visit to Fort Myers Florida, where the Georges had settled after Mike's early retirement. Mike, even more piratical than before, met me at the airport sporting a red bandana round his gleaming pate. We drove for miles through endless suburbs until we reached their new home. What struck me most was the featureless low-rise density of the wide avenues of identikit bungalows, each on its half-acre of 'yard' no fencing, scrub grass and occasional listless palm trees. Ann, lovely as ever; was there something brittle in her smile, something convulsive in her hug? Mike had no work to go to and was determined to entertain his visitor by excursions to shopping malls and trips on his pride and joy, the neat motor boat moored at the end of the 'yard' on the edge of the mangrove swamp and interlacing canals that surrounded the area, and which was the rationale for the choice of the George retirement residence

With the excuse of shopping and beauty parlour outings we did manage to escape and I learned that Ann's ambitions to go back to college, to get a job, even to do voluntary work in the community were frustrated at every turn by Mike's passive resistance. But she spoke hopefully of holidays with friends and Mike's travel privileges, which still meant they could travel the world for free. In essence when I left I saw my friend as a gilded bird in a gilded cage where her free spirit I knew could not endure for long. Always loyal to Mike whom she defended even after their divorce, she returned to Ireland a couple of years later to begin a new life in Dublin at forty much as she had left Cork at twenty, with an international polish adding an extra burnish to the Blarney *blas*. A new life called for a new name, and Ann O'Leary/Aine George transmuted into Anna-Maria George, who became an extremely successful and sought after tour guide. Speaking fluent French, Spanish, Turkish and passable German, her Bórd Fáilte training never forgotten, Anna-Maria enchanted international coachloads of visitors to Ireland with her charm, wit, and repertoire of folk songs, her beauty undimmed, her spirit revitalized.

The Maharishi Mahesh Yogi became an important personage for the staff of La Maison d'Irlande that spring. Barry Maybury had been converted to transcendental meditation some time previously and we happily joined in the organization of the holy man's upcoming visit to Paris, particularly as it was widely rumoured that one or more Beatle would accompany the Master. For three weeks Barry's office became the headquarters of the welcome committee: invitations were printed, posters run off, press releases distributed and a special phone line dedicated to the event. The nearby luxurious Hotel Scribe was the venue althouth many of the guests on the evening in question did not arrive in business suits or cocktail wear. There were a good many floating caftans, comfortably unisex, many minis, some maxis ahead of their time, and a general sense of gentle good cheer. If the scent of eastern perfumes were strangely tinged with other more acrid substances, no one seemed to notice, and the various odd-coloured teas served made a pleasant change from Irish coffees and were not half so messy.

Disappointingly, not a Beatle to be seen, although someone did say a couple of Beatle wives were in attendance. All in all it felt very much like my papal audience experience; the same sense of expectation, of awe, of uplifted devotion. The Master when he arrived was not unlike his Holy Roman compadre: more simply dressed perhaps, certainly more hirsute, the gold and jewels replaced by rose petals. He too sat on a throne-like structure, surrounded by banks of flowers, smiled and even laughed benignly at us all. When he spoke he waved his hands to and fro as if to an inner melody; his voice was soft, his English guttural but fluent and we strained to listen. The more soporific his flow of words became the more we found ourselves in danger of losing not only the drift but whole sections of his address in a kind of pleasant dreaminess. Perhaps after all that was the secret of his appeal. To succeed in lulling large numbers of normally sceptical westerners into a state of peaceful wonder can only be favourably compared to arousing similar audiences to rage or fear by racist demagogues, or the burn-in-hell clerics of my youth. So 'Go with God, Maharishi, wherever you are in the cosmos, and good luck to you.'

Unfortunately, the Maharishi's message of inner contentment did not impinge on my own inner misery, which I did not bear bravely or well. But even my self obsession was distracted by the événements of May 1968. I had at last summoned up the courage to tell Barry I was leaving and was due to depart Paris on 1 June. As mere foreign residents the coming storm had had little impact until the whole fabric of society seemed to collapse about our ears sometime in early May.

At that time I was living in the rue d'Assas, yet another sublet apartment, and taking the number 64 bus to work, along the Boulevard Raspail past the Assemblée Nationale, crossing the Seine to Place de la Concorde and so to the Madeleine and Place de l'Opéra. The route was important insofar that it avoided the danger spots of the 5th *arrondissement* where full scale *manifestations* were a daily occurrence. This shortlived ability to carry on as normal was interrupted by the stoppage of all Paris public transport when the Communists and the unions joined the students in upping the pace and gravity of the social upheaval.

Like the Windmill in World War Two London, La Maison d'Irlande never closed. Barry Maybury said his girls certainly had plenty of *boyaux* and so we walked to work and back every day for an endless two weeks, an hour and twenty minutes each way for me and Anne, who linked up at the silent Sèvres Babylone *métro*. Apart from the sore feet, we thought it all a bit of gas and took to frequenting the Boul Mich area in the evenings to watch the ebb and flow of the action, compare the *placards* for artistic or poetic merit and wait for the arrival of the squealing Black Marias before discreetly fading away down a side street to safer ground. Even in early mornings when demonstrators and presumably *flics* were girding their loins for the next encounter, the Black Marias squatted like malevolent toads lining the Place Saint Michel and adjoining Seine quays until called into action. This practice continued for many months: it sometimes seemed to me on return visits to Paris that they had become fixtures, like a sort of public art memorial of those May *bouleversements* when the youth of France came close to defeating a government and sending de Gaulle into a second and more ignominious exile.

One evening we had carefully removed ourselves to a discreet café on the rue St André des Arts to await the calm after the storm a couple of streets away. Abruptly the patron ran from behind the bar and shouted a warning; we heard the crash of breaking glass as the plate-glass windows shattered before the onslaught of riot police carrying shields and wielding steel batons. We had time only to crouch beneath the tables covering our heads in vain attempt to avoid the flying glass. Great boots and indecipherable threats loomed about us, then it all receded like a tide and we limped our homeward way, less inclined thereafter to sally forth as carefree observers of other people's history in the making. One harmless middle-aged Dutch lady of our acquaintance who lived in a tiny apartment on the Quai des Augustins was caught up in the melée that same evening on her way home from work – she was cut down by a passing gendarme and ended in hospital with concussion and three broken ribs.

Thus my Paris sojourn ended, chaotically and without farewell parties. I returned to Dublin, half hoping for, half dreading what might lie ahead.

19. The Web – and the Webbing

This re-entry into Dublin life was less triumphant and less remarked upon than in the heady days of 1962. Now twenty-seven, without a job, without a home, a more grown-up attitude to life was called for. Joan was living with Mary in Crouch End childminding her two much-loved grandchildren while Mary worked at the BBC and carried on an increasingly discordant relationship with her two-year-old daughter Nancy's father Reg New. Ruth, still surviving in Dublin theatreland occupied Leeson Park where I unpacked my bags until a better offer presented itself.

Without much effort or planning on my part I found myself working with USIT, The Union of Students in Ireland Travel Company. I had met Gordon Colleary and Sean Dempsey in Paris earlier in the year when they were liaising with their French counterparts, setting up student charter flights between Dublin and Paris for Irish students. This created requirements for educational and holiday opportunities in Ireland for French students imminently expected to fill those same charter flights in the opposite direction. Who better equipped to supply a suitable menu of Ireland's attractions than one Eileen O'Mara, late of Paris, France, French-speaking expert in all aspects of Irish tourism?

USIT not only had a young clientele but everyone who worked there apart from Mr Barrett the accountant who must have been at least forty was young too. Anyone over twenty-five was looked on as positively middle aged, although possibly only the big boss, Gordon Colleary, and myself fell into that category. Although not tall, Gordon gave the impression of bigness, his voice, his round curly head on a distinctly rotund frame, his gestures, his gait, all exuded a sense of being larger than life. He was the first person I met who could be said to have that much-vaunted quality of charisma. We all adored him even if he made some of us a little nervous as his ideas came faster than he could verbalize: they issued forth in short bursts of staccato speech with often some stammering in between as if to give his listeners a chance to catch up. I shared the office next door to his on the first floor of 5 St Stephen's Green, the neophyte student tours department, which I shared with my immediate boss Sean Dempsey and his secretary Terry.

Sean was a very different entity to Gordon. Younger than me, he was a somewhat pedantic young man with a dry sense of humour and a gift for sound business management, which the mercurial Gordon badly needed to keep his wilder flights of travel world domination in check. And Gordon did dominate the Irish travel industry scene for the next decade. He had a genius for the charter game and matching political nous in establishing trading partnerships with kindred student travel organizations right across the globe. Gordon had been president of the student union just a few years earlier when he had the idea of setting up a travel company specifically to match students' desire for travel with the charter flight concept then beginning to develop the package holiday market to sun destinations. Many a USI President in those years cut their commercial teeth in USIT where they represented the students' union shareholding in the company: Richard O'Toole, Howard Kinlay, Eamon Gilmore and Pat Rabbitte are a few who come to mind. As a company and as a fast-growing force in the holiday, educational and tourism travel sectors, it was looked on askance by the older, wiser travel chiefs of the day. Blithely unaware of any tut-tutting in the outer world, the band of iconoclastic youth in which I now played a role pushed all the boundaries creating exciting new ideas and forming commercially successful ventures in the process.

My own small part of the grand scheme was to translate all my carefully acquired knowledge of Irish tourism into experiences that would appeal to the new youth market, who, for the first time ever could travel to Ireland by grace of the cheap student flights beginning to criss-cross the cities of Europe. Remembering the popularity of the horse-drawn caravans but finding it difficult to persuade the owners of these fleets to entrust their wagons or steeds to students, we convinced Gordon to buy sixteen of these vehicles, which were entrusted to the care of a cute Kerryman with a bit of land outside Tralee. It was my job to dream up a seven-day itinerary along the Dingle Peninsula of no more than fifteen miles a day but chock full of monastic sites, Celtic crosses and fabulous beaches, while our Kerry friend made deals with friendly cash-hungry farmers at the appropriate intervals to supply feed and water for the horse and allow the caravan to park on their land.

Another venture was to purchase a decrepit hotel in Lisdoonvarna, the Royal Spa, and use it as an international student centre. My scenic tours of the Burren, Connemara and the Aran Islands all began and ended at the Royal Spa. The male denizens of Lisdoonvarna, then undiscovered by anyone except for very old ladies in search of a seaweed cure, could not believe their luck. For the half dozen years or so the experiment in hotel-keeping lasted, the town thronged in July and August with streams of the *jeunesse dorée* of Europe. The West of Ireland programme was particularly popular with the Scandinavian market and, as USIT was operating a weekly return flight to Stockholm, the arrival of tanned blonde Swedish girls on a weekly basis made the town's September matchmaking revels pale into insignificance. The Royal Spa lifted its Victorian skirts and danced the summer weeks away. Musicians flocked to play in the bar, ceilidh were held twice weekly; more was achieved in that shabby hostelry to popularize Irish music across Europe than Ceolteóri na hÉireann ever imagined.

Another notion of mine was to create a series of coach tours especially for students and young people with an interest in Irish history and culture. I soon discovered that even if the students themselves were not overly culturally inclined, their parents and schools were, and there existed a network of earnest study tour organizations, especially in France and Germany, where this kind of travel for educational purposes was government subsidized. Soon I had devised a suite of what came to be known in the industry as special-interest tours of Ireland, ranging from the literary 'In the Footsteps of Yeats and Joyce' to the archaeological 'In the Footsteps of Pre-Christian Celtic Ireland', with some minority hikes towards the 'Footsteps of Ireland's Flora and Fauna' or even the 'Footsteps of Irish Rebels 1798–1916', although the latter fell out of favour as the bloody seventies dawned: with their horrors came a decline of interest in carefree holidays in the green, now red-stained fields of Mother Ireland.

As a side effect of all this activity came the realization that I was supposed to return a profit on my creativity. I learned, and came to enjoy, the process of negotiating prices for the bed and board of my tour passengers together with the cost of a coach and driver per day, divided of course by the number of passengers. Additional items such as entries to places of interest or the services of a tour guide had to be calculated into the mix, and having come to a full total of the cost per person, I, once and once only, communicated this, net, to my French counterpart. Sean Dempsey's horrified reaction to my proud display of mathematical accuracy taught me the cardinal rule of all business transactions: 'Where the hell is the mark-up?' I never forgot again.

The perils and pitfalls of learning to be a handling agent as the role was then known, became apparent over that first year, and had the tours department been obliged to survive on normal commercial criteria my career in USIT would have been shortlived. But the indulgence of an employer whose primary activity lay in transport with tourism seen as a carrot to attract those precious 'bums on seats' allowed the luxury of trial and error to get us through the learning curve and develop the business to a respectable level of competency and quality.

I quickly learned that a good tour guide was the essential ingredient to a successful tour and satisified customers. Practitioners of one of the most underrated vocations, these highly important persons could make or break a coach tour. The good ones were entertainers, historians, psychiatrists and sheepdogs, the bad ones phoned the office three times a day on pay phones to complain about the lunch stop, the driver, the hotel facilities in general and their own room in particular: their groups were always 'difficult' and they doled out the requisite amount of information in boring chunks of facts, dates and historical accuracy. In those early days we naturally gravitated towards recruiting student guides, then as now, in search of summer jobs, they had some expertise, one supposed, in their chosen field of study, literature, history or languages and their native wit supplied the rest.

On one disastrous occasion I hired my old Parisian colleague, Justin O'Mahony, to accompany a group of French teachers on a week's tour of Ireland. All went well for five of the seven days. In fact Justin sober was the ideal tour guide, knowledgeable on every possible aspect of Irish life and culture. On boring bits of the road he sang and played the penny whistle. On the fifth evening his unnatural virtue collapsed under the strain of good behaviour and he got riotously drunk. The teachers from Alsace were not impressed. His drunkenness might have been forgiven had he not tried to get into bed with one of the younger male passengers, but that was a bridge too far, even though he called on Oscar Wilde as a character witness.

My favourite guide that first year was a youth of undoubted flair who was surely destined to become a major success in the world of Irish business. He had one critical and po-faced client on a weekend tour of Dublin and Wicklow who sat in the front seat of the coach daily, underwhelmed by either the scenic beauties of the Garden of Ireland or the Georgian squares of Dublin city, his head buried in the *Blue Guide*, checking everything the unfortunate guide had to say. On the last leg of the City Tour, just before the group were to be decanted outside the USIT office, the obnoxious gentleman pointed to a stone figure astride a horse, just opposite the College of Surgeons. 'Who is that?' he asked sternly, 'I cannot find a reference in my guidebook.' 'Oh that?' said our tour guide, quick as a flash, 'That, of course, is Mr Stephen Green himself'

Another early project set up by Usitours, as our department became known, was the School of Irish Studies, which had an honourable twenty-five year lifespan after its formation in 1969. The school was the brainchild of Sean Dempsey enthusiastically assisted by me. There was an unfulfilled demand from American colleges for a summer school in Irish studies of sufficient academic integrity to be recognized for accreditation within the US university system. Dr Maurice Harmon of UCD became the first Dean of Studies, Patience Ryan the first administrator, the first premises 27 Harcourt Street, an early USIT investment in the property market, acting also as the grace-and-favour home of a struggling radical newspaper *NUSIGHT,* edited by a young disciple of Gordon's, one Vincent Browne.

A considerable amount of Usitours funds went into this fledgling and risky enterprise. Sean, always the perfectionist, insisted on top quality in everything from print production to major marketing campaigns in launching the school to Ivy League colleges across America. The first glossy A3 brochure in full colour on heavy art paper, its logo a perched blue eagle from a detail of a Harry Clarke stained-glass window, matched anything in the racks of contemporary art magazines. Its creator Joe Kelly was a gifted designer and he and his wife Bernie became great friends of all of us for many years. The secret of the school's success was the partnership between the business acumen of Sean Dempsey with the commercial backing of the Usitravel Group and the scholarly integrity of the school's academic content. Respectability was backed by the line-up of its lecturers who were all leaders in the field of Irish studies and attached to either UCD or Trinity College during the academic year but free and willing to take up other opportunities in the summer months. The pampered young Americans who travelled to Ireland in those years, some of whom frankly draft dodgers of the Vietnam War, had the privilege of learning about Irish literature from the likes of Augustine Martin and a young David Norris, to see Newgrange with Michael Herity or Peter Harbison, hear poetry readings from Thomas Kinsella or Seamus Heaney and get their first taste of Irish music from a young uilleann piper, Paddy Moloney and his recently named band, The Chieftains.

In due course Dr Michael Scott, husband of the great short-story writer, Mary Lavin, became Dean and my sister Mary New took over the role of administrator from Patience Ryan on the latter's departure to Rome, another neat loop in the happenstance of our family story. Sadly the partnership between USIT and the School fell away in the early seventies. By now the USIT empire had spread its tentacles all along the west side of the Green as far as Dawson Street: Usitours in number 4 Stephen's Green, Travel Agency and the charter tour operator Blueskies in number 5 next door, in number 6 administration, accounts and the print department (*déjà vu* in Sean O'Sullivan's old studio), Group and Educational Travel in number 7, then skipping the august disapproval of the United Services and Stephen's Green Gentlemen's Clubs, the USIT Flight Department, slightly removed from the vulgar commerciality of its sister enterprises, burst the seams of number 11.

All of these offshoots were set up as commercial companies under the broad umbrella of the USITRAVEL group. USIT alone retained its core identity and status under the aegis of the Students' Union of Ireland, whose presidents, turn and turn about, cut their teeth on the realpolitik of business. By the early seventies Usitravel had grown too large and too fast and even Gordon's ability to keep all the balls in the air was in jeopardy. Bank strikes and oil crises, over-expansion and negative cashflow finally took their toll. Overnight it seemed Allied Irish Banks took over the Usitravel Group including Usitours and the School of Irish Studies. With what was felt to be undue haste, accompanied by a whiff of UDI, the academic directors of the school applied to our banker masters for a divorce on the basis that it was inappropriate to have an institution of such lofty status connected to what was now a purely commercial travel firm. The bankers duly obliged and the school re-established itself with a prestigious board of governors as a non-profit institution, not unlike a co-op made up of academics instead of farmers, with any risk of surpluses painlessly transmuted into fees. Thus the school continued a happy existence, eventually as a year-round college mutually beneficial to students and their tutors, for another twenty years.

In my parallel universe I resumed my obsessive relationship with Owen Walsh. Months leaked into years, the pattern formed and reformed, high tides of passion and hope receding to lows of rejection and regret. Owen spent the winter after my return from Paris in Donegal, caretaking a remote manor-style guesthouse on the shores of Lough Swilly. Every second weekend I would take the evening bus to Letterkenny, which took about five hours with a stop in the Central Hotel, Monaghan, for welcome hot sweet tea and Goldgrain biscuits. Then by taxi the five miles or so to Ardrummon House, where Owen always had a blazing fire and a big plate of Irish stew to welcome me. It was an idyllic spot: the house, well back from the road, was on high ground sloping steeply down to the rocky foreshore. A delicacy was soon added to the somewhat basic household diet – mussels abounded on the low rocks and, shod in wellies, we would gather them by the bucketful, especially when we had guests. My new entourage in USIT were soon included in these Donegal escapes, attracted by the extremely comfortable accommodation available and the freedom its remote location gave to young couples in search of love away from parental or censorious eyes of landladies. One young couple I was especially delighted to entertain in Donegal was Sean Dempsey and his new love Gráinne Sheridan, daughter of Martin and Patsy, who had joined the Usitours team and swiftly, with all her mother's slow charm, won the boss's heart and embarked on a love affair that was to endure for the next forty-five years.

Eamonn Gallagher, late of the Irish Embassy in Paris, was a frequent travelling companion on the bus journey north. He was, he told me 'resting', like an actor between productions, awaiting a posting to an overseas embassy. His family came from Donegal and he often spent his weekends with his elderly parents. I wondered at his filial devotion but came to accept his occasional visits to Ardrummon House even though he made a slightly awkward addition to the younger guests in situ at the time. After some time he asked me to broach Owen with a request to hold a dinner party one Saturday in November for some guests he would like to entertain but for whom he didn't have suitable facilities in his parents' home. He would supply the food and plenty of wine and would even pay us for the privilege, on the understanding we would prepare the meal.

With the promise of help from my colleague Ursula Fox, who had already proved her worth in the kitchen, we agreed. Eamonn delivered the joint for roasting the evening before with strict instructions to keep it 'hanging' until the next day. Intrigued, we were presented with a fine haunch of venison, acquired from a local illicit source. I was aghast, never having laid eyes upon such a beast in Paris. Ursula was made of sterner stuff, saying it looked just like a very large joint of beef, even if darker in hue and bloodier; the oven was plenty big enough and we would just give it an extra hour's roasting. We had collected a fresh bucket of mussels that morning: cleaning so many of them was a major chore but we found a machine in the kitchen whose use we had never established; however if you loaded it with mussels and turned on the switch, they rattled around noisily for a couple of minutes, emerging clean of all sand and grit. Peeling the potatoes was entrusted to me while Ursula perspired over the oven and its contents. She even managed an apple tart of gargantuan proportions. I laid the large table in the formal dining room, never used by ourselves, with the best china, glass and cutlery I could find in the pantry and even added an old candelabra found on one of the shelves and made a last-minute call to Eamonn to bring some candles.

The evening went off splendidly even though we were not invited to join the party. Owen swore he wouldn't have any part in the whole scheme and had retired to the room upstairs he had stripped down for a studio. Ursula and I went in and out a few times with the food, Eamonn taking charge of the wine, and even brandy as we discovered after they'd gone and we sat down exhausted to devour the remains. To be fair, several bottles of wine remained untouched as well as half the brandy so Eamonn's guests were a reasonably sober lot. Sober and serious too – a boring crowd we decided. We had a drink with a couple of them who arrived early and seemed pleasant if not very chatty. Why Eamonn was making such a fuss about these nondescript, crumple-suited young men who told us they were from Derry, we couldn't quite figure out. It was several months later when the whole Donegal episode had ended in farce that I recognized their faces in the *Irish Times*: one was Ivan Cooper and the other John Hume, founder members of the SDLP. Eamonn's mission had a touch of John le Carré about it, his domestic weekends *en famille* a cover for some early cross-border intelligence-gathering with a new breed of nationalists who were marching the streets of Northern Ireland, sowing early seeds of fighting generations of violent prejudice with peaceful political protest.

The beginning of the end of that winter idyll in Donegal had a lot to do with the fire brigade. We had quite a gathering in the house over New Year 1969. Norman and Silvia came with baby Paul, now an extremely lively three-year-old, remarkably like Norman in baldness and rotundity. Mary arrived from London via boat, rail and bus with brown David and blonde Nancy and proceeded to put order on the household. Owen, the genial host, busy with charcoal put the children down on paper for posterity, until, predictably, both they and he got bored, with largely similar reactions of yells and flounces off to seek more congenial company. After a late-night ringing in the New Year, all slept late, Mary alone arose to clean up the kitchen and rake out the fire in the lounge, specially lit for the occasion ... not before time as it turned out. The tiles around the fireplace were hot to the touch and she could see glowing embers and small flames through the gaps in the floorboards. She first called the fire brigade and then roused the household. The doughty men from nearby Ramelton were on the scene within half an hour, doused the fire and a good deal of the furniture, told us we were right to have called and warned against lighting another in that location. However the story was too good to keep to themselves and soon the tale of the buxom redhead in a night-gown, the long-haired brunette in a green caftan, the English lady in jeans and wellies, three children, one of them black, one half-naked artist and one large bearded gentleman went the rounds of the neighbourhood. It might be said to have added fuel to another fire, this one of rumour and delicious innuendos of goings-on in the Big House. The almost weekly succession of 'fine things' downing pints in the pub in Ramelton, coupled with the occasionally pictur-esque behaviour and language of the 'quare artist fella' in permanent residence and glimpses of some of his work on display, led first to the tale of young women being painted in the nude, and in true Chinese whispers, concluded with the shock and horror of 'blue movies' being shot on the premises.

Inevitably the aghast owners sent in notice to quit three months before the due date. Bad enough to have to return to a cold and moneyless winter in Baggot Street, but a summons was also delivered for the caretaker to appear in the local district court charged with conducting a house of ill repute and inflicting wilful damage to the owners' property. Owen duly appeared in court some weeks later. We had time to get some legal advice from good friend and later sheriff of Dublin, Brendan Walsh. Owen was to throw himself on the mercy of the court and produce respectable citizens as witnesses to his good character and blameless record. Norman Stewart and Sean Dempsey, suit-ably suited, with genuine business credentials, spoke earnestly on his behalf, quoting his illustrious artistic career and producing a character reference from Mother Mary Martin, which probably clinched the matter. The case was dismissed, despite evidence being brought of the misuse of a valuable item of kitchen equipment, one potato peeler, which emanated a distinct stench of stale fish. Our hero celebrated his escape all the way back to Dublin, insisting on stopping several times en route, memorably in Omagh, where he was finally bundled back into the car shouting 'Up the Republic, Up Mayo', as wiser and more sober heads headed rapidly for the border.

By the end of 1969 the family chessboard shifted again. Mary had been living in London for most of her adult life: her two children were born there and her father died there. It was a big decision. I imagine that with Power's death, the stability built on that loving relationship fell away and she began to question the rationale of keeping a home going with an incompatible partner and a mother with whom she had never got on, but lived with in a state of mutual dependency, Joan by financial necessity, Power's O'Mara pension having ceased on his death, and she for childcare.

There was also the issue of the family flat in Leeson Park. Matters came to a head when the landlord threatened eviction due to almost a year's unpaid rent. Ruth's employment opportunities in Ireland had completely dried up and she too had moved to London, where she found a clerical job with the Post Office 'just to tide her over'. In those days of secure tenancy rights, the fixed rent in Leeson Park was £3 a week: the flat was old-fashioned but spacious with a fine back garden and in an undoubtedly sought-after residential area of Dublin. Mary took the decision to return to Ireland permanently. Letters sped to and fro between Mary and me and Joan and me, Mary's full of lists of what should be jettisoned and what she would need to have shipped across the Irish sea, Joan's of fretful plaints of what was happening to 'her' home and why she was never consulted. In what must have seemed the sensible thing to do but was in retrospect disastrous for the continuity of legal tenure, Mary changed the lease to her name, taking over responsibility for paying off arrears in the process.

At least Joan returned to home ground and met with a warm welcome amongst friends in and out of familiar Dublin pubs. Mary too found life in Dublin easier to manage. There was plenty of temporary secretarial employment in Ireland's first mini boom and she was soon to find a permanent niche in the School of Irish Studies where she became the lynchpin of the management of its student body and smooth running of its entire administration. The children seemed to slot in easily too, although David's colour and London accent were to attract intermittent bullying in the years to come, none of which reached home circles. David's colour was a no-go area within the family, 'David is David,' said Mary, fire in her eyes, 'I won't hear the word colour mentioned' and that was that. Nancy was only three and attended a crèche – she was a quiet little girl who adored her big brother.

Mary took to life in Dublin with gusto. Our social lives crossed but didn't always meet. Owen painted a fine portrait of her, looking queenly, and also one of David, which now hangs in Nancy's home, a daily reminder of her much-loved brother who died at the age of thirty-eight. Social life as always back then centered around the pub. There were two pubs in near proximity to Leeson Park, which Mary found congenial and closer to home than in the more far-flung haunts of Grafton Street and Baggot Street, where she could be her own person rather than Joan's daughter or my sister. The Leeson Lounge, run by Kilkenny man Paddy Clancy, as its name suggests was a comfortable, soft-cushioned bar, whose prices were always a couple of pence higher than the next-door O'Brien's, hence its more business-suited clientele.

O'Brien's, on the other hand, was old-fashioned and hadn't changed its decor in thirty years. The pint, however, was a superior beverage to what could be found next door and the clientele more eclectic. There was Joe the Gas, retired glimmer man of the war years, rubbing shoulders with Professor Robin Dudley Edwards, who often shared an early evening pint in silence, the vernacular of each being equally incomprehensible to the other; Deirdre O'Connell often joined them sitting up on a high bar stool on her way to the evening show at the Focus Theatre, her red hair and white skin translucent against her perpetually black attire. The inseparables: long-bearded, bare-chested architect Tomas O Beirne and his petite raven-haired wife Marie sipped their gins and tonic, Tomas pontificating, Marie beaming.

Flash forward to the eighties when bright-eyed Michael Hartnett slipped in and out, sipping his brandy and milk like a necessary but unpalatable medicine. On one memorable occasion he enchanted the girls from my office with his sly magic and whispering west Limerick lilt. There's a photograph of Michael, gleaming and smiling, surrounded by young women he bewitched without ever reading a line of his poetry. I have a paperbook volume of his translations of Ó Bruadair with the inscription: 'Eilín, This is the first of the trilogy. I couldn't find the hardback. The next, given O Bruaidaig's blessing, will be Haicead. And then with yours, it will be O Rataille. Love Michael Hartnett.'

In 1970 when Mary entered the portals of O'Brien's, the anchorman in prime position at the end of the bar beside the sometimes odorous Gents was Mervyn Ashman, who held court there 363 days a year. A portly middle-aged Protestant gentleman, he was the final arbiter of who was to be accepted within the O'Brien's inner circle, and who was left to wilt in the outer wilderness of his disapprobation. Owen Walsh was persona non grata, whom he glared upon if ever within range of eye contact. Owen's appearances in O'Brien's were rare enough; it became an unspoken agreement between us that Leeson Street was my territory and Baggot Street his, and, post our final friendly parting, we shared those spaces by invitation only. Mervyn's only challenger for head honcho status was Terenure man Ken Mulvany, who was equally at home and welcome in either hostelry.

At first and also second glance, Ken Mulvany was an unlikely match for

Mary O'Mara New. He was a confirmed bachelor of some forty summers, a successful marketing manager in a major US multi-national and a rugger-bugger to boot. He had the remains of a rugby player's fine physique, somewhat altered by a steady diet of Guinness. His genial personality belied a sharp mind and an unlikely but passionate interest in bird life. He was a popular figure on the Dublin social scene and a certain sound of teeth gnashing was to be heard in some of the more genteel bars and rugby club pavilions in Rathmines and Rathgar during the following few months as Ken fell for Mary like the proverbial poleaxed bull.

But to return to the move back to Ireland of Joan, Mary and her children in autumn 1969, the frail basis for family unity soon showed signs of strain. For a time the ménage in Leeson Park appeared to work. The family had settled into the repainted and refurbished flat but, not far from the surface, relations between mother and daughter deteriorated. Papered over again and again, they were opposites in every way. Love was there but buried by a lifetime of misunderstanding and mistrust.

The end came in the form of tragic farce – a call from an indignant Joan to come immediately and rescue her brought me hot foot to Leeson Park. At the top of the steps Joan sat be-turbanned in lonely dignity on her garden chair, clutching her handbag and a holdall containing the Russell letters, the alabaster Buddha, her silver looking-glass, the leather-bound volume of Tennyson and her King James Bible. A truce of a kind was cobbled together but it was the end of the road. A note from a friend dated 24 June reads: 'I was delighted to hear from Eileen that Count O'Kelly has located a room for you in Leeson Street – what a blessing, and it is so central for you.' Count O'Kelly was a philanthrophic papal count who assisted indigent gentlewomen on the lines of the Royal Society of that name in Scotland. However, my mother was to have a last big adventure of her own making before settling down in her new home. With a surprising burst of energy and courage, she quixotically answered an advertisement for a lady housekeeper on a stud farm in Co. Meath, met the owner in the Shelbourne Hotel packed her suitcase and decamped to Priesttown House in early July. It seems to have been an eccentric household, straight from a Molly Keane novel, which amused, rather than scared, her. She didn't stay long and only a fragment of a letter to me remains to tell the tale:

> It seems nobody stays here, because they get nothing to eat. There is a deep freeze full of meat, which 'your man' warned me not to eat. He said 'it's poison, the animal was diseased'. I wish I could write it all down as he said it. He told me he used to live in the house (I assume with his wife) ... the previous owner who had lived till she was 95, having been widowed 50 years before and being childless. He said it was a real home then, proper staff, parties etc. Now there is only a daily woman and she has not turned up since

last Friday. He warned me they would have me doing the cleaning, and of course this is obvious. I am already doing the washing-up but I am determined not to sweep the floor. You may say I should not hob-nob with the servants but it is <u>too</u> fascinating. There was a frightful row on Sunday with an apprentice jockey who couldn't get his wages. He threatened to beat up the boss and I don't blame him. He has since left and gone back to England. He had stayed longer than anyone – 7 months!

Joan's career in Co. Meath lasted until September when she took up residence in her last home in Dublin, a bed-sitting room on the second floor of number 67 Lower Leeson Street at a rent of £2 2s a week.

20. *Mourning My Mother*

On 13 May 1971 I met Joan for a lunchtime birthday drink in Neary's of Chatham Street. It was a happier time in Joan's life and she was enjoying a new sense of freedom in her Leeson Street bed-sitting room. Fresh circumstances and a modicum of distance had made for a reconciliation and a more balanced relationship with Mary, and, while she was still in regular contact with her grandchildren, she was no longer responsible for their after-school charge. Although it was tough going for a lady on the widow's pension, supplemented by childminding and my fiver a month, a couple of factors kept her spirits up.

She was very excited about Ruth's impending marriage to John Brown. The happy pair had come to Dublin on a visit, full of plans for a future built on Walter Mitty dreams, but nonetheless appealing for that. On her return to London Ruth wrote to Joan:

> As regards us, we are as happy as ever, if not more so. John is now quite determined to buy a house; it will take some time obviously, but if we ever achieve it John says you are welcome any time. (I must point out that John doesn't say things like that without thinking about it and meaning it.) Unfortunately that is in the indefinite future, but it will be happening … I'm sorry you seem to be going through a bad time. The most I can send you at the moment is £2, today is John's birthday, so that has set me back a few bob including a bottle of wine and steaks for his birthday supper.

The O'Mara dynasty, Limerick 1896 (*above*): James O'Mara (*foreground*) with (*left to right*) great grandson Stephen, grandson James and son Stephen.

Joseph and Bríd O'Mara, son Power and daughters Moya, Eileen and Nora (London 1906).

Power O'Mara and Joan Follwell (Salisbury, England, 1930).

The wedding of Power O'Mara and Joan Follwell (Salisbury, England, 13 May 1932).

Left: Power and Joan O'Mara at Cruises Hotel, Limerick (1945).
Right: Eileen's First Communion (Sacred Heart Convent, Roscrea,
Co. Tipperary, June 1948).

Left: 'Mater' and Edward Follwell with Eileen (Bournemouth, England, June 1950).
Right: Power with Eileen (Kilkee, Co. Clare, July 1952).

Mary, Joan, Eileen and Ruth O'Mara (Dublin, September 1953).

Mary O'Mara (1954).   Ruth O'Mara (1954).

Eileen in Paris (March 1960).

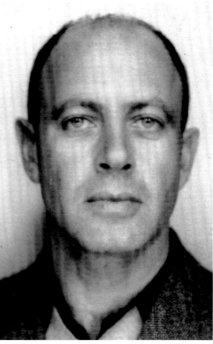

Pierre Catzeflis (Paris, 1960).

Anne Leahy and Joe Hackett (*far right*) at their wedding (Moira Hotel, Dublin, January 1962).

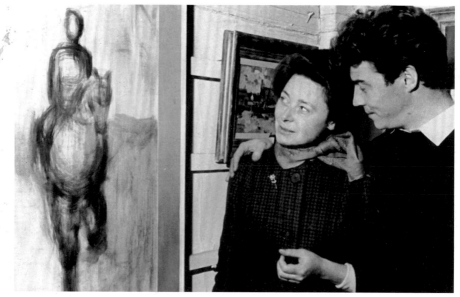

Owen Walsh with Siobhán McKenna (Dublin Painter's Gallery,
St Stephen's Green, April 1964).

Left: Brian Bourke and Michael Kane at the Hackett wedding (1962).
Right: Owen Walsh (1966).

Milo O'Shea and Anna Manahan, in Joseph Strick's *Ulysses*, with Eileen and Silvia Stewart (Dublin, June 1966).

Eileen and Owen on the Clare Island ferry (August 1966).

Eileen in Paris (May 1967).

Owen in Paris (May 1967).

Another plan germinating in Joan's mind for some time also came to fruition. A yellowing article cut out from the *Observer* (31 March 1968) reads 'Russell Letters Sold to Canada' with an account of the sale of Bertrand Russell's vast collection of letters and papers to McMaster University in Ontario for a world record sum of £250,000. Daringly, she made approaches to possible sources of interest, including Christie's, to whom she sent a sample of the correspondence, and received a cautious reply: 'We would be pleased to offer them on your behalf, but naturally the price we quote depends on the importance of all the letters.' In June 1969 she confided in Terence de Vere White, then literary editor of the *Irish Times*, who was most encouraging: 'You should write to Lord Russell while he is still alive and ask for permission to publish them … without that you are spancelled…', and in a later letter: 'Will you think of writing some of your memoir for us? It might get a publisher interested. Think it over, I might be able to help.'

She did meet with de Vere White and showed him the letters and talked at some length about her memories of the great man but never followed up on writing the memoir he suggested. To her chagrin, she learned that he had used her story in a novel written soon after they met. Thankfully she was spared its publication. The character of Rita, central to the plot of *The Radish Memoirs*, is a recognizable but deeply offensive caricature of Joan in shabby old age, down to those 'bockety' shoes and stained smoker's teeth – a cruel and cynical breach of trust.

Bob Bradshaw offered to introduce her to the agent who had sold his letters from Brendan Behan but bruised by de Vere White's behaviour, Joan took no further action until sometime in the early summer of 1970, when, coinciding with the upheaval in her domestic situation, she was fortunate to meet with an honest broker. Philip Pettit was a young Ph.D student in the Department of Ethics and Politics at University College Dublin. He entered into negotiations on her behalf directly with Kenneth Blackwell, the Russell Collection archivist in McMaster University. After some months, many heart searchings from Joan and a great deal of unrewarded patience on the part of Philip Pettit, a deal was struck. Not without a degree of *angoisse* on Joan's part as her letter of 4 November indicates:

> *Dear Mr Blackwell*
>
> *Mr Pettit has forwarded your letter to me and I am sorry to tell you it has made me angry. Possibly the misunderstanding was on my side. I agreed, after much mental conflict, to let you have my Russell letters at a derisory figure in present day terms, because I am a romantic and felt they should be in the Archives, where scholars, after I am long dead, might read and use them. What cheered me up was that I thought you had commissioned me to write a book – an introduction, autobiography, call it what you will. But £50!!*

And my tape-recording, though I say it myself, was marvellous. It seems, according to your letter, the copyright in this is mine and you will send me a copy. I have been waiting quite some time. Also I believe it is customary to be paid for such recordings.

I am sorry to appear mercenary. I believe my letters and my association with Bertrand Russell to be of considerable interest. I have kept them for 40 years and have not attempted to barter them in the open market. I don't understand legal documents. I have no solicitor. I live as best I can on a widow's pension. If and when you send me a copy of the tape-recording I shall probably not have the money to pay the customs duty.

Mr Pettit has acted for me out of the kindness of his heart. I think you might have shown a similar generosity. I refer particularly to the tape, which, guileless as I am, I can see is quite unique. Please send me a copy at your earliest convenience. Meanwhile I shall think the whole thing over.

Yours sincerely
Joan O'Mara

The aforementioned tape was recorded earlier in the year by a young McMaster research graduate named Pollock and Joan was right in thinking it unique. I found it twenty years after her death on a large spool which I had transferred to cassette. I immediately listened to it in my car and both wept and laughed to hear her familiar, slightly posh voice, nicely lubricated by a couple of whiskeys with which I imagined young Pollock must have plied her. She was prosaic, flirtatious, funny, nostalgic and a little pathetic, all at once.

In spite of these hiccups, agreement was finally reached and the contract duly signed in March 1971, the final offer being increased by 10 per cent. So Joan received the sum total of £330 for her treasures, not an unreasonable offer at that time, as Mr Blackwell rather stiffly informed Philip:

> It compares favourably with a recent purchase we made at a New York auction, where we bought five letters by Russell concerning his second divorce and three miscellaneous items, not by him, for $140. This is about £10 per letter, compared to our new offer to Mrs O'Mara of about £12 per letter, with no auctioneers profit to be subtracted...

Considering bank interest on savings was about 15 per cent, this nest egg represented an added security to Joan's perilous finances. Happily, bridges were mended with Kenneth Blackwell, to whom she wrote on 8 May, 'I am glad they are in the archives where they belong and I like the idea of some scholar discovering them long after I am dead ... they present such a contrast to the "permissive" society of today. We believed in "true love" but we were "sérieux" au sense francaise du mot.'

The same ironic deity who seemed to have always overseen Joan's fortunes with a less-than benevolent eye must have taken umbrage at this onset of good luck, because, less than a week after writing that letter, on leaving Neary's, the day of her birthday, Joan tripped on those bockety shoes she always wore, fell and broke her hip. I was alerted sometime later in the afternoon and found her in considerable pain in a ward in nearby Mercer's Hospital. Her hip was duly reset but somehow it did not seem to mend. I would visit her between two and three, Mary in the evenings. Sometimes she would be holding on for dear life to a walking frame, with a nurse on either side, attempting to take tottering steps while pleading to be allowed back to bed. At first hopeful, then increasingly querulous, she was not an easy patient, continually asking the busy nurses to make phone calls and making little lists: 'clean nightie … blue cardigan … *New Statesman* … safety pins, Basildon Bond envelopes … cheese … Goldgrain biscuits … phone Pat Broe … John Jordan … Daisy McMackin'. She couldn't eat the hospital food and her normal thinness became skeletal. One day as I stood at the end of the bed, she stared straight through me out of hard pebble-brown eyes. Walking back to the office passing the Gaiety Theatre, I met Terry, Sean Dempsey's secretary, who stopped to ask how my mother was. I found myself weeping. 'She looked at me like she hated me.' The doctors said she would have to be moved to a nursing home. Mary and I had many councils of war: what to do, how could we pay for it, should we use up her recently acquired nest egg … but what then? Mary, of a more pragmatic bent, wrote to Joan's brother Eddie in England, as far as we knew now comfortably retired from a lifetime in senior public service, and also to Power's sisters. All expressed sympathy but none offered financial help. 'Let's wait and see … Joan has always had her ups and downs … I'll do a novena … let us know what you decide.'

I met a doctor on the stairs as I was going up to see Joan one day in late summer, who stopped me and said: 'You know of course that your mother is mentally ill – we are transferring her to St Brendan's where she'll be well looked after.' Grangegorman! The most notorious lunatic asylum, unchanged since Victorian times; the very word had nightmarish connotations. It was a long bus journey on the number 10 almost up as far as the Phoenix Park. We took it in turns to visit. Mary turned up trumps, fought with the system, cooked delicacies to tempt Joan's non-existent appetite and fed her spoonful by spoonful out of a Thermos flask. Just walking into the building required courage: the smell of urine, faeces and boiled cabbage hit as soon as you entered the long ward. Patients would be wandering about apparently unsupervised in various states of undress, sometimes slumped into chairs with the stuffing hanging out, the seat fabric long since destroyed by urine. Joan's bed was at the far end of the ward with a fairly clean seat in the corner that we tried to secure for ourselves. Strangely she seemed more cheerful, less fretful than in Mercer's, and took a great deal of interest in the other inmates, whispering accounts of their sayings and doings with an amused, if slightly manic glint in her eye. What broke my heart most was to see the gradual disintegration of her sense of self. Her refinement and exquisite prudery seemed to coarsen and fade over the weeks that followed. One evening she asked me quite casually if I would wash her back – she who eschewed nudity and was physically modest to an extreme degree was now oblivious of taking off her vest and allowing me to sponge her down in the full public glare of the open ward.

In October Joan developed a continuous chesty cough, was often feverish and became more and more distracted and confused. Mary kept up a barrage of letters to the doctors – as we could never get to meet one – insisting she have some medical attention. Finally they diagnosed a bronchial condition and transferred her, yet again, to St James' Hospital. Joan was put under medication and a drip installed to add glucose and rehydrate her system, and she seemed to rally both physically and mentally.

With a distinct feeling that the tide had turned and somehow we would never let her go back to St Brendan's, I set out on what was now a regular series of European sales trips, this time to Germany. It was a Monday and an early flight brought me to Frankfurt by lunchtime. I went straight to the Irish Tourist Board office for a briefing and met with Gunther Pulzeimeyer, Barry Maybury's equivalent in the German market. I had hardly reached my hotel later that afternoon when a call came from his office. An urgent message had arrived from Mary. 'Come home. Mummy sinking.' A scramble to the airport, our friendly airline holding the flight by twenty vital minutes got me back to Dublin on the same day I left. When I arrived at the hospital Joan was surrounded by tubes with an oxygen mask over her face, breathing harshly. She died later that night. I don't know if she knew I was there or not. The next day the hospital performed an autopsy. I had to go to the morgue to identify the body. She looked tiny, shrunken, her wispy hair stuck to her skull. They gave me her handbag and her wedding ring. I wear it still. The autopsy report recorded she had died of undiagnosed lung cancer. Uncle Joe said the funeral Mass in Gardiner Street. He was a beacon of gentle light that dark November day as he said the last prayers over her grave in Glasnevin Cemetery, the O'Mara family plot that she shares with Joseph and Brid O'Mara and their daughter Maura, who died in childhood, all strangers and strange bedfellows for her. There is one place left in that plot, which Mary, who wishes to be cremated, has agreed will be mine.

21. Troughs and Travels

A miasma hangs about the months following Joan's death. It swirled around me, through me, infiltrating my mind and even my body with a sense of depletion, of drift and weary days to be got through somehow. Joan used to quote, 'Things fall apart, the centre cannot hold.' I never understood what it meant until now. I clung to my job like a liferaft in a sea of grey. My need for a pay cheque obliged some regular presence in the office and grasp of day-to-day essentials. I lived in squalor: never interested in cooking or housekeeping, my flat in Herbert Place became squalid. I stopped washing up, I stopped washing my clothes, and eventually I stopped washing myself. For the first time I began to understand what Ruth found at the bottom of a bottle of gin, except in my case it was vodka. I sat home night after night with the curtains drawn and my Rentel TV permanently on. If friends called I wouldn't answer the door but watched behind the curtains until they went away. One evening I sat in front of the gas fire going through a bag of my mother's letters to me in London and Paris and, drunk with self-pity, I tore them up: nary a one survived, to my everlasting regret.

The catalyst that spurred me to recovery came in the hirsute shape of a man in the travel business I had always despised. When I woke up beside his snoring body at 3 am one cold March morning I spent the next two hours wrapped in a blanket on the sofa and by the time he sheepishly left for home, wife and children, I had promised myself 'never again'. Owen, whose attitude varied during these months between rough sympathy and rougher intolerance of my self-indulgent grief, took a hand in the cure. I came home one evening to find the kitchen cleaned, the bed stripped and my clothes piled up in a corner of the bedroom. 'You'd better get some of that stuff washed,' he said, 'we're going to Madrid on Friday.' For a week we stayed in Anne and Joe Hackett's apartment on Ferraz and immersed ourselves in the city. Late mornings lounging in cafes, afternoons exploring the Prado and the Reine Sofia and evenings living the life of the *barrio* with Anne and Joe, sipping *tintos*, munching tapas with an occasional more generous *ration* to fill the pangs of hunger. It worked. I came back refreshed, the black depression lifted and I functioned once more as a useful member of the USIT team.

Summer came and with it Mary's wedding to Ken in University Church, St Stephen's Green. Owen gave the bride away. We set out from Leeson Park, Mary in a black-and-scarlet maxi dress, myself in mauve with white plastic boots to the knee, Nancy and David, who wore a bow tie for the occasion, Owen, hair to his shoulders, in the bawneen tweed jacket. Everyone was in the church when we arrived. We hurried through the vestibule and then hovered outside the door, unsure of the etiquette required for the entrance of the bride. We noticed a sacristan also hovering in the vicinity until it dawned upon both parties that each was waiting for the other. Understandably perhaps the poor man had not recognized us as the bridal party. But he rallied and gave the signal to the organist who struck up the Wedding March and Owen Walsh walked Mary O'Mara New up the aisle, where good Uncle Joe did the honours in fine style.

I was then living in a two-room flat facing the canal in Herbert Place just beside the Huband Bridge, a favourite not only for poets and painters but a distinct band of aging Dublin prostitutes, whose patrol stretched from the less-frequented city side of the canal from Leeson Street Bridge to Huband Bridge and around the back of the Pepper Canister Church. Any unaccompanied return home at night was always trailed by a series of slow-moving vehicles that swooshed with pleading or bellicose whispers, 'Are you in business?' 'Any chance of a ride?' 'How much for a quickie?' as I trotted along, pretending deafness and longing for a cloak of invisibility. I had great sympathy for the unfortunate middle-aged ladies whom I saw nightly from my sitting-room window climbing into the cars. Owen and my male guests took a more ribald view, timing their comings and goings and working out the average evening takings on the beat. It was here that I learned to drive in John Brown's stately two-toned Austin Cambridge, which spent most of its life parked beside the canal, brought out only for major excursions, in the meantime providing a substantial cover for pedestrian punters who inveigled the ladies into an exchange of favours behind its comforting bulk. As Oliver St John Gogarty said of other canalside fixtures, it was 'more sinned against, than sinning'.

About this time USIT was expanding its range of charter flights to the USA and Canada, offering Irish students, for the first time, work opportunities in America, vastly more appealing than the traditional canning factory in Leeds or Manchester. Deals were done with the US State Department allowing bona fide college students a three-month entry visa known as the JI Visa, in practice a work visa for the summer months. This entailed the compulsory registration of students for an International Student Identity Card, entitling bearers to travel and other desirable discounts worldwide. The printing and production of the student card itself became a valuable source of income for student union offices on university and technical college campuses throughout the country, all of which also had a travel office in situ, thereby ensuring guaranteed flows of business to the USIT reservations centre in Dublin. I regret to say a modicum of slick forgery was a feature of the early days of the scheme, until more modern technology spoiled the fun. Several persons of my acquaintance who might have been considered somewhat mature for a college education somehow acquired this precious piece of official student status. I, as a USIT staff member, had access to cheap flights in any case, in much the same way as regular airline staff, which privilege Owen Walsh also came to enjoy.

In the summer of 1972 Owen received an invitation to visit the US and paint a mural in a Catholic church in Connecticut. It stemmed from a friendship that had developed with an American couple, the Tavernas. Tony Taverna was a large Italian American: voluble, domineering and greatly in love with his petite, red-haired Irish wife, Mary, whom he had met on a transatlantic flight when she was an Aer Lingus air hostess. He had made a lot of money in what he vaguely described as 'the insurance business'. A Republican to the core, he gloried in the 'American way' and valued little in Europe except his wife, for whose sake he trekked across the Atlantic at least twice a year with their three little girls to visit Mary's family in Dublin. Her sister Eileen was married to an up-and-coming bank manager, Michael Fingleton.

A restless man, Tony always had to find something to do or someone to talk at to make his trip worthwhile. He came across Owen Walsh and they took to each other enormously. Tony eschewed pubs and could not understand the appeal of smelly, shabby premises predominantly peopled by middle-aged men, where, worst of all, no food of any substance was to be had. He was an early foodie and expounded on the infinite varieties of pasta when spaghetti bolognese was still only occasionally to be seen on Irish restaurant menus. When Tony and Mary were in town we met in the Royal Hibernian Hotel for a civilized lunch or in the evenings went to the trendy new Quo Vadis in Suffolk Street or Bernardo's near the back of Trinity where Tony could at least order in his strangled Bronx Italian. Tony had become an art connoisseur since meeting Owen, and indeed a generous patron. He loved the four-by-five-foot portrait of his wife, insisting on a scale suitable for their Connecticut library. Mary's red hair and green outfit, also Tony's choice, were treated by Owen in an oddly lurid way on the canvas and in the process took on some of Tony's cheerful vulgarity, but both sitter and patron were delighted with the result so I kept my reservations to myself.

Hence the letter inviting us to come to the States in September and spend some time at their home in Greenwich, Connecticut. Tony, a devoted church-goer, had commissioned a mural on the raising of Lazarus to be executed by the famous Irish artist, Owen Walsh, in honour of his endowment of the church's Medicare Trust for the underprivileged. With the confidence of Mother Mary's Drogheda murals under Owen's belt, so to say, we booked our flights. A special staff offer on one of the last flights of the season cost £12.50 round trip apiece. Finances and the dollar exchange rate were not in our favour but as we were to spend the first night on a complimentary basis at the Penn Garden Hotel in Lower Manhattan, the USIT New York headquar-ters, and were to travel out to Connecticut by train the next day, we felt secure enough with our joint stash of $60 to see us through. To our great dismay, there was an apologetic note from Tony awaiting us at the hotel, putting back our visit by forty-eight hours due to some domestic crisis. We knew no one else in New York apart from a Westport friend of the Walsh brothers who worked in an uptown Irish pub. Our $60 was already reduced to $50 after the bus fares from the airport and a hamburger dinner and we knew we could not afford to stay even for one more night at the Penn Garden at $25 for the cheapest room. Ever the pragmatist, I decided that Greenwich Village would be the cheapest place to stay and to this end we scoured the ad section of *The Village Voice,* where I found a bed and breakfast advertised in West 22nd Street for $14 a night, double.

We sallied forth next morning, leaving our luggage in the hotel, and walked the ten blocks or so to 22nd Street, which we assured each other seemed fine, if a little run down. The rooming house, identified only by its street number, had a sign on the door 'Walk Up', which we did to find a well built Afro-American lady sitting on a high stool behind a counter on the first landing who looked at us dubiously when we said we had reserved a room by telephone. However, in exchange for one night's down payment, she gave us a key to Room 17 'Up two more'. The room possessed a large bed but the rest of the furniture consisted of a plastic swivel dentist's chair complete with headrest, a three-legged table leaning against the wall and a bare bulb hanging from the ceiling. We sat on the bed for a few minutes listening to some myste-rious grunting and groaning next door and then went downstairs. The lady had gone and so had our $14. Wordlessly we turned into the bar beside the 'hotel' to find sustenance and discuss the situation: it was down a few steps, dark and very dimly lit. Owen ordered two beers, we looked around conscious of the sudden silence that had greeted our arrival and realized we were the only white faces in the place. A hum of conversation soon took up again. We sipped our beers, saying little, and left, walking quickly back towards the hotel. Somewhat subdued neither of us mentioned our doubts to the other but tried to keep our spirits up by planning the great shopping spree Owen was going to treat me to when he got paid for the commission.

That afternoon, before collecting our luggage, we decided to track down the Westport man in the Blarney Stone Pub. Not daring to venture into the subway we found a bus going all the way up to 95th Street and with great good fortune Jack Hoban was on duty and delighted to see us. He served us big pints of beer and pastrami sandwiches, which we devoured while pouring out our story, half laughing, half fearful of our predicament. We never did discover whether our 22nd Street experience was to end in laughter or tears. Jack, visibly shaken, sternly forbade us to go near the place again and pronounced we had got off lightly with the loss of only $14. He promptly insisted, with true Mayo hospitality, that we move into his apartment for the two nights. Not only that, he pressed a $20 dollar bill into Owen's hand and insisted he take a yellow cab to the hotel and back for our luggage.

I enjoyed this small window into Manhattan life, rode the buses up and down Third and Fifth avenues, found my way to Macy's and Gimbel's Bargain Basement and walked through Washington Square in memory of Joan's revered Henry James. I also had time to squeeze in a real James Cagney experience of my own. Leaving the two men in bed on our last morning I headed out from our Riverside Drive apartment house; halfway down the long flight of steps from the hall door a squeal of brakes, a popping sound and the noise of shattering glass stopped me in my tracks. Two cars had mounted the pavement before the house: the occupants of one were held straddled across the bonnet of the other by one pistol-brandishing gentleman while another, looking straight, as I thought, at me, pointed his pistol in my general direction and said the immortal words 'Hold fast, there!' As I wordlessly backed up the steps I had descended so lightheartedly, his eyes turned away and I turned tail, arriving breathless minutes or hours later to bang on the door of the apartment, pleading entrance. By the time the Mayo men had heard me and let me in, the scene on the street had disappeared. Was it a heist, a drug bust, or just a local scrimmage? It made my day and many a pub and party story in the weeks that followed. The Tavernas at least were impressed when we finally met up – in fact Mary confessed she had never been on a New York bus or travelled beyond 34th and 59th Street in any direction and now never intended to after my adventures in the outer wildernesses of Manhattan.

Our stay in Connecticut was tame by comparison but nonetheless memorable. The Tavernas lived in what came to be known as a 'gated community' with an armed warden permanently on duty at the entrance, for all the world like a sentry at an army post. Inside all was green, pleasant and open: large sprawling bungalows and two-storey mansions set well apart surrounded by extended yards bounded by tree-lined walkways. Interiors were very 1960s with a sort of Doris Day/Rock Hudson decor, all pastels, cushions, drapes, sofas and labour-saving open-plan kitchens. The artist was set to work immediately. Mary Taverna drove him to the church every morning, where the twelve-by-eight wall space waited to be covered in oils. Owen, ever precise – not to say prissy – about his preparatory work had all his sketches with him, duly drawn to scale, and had sent on an order for paints that Tony had collected in advance. During those pleasant late September days, Mary drove me round to visit neighbours or the pretty towns nearby, carbon copies of each other with their streets of quaint shops selling art or antiques or books, stopping now and then in equally quaint coffee shops for 'coffee and cookies' before heading back home to prepare dinner from the contents of the enormous fridge freezer. I learned that Tony did most of the food shopping. He took me with him one day all the way to Little Italy in Lower Manhattan where he bought his Italian groceries. I was fascinated not only by the shops teeming with Italian voices and Italian smells but by Tony's effortless metamorphosis into a quintessential Latino, complete with waving arms, rude sign language and raucous exchange of insults. Forty years later I was to see him come to life on the small screen, playing another Tony, Tony Soprano.

The following year, 1973, Mary and Ken bought a house in Sandymount, the first property owned – or at least half owned – by an O'Mara for thirty-odd years. It was an opportunity for me to take possession of Leeson Park, which I gladly did, a real home after a series of pokey flats or the dubious comforts of intermittent lodgings at 108 Lower Baggot Street. It was full of memories of teenage years, and of Joan, battling with the rat in the kitchen, confronting Marie Conmee, hosting the brown-paper-bag brigade, or just sitting in her dilapidated deckchair in the neglected back garden enjoying the sun, gifted with that Protestant skin of course.

The move coincided with another low period in my life with Owen who had been quietly supportive in the year after Joan's death but was once again straining against the leash of my devotion. My diary of this time reads:

> Owen's obsessive sexual tenderness, as if he wants to possess me to a state where he can anesthetise me … I think it's his way of comforting me for his infidelity, as though I become sexually more attractive through his sleeping with someone else. Out of the blue he brings up the subject I've been brooding about since Mummy's death – having a child. I had never considered it seriously before. I knew Owen would leave me. Now I feel differently but thought it would mean deceiving him. In this long night he talked about it for the first time, said if I had the courage, he would stand by me. But would he – how much of this is the sentiment of the moment?

These seesaws of breakdown and renewal were increasing the dichotomy between my chaotic private life and my growing professionalism within the mainstream tourism industry. I began to travel extensively on behalf of the company and expanded the range of the Usitours youth clientele to the more lucrative adult tourist, shifting focus to the North American market. To this end, I became the company representative on a number of travel trade associations, such as ASTA (American Society of Travel Agents) and their British counterpart ABTA, which entailed attending their annual conventions as part of an Irish sales team of airlines, hoteliers, tour operators, car-hire and bus companies and the many other variegated strands that made up the Irish tourist industry. So it was I found myself in Las Vegas, Hawaii and Acapulco, surreal experiences for a young woman who was looking forward to going home to a cold-water artist's studio in Baggot Street, Dublin.

Returning to Dublin from these sorties into high living was inevitably a shock. I found myself more and more alienated from the spartan comforts of Baggot Street and settling with increasing domesticity into Leeson Park. I even acquired a cat, named Sophy, given to me by Deirdre Kelly for my thirty-third birthday in 1974. Somehow with Joan gone and with Ruth only a summer visitor, I found less reason to spend my leisure evenings in McDaids or Nearys. When I did so, it more often than not depressed me to see the same tight group performing the same minuets of glower and grimace, with the ghosts of Behan, O Nualláin and Kavanagh hovering at their shoulders. It made me sad to see John Jordan becoming more like an El Greco figure than ever, his boyish head, white face and slim frame attached somehow to a bar stool gazing mournfully into a gin and tonic cupped in those long tapering fingers. Sometimes he would rouse himself to come over and talk about 'dear Joan' and tease me gently about her constant refrain of 'my beautiful Eileen'.

It must have been around this period that my professional access to cheap travel became of interest to the McDaids set. Kevin Monaghan spoke wistfully of attending the twenty-fifth anniversary of D-Day celebrations on Omaha Beach, but the antique business was at its perennial low ebb so I organized a cheap return boat and rail ticket to Calais via London and we launched him from the North Wall one bright June day. Less than a week later Kevin turned up again in McDaid's. We hung on his every word to hear the saga of meeting old comrades in arms, treading in the sandy footsteps of his former glory and saluting the stars and stripes through the mists of nostalgic tears. Alas, a short stop off in London hostelries and other vague mishaps en route resulted in him landing in Calais without the wherewithal to go any further so after a fruitless and largely foodless, if not wineless, twelve hours on French soil, Kevin was forced to beat a tactical retreat, returning non-stop this time to Dublin. Initially somewhat crestfallen, gradually the oft-told story of those twelve hours, where Rodin's burghers, the hôtel de ville and the bistro whose *patronne* treated him to a bottle of her best cognac and a *baguette au fromage* in honour of les *braves soldats americains* became his field of dreams and the failed mission to the fields of war mattered not a jot either to Kevin or his listeners.

Another episode that nearly cost me my job. One evening in McDaids I foolishly recommended a bargain basement student flight to Corfu, seats available to staff and friends for £10. How Bob Bradshaw got hold of a passport is a mystery but he and two friends duly set forth on a Greek odyssey, the friends in question being John Jordan and McDaidian honorary medical doctor, Richard Riordan. I should not have been surprised by a call three days later from the Greek police department on Corfu to say they were holding three Irish men for repatriation on the next available flight. Drunk and disorderly was a tolerable offence but the attempted seduction of Greek boys on lifeguard duty was not, at least in the time of the Colonels. Bob was most upset, more at the slur on his heterosexual reputation, than any embarrassment on my behalf. The others had had a wonderful time and were blithely unrepentant and their experience soon took on the legend of a brave three-man protest against the colonels and the Junta.

I mainly went to McDaid's to meet Pat Broe, now my closest woman friend, whom I admired for her struggle to survive as a woman poet while holding down the role of mother and recent widow in a male society Her husband Des, stonemason by trade and sculptor by aspiration, had died a macabre death in 1969, choking on a piece of food hurriedly eaten one ordinary weekday lunchtime as he ran down the stone steps from the hall door. Pat was some ten years older than me, a *jolie-laide* who could drink any man under the table and often did. Her tongue never failed her. Even when her other faculties deserted her she had an unerring instinct of spearing just the right pimple of the soul's anatomy, impaling her victim till he or she bled for mercy. Sober, she was lovable, loyal, hardworking and a fount of understanding and wisdom at least for me. Pat loved her three sons, Damien, Dimitri and Darryl, with a fierce maternal pride, and it was for them that she took on the management of Broe Monumental Sculptors in Harold's Cross where she kept the books, took the orders and dealt with mourners while her brother-in law-Noel, and eventually Damien, hewed the stone and etched the inscriptions in the small stoneyard adjoining Mount Jerome Cemetery.

In the immediate aftermath of Des's death Pat took several lovers more in a sense of bravado than any real lust or love for the recipients of her favours. It became clear that Pat's real sexual preference lay with women and her friendship for me changed in nature to real if unrequited passion. Sober, she would discuss the superior virtues of Sapphic love quite dispassionately, drunk she became tearful and importunate, which in later years estranged us, although not so finally as her maudlin espousal of Provisional IRA obscenities in Northern Ireland.

If Pat Broe was volatile, even ambivalent about many things including her own sexuality, she was unwavering and obstinate in her self-belief as a writer and poet. She wrote under the name of Patricia Reid Broe and all the years I knew her, jealously hoarded time for writing – with three young children, no mean feat. I wasn't sure to be shocked or envious when she proudly displayed the Yale lock she had fitted to her bedroom door, behind which she remained, impervious to the roars of the boys in permanent danger of breaking one or several limbs as they rampaged throughout the rest of the house, their daily battleground. An extrovert in most other dimensions, she was shy about her work and I saw little enough evidence of it, although she did publish occasionally in one or other of the poetry broadsheets that abounded at the time under the editorship of Hayden Murphy or James Liddy. Her great friend and mentor was the poet Pearse Hutchinson, who encouraged her to write in Irish, and in the mid seventies she took on the self-appointed task of translating the short stories of Pádraic Ó Conaire and decamped for a year to Maoinis, a tiny almost-island near Carna in the Connemara Gaeltact, with her youngest son Darryl.

It was on one of these visits to Maoinis that I met the Fennells. Pat brought me to meet her neighbours, Desmond and Mary Fennell, who lived on some high ground nearby in a newly built bungalow, filled to bursting, it seemed to me, with innumerable energetic children all speaking at once in indecipherable Irish at the tops of their voices. It was indeed 'the high ground'. Desmond Fennell at that time had all the attributes of a latter day High King of Connaught, writing voluminously and persuasively about the logic and merits of a federal thirty-two county Ireland with Connaught standing alone and self sufficient in its Gaelic pride and purity. That first evening he lectured Pat and me on the unassailable merits of *Eire Nua* and the cause of the Provisional IRA. I felt more at ease with his wife Mary, especially when we figured out that her mother, Dr Troy, had been our family doctor in Limerick in the 1940s. The fact that Mary worked, teaching Irish and French as the *Banisteóir* of the local school, while Desmond stayed at home, seemed at odds with his position as head of the family and anti-feminist views; I was convinced that neither Germaine Greer nor Betty Freidan were to be found on the Fennell bookshelves.

22. 'Babies and 'Bathwater

I was overcome with terror and delight when I realized I was pregnant in autumn 1974. If a miasma surrounded me after Joan's death, quite a different mist enveloped me during my pregnancy: light filled, it was a fog nonetheless, through which the outside world seemed insubstantial and remote. Owen had spent most of the late summer in a friend's house in Ballinskelligs, Co. Kerry. He had been commissioned to paint some Kerry landscapes for the dining room of a new Waterville Beach Hotel under construction at the time. The developer was his friend Padraic Burke, an entrepreneur of the best sort, young, energetic and prepared to take risks, both in business and as a patron of the arts. As I worked flat out during our busy summer season, we didn't see much of each other and Owen, in a reversal of roles, seemed to feel the separation more than me. I then set off to the USA on one of my regular sales trips just as he was heading back to Dublin. On my last day in New York, I was handed a telegram as I stepped into the elevator at the Irish Tourist Board's offices in 590 Fifth Avenue. My heart sank – telegrams could only mean bad news. It read: 'Longing for home, bed and you. Owen.' I must have blushed up to the roots of my hair. My companion, a rather straight-laced Bórd Fáilte executive, asked was I all right. I muttered something inane and clutched the precious piece of yellow paper tightly. I found it recently along with some of my other more heart-scalded notes.

I knew straight away I was pregnant. I didn't have to wait for an overdue period – it was a sensation I had never felt before. I had given up taking the pill at least two years previously, but convinced myself (or had I?) that having taken lots of risks in my twenties it was unlikely to happen in my thirties, when I believed both my fertility and Owen's would be on the wane. Owen's first reaction was stunned silence, then before I had time to say more than it was my right to decide he rounded on me and declared that if ever I tried to get rid of *his* child, I would never see him again. That settled, I set about planning the future, first and foremost securing my economic survival and ability to hold down my job. Not an ideal job in the circumstances: too much travel, uncertain hours and weekend work only too frequent. Within a month I had produced a new company strategic plan in which I suggested merging the travel agency and tours department with me taking over as operations and programmes manager, while a new post would be created for a marketing and sales manager. It would mean a largely nine-to-five office based routine with minimal travel involved. Now under AIB ownership, Sean Dempsey, Usitravel's general manager, approved the plan and recommended it to the board. By January 1975 I had changed positions, perhaps to a less glamorous role, but one that would suit my coming change of lifestyle very well.

Not for me a wretched pregnancy, skulking under the disapproving eye of Catholic Ireland. I was unaware or unconscious of any social obloquy. I had the support of the man I loved, a secure and convivial job, and an enthusiastic if startled circle of friends. Mary and Ruth, in their different ways, were joyful on my behalf and even my one remaining aunt, Nora, was congratulatory, albeit in a regretful tone. An occasional missile came my way, but they were too unimportant or irrelevant to be angry about: the male colleague who laid bets on the parentage among his peers; the Bórd Fáilte executive who invited me to lunch, begged me seriously to consider adoption for the sake of the infant, and warned me about the taunts of ille-gitimacy awaiting him or her when they went to school. That last observa-tion, however, gave me to think, and a young solicitor, Brendan Walsh, son of my parents' old friend and legal adviser Brendan Snr, was surprised to get a visit from me one day, instructing him to change my name by deed poll to Eileen O'Mara Walsh. He pointed out I could call myself whatever I liked, but no half measures would do. I wanted it legal, so that when this yet unknown offspring was going to school, it would bear both its mother's and its father's names. Similarly, I decided I would undergo the coming ordeal as a private patient and so consulted a gynaecologist in Fitzwilliam Square: the fee (including hospital stay in Mount Carmel) was to be £1000, about 20 per cent of my annual salary at the time. This dapper gentleman took me smoothly under his care, asked no questions and gave me a cursory examina-tion once a month until June and then at two-weekly intervals. I was healthy as a trout and developed no particular oddities, unless eating green olives as if they were Smarties could count as peculiar.

I was indifferent to any gossip or raised eyebrows in the world outside my immediate circle and carried on in my job as usual. Full of energy during that spring and summer, in May Owen and I travelled to France on the new Rosslare–Le Havre ferry, driving my recently acquired white Peugeot. This, a badge of my new management status, gave me great pleasure and I had no qualms about venturing into the unknown realms of left-hand drive on the Continent, as Europe was referred to grandly by the travelling elite. The purpose of the trip was to research a tours programme to Europe, with France first on the list. I was going to inspect and select a number of routes, hotels and campsites in Normandy and Brittany that, coupled with a deal with the ferry company, would be the basis of package holidays for Irish motorists. It was an idyllic time for us both. As I was dutifully trekking around hotel bedrooms, Owen, his travelling easel over his shoulder, sketched and painted a series of luminous landscapes, once more imbued with the blues and golds of French sunlit days. Damp canvases and crayoned sketchpads tracked our journey: Honfleur, Caen, Mont St Michel, St Malo, and Dinard on the first leg, then to the wilder, more familiar coastline of Brittany, a sunnier Donegal in un-French-sounding Breton villages such as Plougastel and Douarnenez.

A door to the past opened briefly in Pont-Aven where we stopped in tribute to Gauguin. Tired and a bit cross due to our competing navigation skills and sense of direction, we pulled up at an anonymous-looking Hotel de la Poste in the centre of town. We settled for a dull room with no view and went down to the bar for a drink. It was lined with paintings, but not the usual gay tourist daubs – these were of a period of thirty or forty years previously, mainly dark and heavy landscapes interspersed with portraits of robust girls in peasant dress. A taciturn, middle-aged woman served us silently and we were glad to leave for a well-lit and lively bistro nearby. Later on Owen come to life after a long day on the road, insisting on a nightcap, again served by the silent lady of before. Owen, loquacious and ready for a chat, learned the hotel had been in her family for two generations and that she had sat for her father – the artist in the family – for many of the portraits on the walls. She spoke glowingly of the handsome young Irish writer who stayed in Pont-Aven for some weeks after the war and spent evenings drinking with her father and beguiling his daughter. She insisted on taking down a framed black-and-white photo from behind the bar. We tried to match the slim laughing girl with the matronly figure before us, but there was no mistaking the six-foot figure with his arms around both the girl and her father: Liam O'Flaherty.

The Liam O'Flaherty I knew in old age was still a handsome giant of a man, who nowadays manifested no *grá* for young women such as myself, whom he often dismissed from the company, preferring to be alone with Owen in whom he saw a reincarnation of his own rambunctious youth. Whenever his faithful companion, the gentle Kitty, was cajoled to walk him over to Parson's bookshop from their apartment across the canal on Wilton Place, he would, without much effort, inveigle Owen, often to be found in the same emporium, to drink whiskey with him in the Waterloo Lounge or Mooney's at Baggot Street Bridge and listen to his tales of macho prowess. A footnote to this memory sits on the bookshelves of the unborn son who was a third presence in that Pont-Aven bar. When he was about seven years old, he was brought to meet a very very old man indeed, who gave him a book, *The Test of Courage*, and scrawled his name inside in a shaky hand.

Pont-Aven was the farthest extent of our journey. Running out of both funds and time we headed back inland through Normandy to Le Havre. One last stop was in Deauville, within a couple of hours' drive of the ferry, where careful husbandry left us with exactly twenty francs, having eaten our last *repas*, covered the hotel bill and with enough petrol to get us back on board the *St Patrick*. The only cloud of dispute to mar the harmony of the past weeks concerned the spending of this twenty-franc note. Owen wanted to go on the town and enjoy a last few vinos on French soil, I wanted to go to the casino; we both got our way in democratic fashion and split our cash equally between us. Was it to be a mirror of our changing lives, me the gambler, he the old dog for the old road? Whichever or whatever the choices meant, we were both penniless but happy when next we met and headed for the ferry back to Ireland next day with no regrets and I, at least, full of expectation.

I had planned to continue working as late as possible in my pregnancy so as to make the most of my six-week maternity leave after the baby was born. I left work on Friday 18 July in the hope of the baby arriving within the next ten days, but not to be hurried; it was in the early hours of 4 August that my son stirred himself to make an appearance. No telephone in Leeson Park was a disadvantage – I had applied for one about six months earlier but the average waiting time for a new installation in those days was about twelve months so the plan was for Owen to dash down to the nearest telephone box on Leeson Street to order a taxi. In the euphoria and sense of invincibility that overtook me in those early morning hours I pooh-poohed the notion of having to wait for a taxi. Fully dressed and accompanied by Owen, cursing the gods, himself and the forces of nature, I took my carefully packed suitcase and drove through the empty streets in my white Peugeot arriving at Mount Carmel Hospital, perfectly self possessed and in command of the situation.

Some six or eight hours later I understood completely Patsy Sheridan's comments on giving birth: I yelled like a fishwife, wept like Niobe, told Owen to go to hell, and generally abandoned the veneer of self control that had kept me going all the long months and even years up until I met Mother Nature, red in tooth and claw, for the very first time. Things were never the same afterwards. The red tide receded, calm restored, babe and mother slept peacefully, but the raw me had found not only a voice but a purpose in being, and was not to be gainsaid thereafter. The bathwater, containing all extraneous matters of importance in my former life, went out with the afterbirth.

Day one of the rest of my life dawned, another fine August morning. Owen enlivened the hallowed precincts of Mount Carmel by telling my sprucely shaved and bank holiday rested gynaecologist who offered his smooth congratulations at noon, an hour after the birth, to 'Fuck off, you bastard – no fucking thanks to you for a safe arrival!' Mary and Ken arrived with a bottle of champagne, the baby's head was duly wet and father's thirst slaked, while mother lay and smiled between groans. The baby, secretly known by me as Daniel, inexplicably became Eoghan Joseph in the birth notice in *The Irish Times*: 'To Owen and Eileen, a son, Eoghan Joseph, August 4th, Mount Carmel Hospital *Is fada linn do theacht*', a garbled gaelicization of the sentiment 'You were a long time coming to us.'

During the precious month remaining of maternity leave I cocooned self and baby in an odorous nest of bedclothes and breast milk: no one who has not been benighted by under-developed mammary appurtenances can appreciate the delight in displaying a fully rounded bosom to the world, not to speak of the sensual delight of breastfeeding. A friend who called one afternoon was shocked to find me sleepily emerge in my night attire, detritus scattered in every room, nappies steeping in the bath or draped to air on chair backs and a rickety clothes horse – she hurried away to warn of my impending physical and mental collapse. I remained oblivious and the surrounding squalor had no long-lasting effect on the infant's health or happiness. Owen Senior, as he became known quite quickly after Eoghan's arrival, took over the kitchen, brought me breakfast in bed and chopped up his speciality salad every evening accompanied by a limited but nutritious menu of cold meats, chops or fish wrapped in tinfoil and cooked in the oven. He was not a 'new' man and proffered no assistance in baby changing or baby minding though he did take full advantage of a captive mother and child sitters, reverting to his favourite theme of the early sixties in a series of paintings and drawings of full-breasted women nursing either an infant or a cat, or both.

Sophy, by then an important member of the household, was a magnificent half-Persian tabby. In a touching display of solidarity, she too become pregnant and produced a fine, if suspiciously multi-toned, litter of four in the early summer. These we christened Casey, Lucey, Newman and Mac in homage to the bishops of Ireland. Sophy reigned supreme for another seventeen years, dying quietly in her favourite spot, under the warmth of the lamp above the kitchen counter during the month Eoghan did his Leaving Certificate in 1993.

I had found an ideal childminder in Olive Smith, my old neighbour in 62 Pembroke Road, who had been looking after baby Ben, toddler son of Patience, my friend from USIT days, now married to Bill Jerman, before their departure to live in Rome and work in the Vatican City.

My five-week-old Eoghan presented no challenge to Olive, whose strident voice, far too large for her diminutive frame, effortlessly controlled her own four sons and husband Willie. Lack of sleep and milk-stained blouses were my primary concerns those first few weeks. I was less affected by the daily parting with Eoghan than I had envisaged, or perhaps buried it below more immediate priorities. He throve on his daily excursion to Pembroke Road and back and took to the bottle without a backward glance when my supply of sustenance ran distinctly low and my bosom reverted to its normal petite contours. Ruth and John Brown paid us a visit soon after I went back to work. A photograph taken on the steps of Leeson Park shows myself, long hair swinging, Laura Ashley dressing-gowned, a grinning Owen stripped to the waist and John Brown and Ruth with baby Eoghan displayed like a rugby trophy between us.

23. Beginnings and Endings

Determined to cut a dash on my return to work and imbue respect among my seniors and peers, I paid a visit to Brown Thomas in Grafton Street. Known for my panache (rather than good taste) in dress code, I rigged myself out in a faux-leopardskin midi coat, red suede boots and a rakish red hat, all of which I wore to Eoghan's Christening in University Church in St Stephen's Green. The sacristan blanched once more at the motley crew in attendance. Rotund, bearded Norman Stewart and once again heavily pregnant, red-haired Silvia, in emerald maxi dress, were godparents. Mephistophelian Kevin Monaghan, Pat Broe and Deirdre Kelly were in attendance. Mary, her scorn for Mother Church resurfacing with a vengeance, refused to have anything to do with this ridiculous ceremony of rank hypocrisy. Fortunately she didn't hold it against us for long, and certainly not against her darling Eoghan, whom she doted upon, as did his big cousins David and Nancy, readily available as babysitters.

In the spring of 1976, just when the immediate frantic spinning of job and baby had settled into semi-manageable proportions, a registered letter from the landlord of 28 Leeson Park arrived giving me three months' notice to quit. It transpired that the change of tenancy from Joan's name to Mary's on the family's return from London meant I had lost the right as a daughter of inheriting the family lease – a mere sister of the current lessee, no longer in residence, had no such inbuilt protection. I put my trust and fate into the hands of a supposed expert on tenancy rights who assured me that the family history of over twenty years would be taken into account by the judge who would be loath to evict a lone mother and child. So one morning in June I stood before the District Court judge and made my case, to no avail. The judge, his ruling strictly on legal grounds, was scathing in his opinion of squatters taking advantage of tenancy laws, which gave the landlord no rights to his property; as a concession to my situation, he extended my eviction order by a further three months.

Thus was I catapulted into the property market. It did not take long to realize that finding another flat to rent of decent size and location was not going to be easy. Apart from difficulties relating to my unconventional status and credit rating, tenancy laws were changing in favour of the landlord and searching the *Evening Press* 'Flats to Rent' section proved fruitless. A latent pragmatism and solution-finding propensity began to manifest itself. If I couldn't rent, I would have to buy. To buy meant taking out a mortgage: how was that to be done, who would lend and how much? I was a quick learner and based on my good employment record I found a building society to accept me as a client. The maximum loan on any property was limited to 75 per cent of its value, therefore task number one would be to fill the impossible 25 per cent gap in the total sum. Based on my annual salary at the time of £4800, the Building Society was prepared to offer a mortgage of £6000 provided I found a property that passed the dreaded surveyer and I could raise another £2000, all within a rapidly narrowing time scale. Most evenings and weekends Eoghan was strapped into his car seat and we toured the near southside suburbs; the thought of crossing the Liffey never entered the equation. Ranelagh and Rathmines were soon off the list, too expensive and too few small houses. The search centred on Sandymount and its poorer neighbour Ringsend. I wrote to the only rich friend I had, Tony Taverna, seeking the loan of £1000. True to form I got an immediate affirmative reply and a banker's draft soon followed. I then approached three others, Norman Stewart, the Leahy sisters and my brother-in-law, Ken, for £250 each: all were forthcoming and I figured I could put together the rest myself on a short-term office loan. I found the house of my dreams, a bijou cottage just off Sandymount Green. Alas, the vendors were looking for an immediate cash deal and there was a competing bidder waiting in the wings. No time to wait for mortgage approval. In desperation I wrote to some cousins whom I knew had recently sold a 400-acre farm adjoining the proposed Naas dual carriageway for a cool £4 million, but a kind letter turned me down gently due to 'liquidity' problems. I was learning a new word in this strange world of finance every day.

In October 1976 I moved into 9 Malone Gardens, Bath Avenue, Irishtown, Dublin 4, neither as salubrious an address nor as picturesque a property as Sandymount. I never liked the house, a narrow concrete box midway down a terrace of other concrete boxes, just off a busy thoroughfare between

Ballsbridge and Sandymount. There were compensating advantages: it was convenient both for depositing Eoghan in nearby Pembroke Road and within fifteen minutes of St Stephen's Green. Best of all I discovered a warm and friendly neighbourhood. In leafy Leeson Park neighbours were remote and largely unacquainted with each other, the very size and extent of the houses and gardens lending an automatic distance. In contrast I had hardly moved in the sofa and a couple of beds salvaged from Leeson Park when two little girls knocked at the door to ask 'could we take the baby out for a walk, missus'. Like dogs, as I discovered in later years, babies are a passport to getting to know people. Eoghan was soon the pet and plaything of the dozens of kids who played hopscotch, skipping and chasing in perfect safety up and down our cul-de-sac.

It may be noticed that Owen Walsh has slipped a little from the narrative. In truth he had slipped a little out of focus during those early months and never regained his central role in my life. He was a moody parent in the early months and I feared his sudden outbursts of rage, never violent but terrifying nonetheless, and imagined it affected Eoghan's normally sunny temperament. We never fully lived together again after I moved out of Leeson Park – Owen felt hemmed in and claustrophobic in Malone Gardens and took to calling at odd hours or insisting we spend weekends in Baggot Street, neither of which was conducive to keeping up any sort of routine and I began to dread late-night visitations with amorous intent as much as I had yearned for them in the past. 'Have you no lust in your loins woman?' he yelled at me once, before banging out of the house in disgust. Gradually his demands waned and we found ourselves reaching a plateau of respect and kinship that endured as the years passed. As Eoghan grew from babyhood to toddler and childhood, his father became very attached to him, took him on long walks, brought him to the studio and showed a surprising dexterity in football and ball games in Merrion Square.

An agreeable pattern of work, motherhood and companionship charac-terized that first year in Malone Gardens and midway through 1977 more change beckoned. It was the year of the putsch, the takeover, the sell-out, depending on the position or stance taken by Usitravel management and staff towards Allied Irish Banks' decision to get out of their disastrous forary into the travel business. The Irish Travel Agents Association gloried for years afterwards in their successful campaign to prevent the bank from setting up travel desks throughout their branch network. It is doubtful if such was ever AIB policy: their main interest was in the opportunities they saw for foreign exchange transactions. It became ever clearer that the inherent risk endemic in the travel industry did not sit comfortably with the caution and prudence then characterizing Irish banking. Oil and water, fish and fowl, made for poor business partners.

The battle lines were drawn within days of AIB's announcement of the sale of the Usitravel Group as a going concern midway through 1977. Fully union-ized following the AIB takeover, the staff's preference was to sell the company in its totality to Aer Lingus, another safe union house, with an added incentive of inbuilt redundancy payments to all. Management on the other hand had quite different ideas, with a management buyout heading the list. The union representative was a highly skilled negotiator of impeccable lineage, James Larkin Jr, who organized meetings, balloted staff and rallied support from the IBOA. Sales figures plummeted that summer when time off for union meet-ings, huddles in the back of the shop or in the more private precincts of the print room disrupted the daily routine considerably. Equally management met in frequent confabulations, either in Sean Dempsey's office or in the privacy of the snug in Rice's Pub on the nearby corner of Stephens Green.

I thought long and hard about the choices open to me. A redundancy figure of a year's salary, tax free, was on offer to management; with holiday pay this would net me about £7000, a huge sum as a nest egg for the likely rainy days ahead although I knew I was highly employable to a number of compa-nies in the travel industry, having valuable overseas business to bring with me. On the other hand, I yearned for a future where I could be in control, not answerable to a boss or board of directors. So I submitted a bold, possibly reckless proposal to the powers-that-be: I would take over Usitours as a going concern in its present location in 4 St Stephen's Green and accept a lesser redundancy figure in return. Whether because Usitours was too insignificant to be of any great interest, or because the bank negotiators saw it as a neat solution for one member of the management team at least, my case was met with approval in principle.

Before I finally reached agreement on severance arrangements with Usitravel, I made a trip to London. Confident and passionate though I was in my belief in the future of Irish tourism, and the part my new company could play in its growth, I nevertheless sought another source of revenue and targeted Club Méditerranée as a valuable trading partner. In my time with Stephen's Green Travel, I had had regular dealings with their London office through whom we booked holidays, in the main, to their 'straw hut' resort in Corfu. It was a fairly loose arrangement covered by an annual letter of agree-ment between the two companies but now I aimed to establish myself as Club Med's exclusive sales representative in Ireland. I had a good working relation-ship with Thierry Brener, the large, lazy head of the UK office.

Already I was a couple of steps ahead of any potential rivals; I spoke good French, had lived in Paris and knew the product. I was also armed with an incontrovertible persuader: a photocopy of the Certificate of Registration of 'Club Méditerranée (Ireland) Ltd.', the non-trading shelf company that was the vehicle to be used to transfer the current and pre-booked incoming tour business to me. For a company that was a household name in France, soon to become a PLC with shares floating on the Paris Bourse, any chink in the global ownership of its name and brand was extremely serious. A more grasping or perhaps astute entrepreneur could well have looked for a hefty financial consideration for parting with such a valuable legal entity but since I saw the opportunity in the shape of a useful negotiating tool, I was only too happy to receive a letter appointing me general sales agent for Club Mediterranée in the Republic of Ireland for 1978, renewable thereafter on satisfactory sales performance. So began a thirty-year relationship between Club Med and O'Mara Travel.

I also came to know and greatly admire the Club Med founder, Gilbert Trigano, who had set up the company soon after the war, although I had less respect for his son Serge who took over in the 1990s. My own connection with Club Med reached its apogée in 1990 when I flew low in a helicopter over the Ring of Kerry with Gilbert Trigano to the Great Southern Hotel in Parknasilla when Club Med was exploring the concept of a golf resort in Ireland. Bewildered observers asked why Club Med would wish to change its exotic image: ' *Mais, voilà,*' he replied, '*Irlande*, she is "*exotique*"!'

As on other occasions, the great wheels of government approval were slow to respond and Club Med ended up by signing a far less attractive deal with a youthful Ryanair who had pipped them at the post with the purchase of the Waterville Lake Hotel, a few miles west of Parknasilla. The deal between Ryanair and Club Med might have been a little more favourable to Club Med had I been allowed a role in the negotiations. I was told later that the Club Med lawyers were mystified when an executive acting on the part of Mr Tony Ryan, founder and owner of the airline, objected to my presence at the table. It seemed that this young man, Michael O'Leary, based his objections to me not on any personal prejudice but on my recently vacated seat on the Board of Aer Lingus. The joint venture, although not a success and lasting only five years, did afford a taste of the unique Club Med style to Irish home holiday-makers, and many a memorable weekend for O'Mara Travel's staff outings.

And so it was that early in 1978 I reached an agreement with the Usitravel Board, which included a lump sum *ex-gratia* payment of £3000. It seemed wealth indeed until I thought about the mortgage, Olive Smith, and all the attendant ropes that kept me earthbound. Frank Burke, my canny accountant and soon to be co-tenant in 4 St Stephen's Green, advised me to draw up a business plan and approach the company bank, AIB for a working capital loan. Determined but not hopeful, I went to see my bank manager, aware that my own personal account was nakedly available for perusal in that same bank branch and, without any assets other than a heavily mortgaged small house, I might appear a dubious candidate for consideration. Gerry Nolan, many years later and in safe retirement, boasted that he was the first bank official to extend loan finance to a woman without a male guarantor behind her. He didn't regret it. I never let him down and kept my account in that same branch for over forty years, a lesson in the old dictum, business works on trust, but trust backed by good case-making and sound risk assessment. My first year's budget showed an operating profit of £30,000, minus salaries and overheads of £28,000, projecting a net profit of £2000. I was on the right side of Mr Micawber's lesson for a happy life. I knew I could do it; more importantly, Gerry believed I could and approved a loan of £5000.

What to name this new entity? I had several meetings with Brendan Walsh, appointed company solicitor, to go through the complexities of Memorandum and Articles of Association, appointment of Directors, issue of Share Certificates, all a foreign language to me, but which had to be rapidly understood and signed into fact within a few short weeks. With no one to consult, it was a lonely if not terrifying interim between the cessation of my life as employee on 31 January and the start of my life as employer on 1 March, the date set for the handover of business by AIB. Finding a name was akin to inventing a title for a book I had not read. I filled notebooks with names ranging from the sublime Emerald Tours, to the ridiculous Toor-a-Loora Holidays, suggested by helpful friends. Eventually I settled for the unpoetic but dynastically precise. The O'Mara Travel Company would follow in the footsteps of The O'Mara Bacon Company and The O'Mara Opera Company. The first had originated in the nineteenth and the third would last until the twenty-first century.

Thus in spring 1978 O'Mara Travel began life with some hiccups and a good deal of trepidation on the part of its managing director. I took up residence in the front office of 4 St Stephen's Green, along with three desks, two electric typewriters – oh the bliss of electric typewriters – and a filing cabinet. My single employee and I spent the first three days unpacking boxes of files and stocking up on office supplies, which included the first ream of our new headed stationary, *THE O'MARA TRAVEL COMPANY LTD* tastefully scripted in green with accompanying Celtic brooch emblem. Two vital telephone lines, one dedicated to Club Med reservations, three handsets (I was already planning for expansion) and the most vital tool of all, a telex machine, were duly connected and we were open for business. 'We' comprised Anne (Hadji) Stewart, youngest daughter of Norman Stewart by his first wife Dora, who had loyally served me in the run up to the changeover when she had worked as telephonist/typist in Stephen's Green Travel.

There was little enough of a honeymoon period, doing everything and deciding everything alone, with Hadji, willing and energetic but unschooled in either the mysteries of booking a Club Med holiday or the intricacies of writing up a coach tour itinerary for a prospective French Garden Club. The latter came by way of a request passed on by a French travel agent I had met in Nice a couple of years ago and for whom I had made occasional hotel bookings. At the outset it presented an innocuous though welcome piece of group business. I soon sent off an outline of the four-day Dublin-based tour with appropriate visits to gardens of note in Dublin and Wicklow and quickly received confirmation and go ahead from Nice, indicating the group would arrive in Dublin in mid May.

The first intimation of anything untoward came from a phone call from my old boss Barry Maybury in Paris. 'My dear Eileen, congratulations but are you sure you have the *boyaux* for taking this on so early in your new enterprise?' Slightly annoyed I reassured him that it was a simple programme with few special requirements, at which he gave a bray of his familiar laughter, wished me luck and rang off. It rapidly emerged that my French group consisted of members of the Garden Club of Monaco and that their President, Her Serene Highness Princess Grace, had unexpectedly expressed a wish to travel with the group to the home of her ancestors. Both Bórd Fáilte and the Department of External Affairs were extremely desirous of taking all the arrangements off my hands – after all, it would present enormous challenges for a 'small' company, protocol, security, media to handle. I remained firm, my client was the travel agent in Nice who had confirmed the business to me and I would take instructions only from her. Although I had my mandate: there was to be no press, no formal receptions, no photographers, and was able to proceed with arrangements as officialdom breathed down upon me. For the sake of peace I allowed Bórd Fáilte to check the group itinerary to ensure Irish tourism would be seen at its best and we all prayed for good weather.

It was a beautiful May day when the Monegasque group finally arrived. It appeared that democracy in Monaco worked in much the same way as anywhere else. The princess travelled incognito, first class, and was whisked away on arrival to a suite in the Shelbourne Hotel while the group made their way through customs on to the awaiting coach to be ferried to the more modest surroundings of the Mount Herbert Private Hotel in Ballsbridge, which is what their budget and my best quote could afford. However, over the following three days Princess Grace accompanied the group on the coach, sitting up front with the Garden Club lady secretary when we picked her up at the Shelbourne each morning and evening, and descending at every visit and lunch stop just like any other passenger. Although I had hired the services of an excellent French-speaking tour guide with a special interest and knowledge of horticulture, I naturally accompanied the tour myself. I think Her Highness was a little puzzled as to my identity but was far too polite to ask and I kept well in the background at all times. She usually came out of the hotel wearing a light mac, headscarf and dark glasses, but safely aboard she divested herself of these and wandered through Powerscourt and Mount Usher Gardens in flat shoes and simple summer dress, her ash-blonde hair pulled back into her signature French pleat style. Just, but not quite, like any other passenger, smiling and chatting to those she knew, she retained a kind of hauteur, a *noli me tangere* look, probably first perfected in Hollywood. She also proved to be both gracious and diplomatic when the occasion arose.

On the last evening of the tour we had the addition of Prince Rainier to our coach party. I preceded the group to the Abbey Tavern in Howth, the only venue in those days where visitors could attend an evening of Irish music and eat dinner at the same location. I ensured our reserved tables were in the best position in the house, as the evening was open to other guests, and was waiting in the bar for the coach to arrive when to my horror the door opened to two couples in full evening dress – black tie, ball gowns and mink capes. The Chairman and Chief Executive of Bórd Fáilte and their respective wives had come to gatecrash the party. I could do no more than say I hoped they had reserved a table when the coach drew up outside. Prince Rainier was the first off, in a Donegal tweed sports jacket and polo-necked sweater. He handed down his wife, wearing a pink cotton skirt and blouse with her hair in a pony-tail. Suffice it to say the royals were graciousness itself, greeted the uninvited foursome, then proceeded to have a splendid evening, singing the choruses and clapping the 'spoons' along with the rest of the happily plebian audience.

The following Monday it was back to the desk, all vestiges of the royal visitors gone except for a few badly focused surreptitious photographs I had taken with my small camera in Powerscourt. But my stock had risen among my peers and I was now accepted as a *bona fide* operator. I retrieved Eoghan from his holiday home with Mary and Ken in Sandymount. He showed no ill effects from being passed around like a parcel, he welcomed all comers, was fast losing his baby fat but compensating by replacing his sparse wisps with bright shiny guinea curls and was beginning to love hearing about Peter Rabbit and the Two Bad Mice almost as much as I relished the telling. I both loved and hated wheeling him in the buggy because I could only look at the back of his head and was to be seen stopping every so often to run around to the front for precious smiles and exchange of chat.

I was continually surprised by his stoic acceptance of our ups and downs, especially when they affected him directly as when his much-loved childminder in Pembroke Road abruptly terminated our cosy arrangement on Willie's onset of scruples about 'the taxman cometh'. The following Monday Eoghan found himself marching into a cacophony of children's voices at the nearest crèche, clutching his lunchbox. I looked anxiously for signs of emotional distress but he weathered the change with nothing more than some slight clinging to my coat on the morning handovers. Early in the New Year I had found a much more agreeable solution, a little farther away in Ranelagh. Miss Betty ran a small playschool for children, supposedly from three years old, but she took Eoghan on as an exception to her rule. And her rule was law. She was a large hatchetfaced, middle-aged lady whose big redbrick house on the Sandford Road was kept in pristine condition. The hatchet face I discovered was strictly for parents, whom she disapproved of on principle for handing their precious offspring over to strangers. To the children she was a cross between a fairy godmother and Mrs Do-as-you-would-be-done-by: she kept perfect order, taught them to say 'please' and 'thank you', to wash their hands, comb their hair and put on their shoes, coat and gloves ready for collection by her equally obedient parent clientele.

I had now developed a valuable talent, or excavated a dormant one, of compartmentalizing my life. I would leave the office, jump into my flashy yellow Volvo (another public declaration of confidence) usually (in pre-meter days) parked right outside the office and tear out to Ranelagh. Having braved Betty, with Eoghan strapped in to his car seat, stopping off for cat food or briquettes, I would reach home with all vestiges of O'Mara Travel wiped clean from my mind and settle in for a blissful couple of hours in perfect harmony with my two favourite companions, Eoghan and Sophy. For a few weeks our peace was much disturbed by the advent of a large white rabbit with pink eyes that had been adopted for an overnight stay but then abandoned by his rightful owner. That rabbit although white was black at heart. It was a demanding and aggressive guest who chased poor Sophy hissing under the stairs, dropping little black pellets behind him whenever released from his hutch in the kitchen, it being too cold to leave him outside. Evenings and early mornings were the best times of the day and weekends should have gone on for ever, but once Eoghan was safely deposited with Betty, I switched effortlessly to thinking about the day ahead and leapt into the fray of phones hopping and telex rattling without a backward glance.

A year passed rapidly by. In April 1979, emboldened by one season of profitable business, I decided to move house. A positive cashflow through Club Med deposits looked likely to be the basis of a beneficial cycle of operations for the foreseeable future, it was time to put my money where it would be most effective. Knowing I was likely to require a considerably higher mortgage, I approached my old friend Tony Taverna's brother-in-law, Michael Fingleton, then heading up one of the more innovative building societies. The property I had in mind was on Mountpleasant Avenue, near the canal between Ranelagh and Rathmines, its asking price £17,000, almost double that paid for Malone Gardens. I had an offer for Malone Gardens for £12,500, leaving a healthy margin on the loan repayment to Irish Permanent. Mr Fingleton, a man of obvious probity, indicated it would be inappropriate for him to have financial dealings with a personal or family acquaintance and my application was rejected. Fortunately Irish Permanent agreed to increase my mortgage to £14,500. Coincidently the sum borrowed matched the current rate of interest of 14.5 per cent.

56 Upper Mountpleasant Avenue was a mansion in comparison to Malone Gardens. It was a fine late Victorian redbrick in a terrace of similar houses,

only a few yards from a busy stretch of the canal leading up to Portobello Bridge. Far too big for us, I luxuriated in the space, using the large upstairs bedroom that stretched across the width of the house as our sitting room, with my bedroom next door looking out on the rear, and Eoghan in the small return room beside the bathroom, halfway up the stairs. The normal reception rooms, front and back, remained unused until I was able to afford to transfer the ugly low-ceilinged kitchen facing the yard into what would have been the traditional dining room, knock through the wall into the front room and make an open-plan living space of the ground floor. But that was to come – in the meantime we settled in comfortably and found we had landed quite fortuitously next door to an angel.

Bridie Byrne was her name and she was surrounded by a number of lesser angels: Jim, her meek little husband and their children, Marie, Susan, Elizabeth and Stephen, all built more in Bridie's robust style. Within three months of our move, Bridie had taken over from Betty and there were no more morning and evening time-clocked dashes through morning and evening rush hour. I handed over Eoghan to Bridie-next-door where he spent a busy day following her round as she scrubbed and polished her already spotless house, sitting up in his high chair as the family all arrived for their lunch. Bridie was also from Limerick, but from a West Limerick rural background where she had learned the best of Irish cooking, a tradition she kept to as religiously as she kept the holy water font full in the hall. Bridie expressed her fierce love of family, including us adoptees, through food and her abundant lunches of stews, roasts and boiled meats and vegetables, followed always by delicious tarts, trifles, sponges and pies, all gloriously calorie-and cholesterol-packed. I would often come home to find she had kept me a plate full of goodies, secretly convinced that someone who spent all day in a pokey office could not possibly be capable of feeding herself or her child properly. She was probably right.

Owen Senior also became a more regular visitor than he had been in Malone Garden days, often picking up Eoghan from Bridie to walk down the canal to Baggot Street where I could drop in on my way home from work. Life took on a gentler pace as the frantic summer season moved into autumn. I planned our tour programme for the following year and worked on a Club Med Irish price list to be inserted into the artistic and expensively produced Club Med holiday brochures that would get delivered in bulk to Stephen's Green and dispatched to our small but growing list of clients and enquiries. I made sales trips to France, Italy and London but kept them as brief as possible and depended mainly on Mary for looking after Eoghan in my absence, not being quite brave enough as yet to call on the Byrnes next door for twenty-four-hour care of a lively four-year-old.

It came out of the blue, that telephone call from London on a cold grey October evening in 1979. At first I didn't recognize John Brown's voice. Who was this man weeping down the phone? The same feeling of blood rushing from my head as that time in Brussels buckled my knees and I sat down heavily on the stairs. Ruth was ill, collapsed at home, in hospital, outlook bad, when could we get there? I scribbled down as many details as I could, hospital name, ward, telephone number. I must have phoned Mary; I know she arrived with Ken, calmer than I was. I ran into Bridie and gabbled out the story, she told me to get going, not to worry, everything would be all right, Eoghan would be fine, they would all pray for Ruth. I must have phoned Aer Lingus. Ken drove us to the airport and promised to stop off and tell Owen we had gone and to visit Eoghan. The next two days remain hazy – strange I can recall all the circumstances of Power's and Joan's death but not Ruth's. Mary and I sat on each side of her bed surrounded by tubes, her breathing stentorious, face pallid, abdomen huge. We talked to each other and to her, we held her hand, we tried to remember funny stories about Limerick, we sent her love from David and Nancy, from E.J., from Michael and Hilton, from Paddy and Pat Broe, even from Marie Conmee, anyone whose name we thought might penetrate through the coma to the Ruth inside that swollen body. We stayed until they removed the tubes and told us she had died. An autopsy would be required but hardly necessary. She had suffered a massive haemorrhage of the oesophagus artery and her liver was too badly damaged to recover. John was a silent wreck, we had little enough to say to each other. He would go back to their flat and we would return to Dublin.

We agreed there was little point in returning for the funeral ten days later. Instead, we put a death notice in *The Irish Times* and on the day of the funeral organized a memorial service for Ruth in University Church, loyally and sadly attended by Dublin's theatre world. Mary spoke movingly from the altar, holding a red rose, and we walked across the Green to Neary's. My heart wasn't able for the reminiscences and well-meant condolences. I went home to Mountpleasant Avenue and hugged my son. I would tell him my own stories about his Auntie Ruth, She-who-must-be-obeyed, she of the grey eyes and translucent skin, the skilled poker player, the shy chuckler, my gifted, flawed beloved sister. Owen was stalwart in my absence, moving into the house so Eoghan could sleep in his own bed, and a solid reassuring figure on my return. He and Eoghan presented me with a loosely wrapped brown paper parcel. It was a freshly painted unframed canvas of a small smiling boy with blond curls in a brown-and-white striped t-shirt. The inscription at the bottom of the painting read 'To Mummy, from Junior, by Senior'. John was distraught after Ruth's death and left England to work in the oil fields in the Arab Emirates. A few days after Christmas a year later he arrived unannounced in Dublin. Mary could not face him so I took him along with me on a New Year trip to friends in Co. Clare. John, very much off the wagon, proposed marriage several times en route, promising to look on 'E.J.', Ruth's pet name for Baby Eoghan, as his own son. It was the height of the Northern Troubles and John took the floor in neighbouring hostelries expounding on what ought to be done with those 'murdering cowards'. His hosts were less than impressed. Three days later I brought him on a mystery tour of the beauties of Co. Clare, ending up in Shannon airport where I thrust an airline ticket and his bag into his arms and bade him farewell. It was the last we ever saw or heard of John Brown.

I was not prone to introspection but Ruth's death felt like the coming down of a curtain on part of my life, my youth perhaps, a youth that had lasted well past the halfway mark of my allotted three score years and ten. Even the advent of Eoghan had not entirely shaken me out of my dream of taking the road less travelled, but somewhere on that road, the wind had shifted and was blowing me onto a new course. The way ahead beckoned, more prosaic, less chaotic, more peaceful, less passionate. The way back could only be reached through the looking-glass.

24. Other People's Business

On my fortieth birthday, with sweaty hands and trembling knees, I found myself on a podium reliving my Flanders nightmare. I got through my twenty-minute slot at the National Tourism Conference held in the Great Southern Hotel, Bundoran. It was to be a forerunner of the more public character of the next stage of my life. Looking back now not through my looking glass but at grainy black and white newspaper clippings of business events, board meetings and conferences, what is striking is how little these concerned O'Mara Travel and how much applied to other people's businesses.

After the first exhilarating period of running my own company, I realized it was a lonely place to be, isolated from the wider world of business when I needed to be aware of what was happening in the tourism and travel industry: what were the coming trends, where were the best opportunities and how could I access them? I made a conscious decision to become involved in tourism on a national level and gain an insight, if not an influence, on that sector of the Irish economy on which I had hung my hopes and Eoghan's future: hence my first public-speaking engagement in Bundoran in January 1981. This outing led to an invitation to join the National Tourism Council, then headed by Harry Murray, eponymous founder of Murray Chauffeur Drive and Car Hire, who began his career driving a hearse. He took me under his plump wing; not only did he entertain me with ghoulish stories of breaking the legs of corpses to fit the coffins, he coached me in the politics and ethics of my trade: who was who in the powerful Irish Hotels Federation, Aer Lingus, CIÉ and other industry leaders I was to get to know and respect. I was a small minnow amongst friendly if voracious large fish in the tourism sea but I had been well schooled by then.

Two years later I took over as President of the National Tourism Council and experienced my first direct brush with the political system when I led a delegation of tourism colleagues to meet the then Minister of Industry and Commerce, Desmond O'Malley, in the autumn of 1982 with a list of demands for the forthcoming budget. Somewhat put off my stride by finding the Minister at his desk in shirtsleeves, I launched myself into my prepared speech. No eye contact and no reaction from the minister. I ploughed on to the end and stopped. Mr O'Malley raised his weary gaze to mine: 'Miss O'Mara, are you aware that when you leave this office, I will be obliged to meet at least three other delegations representing tourism interests and each will have a different axe to grind and will without doubt contradict at least fifty per cent of what you have so ably put forward for my consideration today? Frankly if you shower of dissidents don't get your act together on what it is you stand for, you'll get no respect from this office ... good day.' This sowed seeds that resulted two years later in an invitation to Desmond O'Malley to open the inaugural conference of the Irish Tourist Industry Confederation in Kilkenny and to eat his words. He graciously did both. By then, he, too, had seen the light, broken with Charles Haughey and Fianna Fáil and was soon to lead the new Progressive Democrats into coalition with his erstwhile boss.

The Irish Tourist Industry Confederation was to be a much strengthened, unified representative body of the tourist industry, then labelled the 'cinderella' of the Irish economy, and got scant respect or support from government. The position paper I proposed to industry leaders was favourably received by the only powerful private sector, the Irish Hotels Federation. Tourism was dominated by the state sector, Aer Lingus in the air, B&I at sea and CIÉ on the land, any of whom might have looked askance at an approach from a competitor. I was a bit player, representing an insignificant sector of the industry – and a woman to boot, not a threat to the big guns, but a possible catalyst to spur government action in the national interest of tourism and its strategic objectives. Under protective cover of a broad-based representative body, issues could be pursued and government policies challenged.

By the end of 1983 the Irish Tourist Industry Confederation seemed set for a fair wind with all the big and little, public and private companies agreed on its functions and steering instructions. But as in all good fairy tales, the wicked witch, or, in this case, wizard, made a dramatic entry and threatened to spoil the party. The wizard in question, Mr P.V. Doyle, was already a legend in the Irish hotel business and also chairman of Bórd Fáilte. It appeared he did not take as sanguine a view of the coming together of tourism leaders as his chief executive – an early and enthusiastic supporter – had done. For over twenty years tourism policy began and ended in the Baggot Street Bridge offices of

Bórd Fáilte Éireann, who advised successive ministers on the best interests of the industry. At the eleventh hour Bórd Fáilte withdrew its support as a participant and co-funder of our new body – happily restored in later years.

But the commitment had been made by the state sector, the Irish Hotels Federation and the smaller players in the industry, from B & Bs to boats on the Shannon, who were eager to have a voice. ITIC was given a quiet launch at a meeting in the Shelbourne Hotel in February 1984. The first elected Chair for a two-year term was Eileen O'Mara Walsh. An unfortunate by-product of the paucity of funds was the lack of an office to call its own and the non-appointment of an executive director. For the next five years it took up residence in the back office of O'Mara Travel, previously the domain of the Club Med side of the business, which had transferred to the elegant Powerscourt Town Centre off Grafton Street. At least ITIC had the funds to employ a most capable administrator in the person of Stephanie Byrne, who simultaneously prodded and petted successive Chairmen of ITIC over the next twenty-odd years, beginning, after my tenure, with David Kennedy of Aer Lingus.

I was first introduced to Ruairi Quinn in my business capacity at a formal lunch in the Powerscourt Town Centre. As my mother's daughter, I'd always supported Labour but I could never have been described as an activist until the three rapid elections of 1981 and 1982 when I canvassed for Labour in and around the Ranelagh area of Dublin South East, keeping up a family tradition for supporting the Labour candidate in that constituency, begun by my mother almost fifty years previously. As the new chair of ITIC I found myself sitting beside the guest of honour, the Minister for Labour. I doubtless bent the Minister's ear on my favourite subject, tourism, but I found him an interested and well-informed listener. I was surprised, however, to get a call from Minister Quinn some weeks later: 'Eileen, I'm phoning you in relation to Great Southern Hotels – I wonder could you drop over to my office this afternoon about three o'clock … oh, and on your way over would you consider taking on the chairmanship?'

Fame at last – or so I thought when my photograph adorned the front cover of *Hotel & Catering Magazine* the following month, wearing the fetchingly discreet grey coat and skirt I had hurriedly bought for the first meeting of the new Great Southern Hotel Board. Emblazoned across it was the heading: 'Can this woman work miracles?' The leading article outlined the challenges facing the most recently formed commercial state company and the first to be chaired by a woman. The heavily loss making company, aggravated by the bombing of the Russell Court Hotel in Belfast the previous year, was the subject of much debate in the press. Pressure from the unions had finally resulted in the government paying off the debts and injecting £4m working capital into the company but the hotel group was to remain something of a political football over the years that followed, with changes of coalition partners in successive general elections dictating government thinking on the rationale for state involvement in operating a hotel business, profitable or otherwise.

The first meeting of the Great Southern Hotel Board found me and eight strangers eyeing each other with trepidation and good intentions. It was our great good fortune to have Eamonn McKeon seconded to us by CIÉ for a three-month period. In his inimitable way he was realistic and reassuring, leading board members through the labyrinthine complexities of company accounts and current state of health. He was a rock we were to depend on more and more as weeks went by.

I learned fast: the only essential job of a chairman is to hire and fire the chief executive. For this vital task I had the advice of CIÉ's auditors Stokes Kennedy Crowley, now KMPG, through the services of a senior executive in human resources. This gentleman, soon to be known as Uriah by Stephanie, my self-appointed guard dog, became my most assiduous courtier. Day after day he would call my office from his smart airy equivalent across the other side of St Stephen's Green. Couriers would arrive bearing much-annotated CVs of potential candidates, to be followed up by lengthy telephone conversations on their merits or failings. All calls were liberally spattered with phrases like, 'Now, love, I must draw your attention to…' or 'Yes, love, I think we should definitely interview X' or, to vary it slightly, 'Goodbye, dearie, I'll call you tomorrow'. The worm turned at last: 'Mr Heep,' I intoned, 'you may call me Eileen, Ms O'Mara Walsh or even Madam Chairman, but never again address me by *love.*'Not long afterwards, we managed to persuade Eamonn McKeon to leave the secure stable of CIÉ for a more precarious but hopefully exhilarating ride holding the reins of Great Southern Hotels.

My love affair with Great Southern Hotels firstly as Chair and subsequently as Director for fifteen years is best encapsulated by my first encounter with the culture of service passed down through over a century of hospitality to generations of guests. My initial inspection tour of the then six hotels in the group was a depressing experience until the afternoon I crossed the threshold of the Great Southern in Parknasilla. Dismay turned into respect and then hope when I made the acquaintance of three men who were infinitesimally shifting the stair carpet, one step at a time, to hide the worn treads. Brendan Maher, the manager, was both gracious host and martinet, but it was universally accepted that Parknasilla owed its reputation for fine hospitality to Sonny Looney, the head barman, Jackie Moriarty, the head waiter, and Tom Doyle, the head porter. Managers came and went, bringing innovations and 'new' ideas; investment came with additional bedrooms and smartened decor; but it was Sonny, Jackie and Tom who kept the guests returning year after year, season after season, who in the worst of times spent their off-duty winters painting and cleaning, repairing and fixing up the old building, so that when Easter came and the doors opened again no one noticed how worn the carpets were or how threadbare the curtains – Tom, Jackie and Sonny smiled their welcome and the new season began. My most treasured press photograph is at a function, oddly enough in Dublin, with me flanked by all three of Parknasilla's Wise Men.

By year end 1986 the board's strategy of bringing the hotels around from loss-making to profit had proven itself. The *Irish Press* reported:

> Pre-tax profits at the State owned Great Southern Hotels group rose 22% to £0.7m over the year to December 31 last, continuing a recovery from the £1m. loss suffered in 1983. The improvement showed a 6% rise in turnover to £8.3m. which was achieved on higher tourist bookings and continuing cost control. Growth in the home holiday sectors also helped. The group which operates 6 hotels around the country, has spent £2m from its own resources on refurbishment in recent years and is now poised for expansion.

With Bertie Ahern taking on the mantle of Minister for Labour in 1987, I had expected a certain amount of reserve, but quite the reverse occurred. The new Minister for Labour was eager as a puppy to involve himself in company affairs and would call me in for confidential chats about the hotels' future. These sometimes took on a conspiratorial hue as he would ask me to respond to approaches made to him, or through ministerial colleagues, by business interests keen to acquire a slice of the now profitable hotel company. For instance I was dispatched under a vow of *omertà* to meet Dermot Desmond, then high-flying owner of NCB Stockbrokers and inspiration behind the establishment of the groundbreaking International Financial Services Centre in Dublin's docklands. These one-to-one meetings came to an abrupt end when the rumour mill stirred the unions to protest. Industrial strife was to be avoided at all costs by a nervous government clinging to office and it officially rescinded the previous decision of the short-lived Fine Gael minority government to sell the hotels in September 1987.

In 1989, Bertie Ahern – generously with no sign of partisanship – reappointed me to the chair although this second term was to be short-lived. In yet another twist of government policy, and despite innovative proposals from the board to raise much-needed investment finance through a public flotation of shares on the Irish Stock Exchange, responsibility for the hotels was devolved to Aer Rianta (the Irish Airport Authority) in 1990 with the crucial approval of the trade unions who were, after all merely exchanging one state company for a larger one. *Business & Finance* took a caustic view in their August issue: 'GSH may be an excellent deal for Aer Rianta but it is a lousy deal for the Irish taxpayer.'

If there is a tide in the affairs of men (and women) mine was surely at flood throughout the 1980s. An ITIC meeting at the Burlington Hotel in 1985 was interrupted by an urgent call for me from 'the minister's office'. I left the meeting to take the call, not from Ruairi Quinn's office as I had thought, but from Jim Mitchell, Minister for Transport, who invited me to join the Board of Aer Lingus. My dual role with ITIC and Great Southern Hotels, my gender and acceptability within a Fine Gael/Labour coalition, brought my name to the top of the pile. Nuala Fennell, Fine Gael's Junior Minister for Women's Affairs, was placing feminist issues firmly on the floor of Dáil Éireann; one of the virtuous commitments made by her cabinet colleagues was to espouse the principle of 40 per cent female membership on state boards, one quietly shelved by most ministers of any and all parties as the years passed since then.

My term on the board of Aer Lingus ran in tandem with my first five years with the hotels. Not being chair, the role as director patently called for less in-depth involvement and fortunately less of my working time. I was appointed to the Subsidiaries Board Committee about a year after joining the board, chaired by a senior and much respected member of the main board, Desmond Traynor. I grew to like him very much; he was shrewd, unfailingly cheerful and a true Dub. He took a benevolent interest in me, admonishing me occasionally for time spent away from my own business. He once said to me, 'Watch the cash flow – you can run up losses, you know, but you must never run out of cash!' I was delighted to find he could give me advice on a trip I was soon to make to the Cayman Islands where I'd been invited to speak at an international tourism conference. It appeared that Des Traynor was a frequent visitor to the Large Cayman and told me the Grand Hyatt was definitely the best hotel and not to miss a trip in the glass mini-submarine. I followed his advice to the letter and we swopped stories of best cracked crab and cocktail spots over ensuing boardroom lunches. However, he proffered no advice on Cayman Island's financial services.

By this stage I was beginning to read between the lines and understand some of the sub-text of boardroom politics. All boards have special agendas and alliances. The sensitivities of industrial relations on the Great Southern Board paled by comparison with the intrigues of board-union and inter-union relations in Aer Lingus at that time, often exposing the worker directors to a clash of loyalties between their responsibilities as company directors and those as union representatives. Undercurrents on the Aer Lingus Board were not confined to industrial relations. Frissons of unease appeared in the late 1980s when a brash newcomer to Irish aviation, named after its founder Tony Ryan, began to disturb the cosy cartel existing between the major national airlines serving Dublin from the UK and Europe. The Department of Transport, known fondly in the national airline circles, furiously in others, as 'the downtown office of Aer Lingus', was showing signs of a change of attitude. The Irish Tourist Industry Confederation was flexing its muscle and winning the economic case for tourism interests and Ryanair was finding friends in high places. Two of these friends came into my periphery about this time, Padraig Ó hUiginn, Secretary

General of the Department of the Taoiseach, and Charles J. Haughey, and I was eventually to conclude that the former was the more powerful of the two.

I first met Padraig O hUiginn in the Horseshoe Bar of the Shelbourne Hotel when I was drawn into a discussion – a better word would be diatribe – he was having with a young Trinity professor, Sean Barrett, on the subject of Aer Lingus. Such was the invective expressed, I felt obliged to disclose that I was a director of the airline, something already known to that wily, most civilized of civil servants. I reported the views expressed to Brian Slowey, then chairman of Aer Lingus, presumably the required result of our encounter. Another strand in the battle for influence in high places dawned more slowly. I knew how respected Des Traynor was for his ability and financial judgment but during the always sumptuous board lunches served with elegant old silverware and Waterford crystal decanters I learned that Des had afternoon tea almost every Sunday in Abbeville, Kinsealy, where he would raise matters of particular sensitivity informally with Mr Haughey and hope to counteract any negative voices coming from other quarters.

I was invited to join the first Tourism Task Force, a new and popular ploy to delay decision-making in high places, by a personal letter from the Taoiseach, Charles Haughey, in November 1987. I had no idea why or where my name had come to his attention except that I had served on the Dublin Millennium Committee earlier that year. The first meeting of the Task Force under the chairmanship of Gillian Bowler took place in the Taoiseach's office in Government Buildings. Although not yet refurbished to its final glorious condition, the Chaz Mahal was nonetheless imposing, as was my first impression of the Taoiseach himself. Charles Haughey was not a big man but his presence filled the room as he entered and moved slowly round to greet us all. He had an edgy magnetism, a lazy alertness that evoked a matching sharpening of the senses in his presence. He was prone to physical contact as if to imprint his personality – taking a hand in a long clasp, holding an arm, patting a shoulder. I found him at once repellent and attractive, his touch warm and reptilian.

Some months later on the conclusion of our endeavours he invited us to lunch in Iveagh House on St Stephen's Green. It was a convivial occasion. Mr Haughey entertained us with risqué anecdotes about colleagues and foreign dignitaries. A cloud briefly appeared when Martin Dully, new Executive Chairman of Bórd Fáilte, raised the issue of the Rod Licence dispute, then giving the tourism industry extremely bad press in British newspapers. 'We will not spoil the occasion by mundane concerns,' said the Taoiseach. 'Let us enjoy our lunch.' The wine flowed, the food was delicious; liqueurs and chocolates were handed around when he rose to his feet to give us some gracious words of thanks and congratulations. As he sat down to our polite applause, Martin Dully rose to acknowledge, equally graciously on behalf of the industry, the Taoiseach's valued interest and commitment to Irish tourism but fatally renewing his appeal to the Taoiseach to intervene personally with the protesting anglers of Connemara and rescue the remainder of the fishing season. He sat down to an icy silence. For the first time I witnessed the fear Haughey inculcated in his ministers at his weekly get-togethers in Kinsealy. He raised his hooded eyes briefly to the unfortunate Dully and spoke slowly and quietly, administering a devastating rebuke for what was termed bloody impudence and lack of respect for the office of Taoiseach. I was reduced to gazing at the floor, afraid to meet anyone else's eyes. After the Taoiseach left we all skulked away about our own business, thankful we were not going back to an office at Baggot Street Bridge.

The next time I met the Taoiseach was at the launch of the Fianna Fáil National Development Plan at the Burlington Hotel in the spring of 1988. I sat down, a few seats in from the end of a row to the left of the hall, clasping the maroon-bound document I had been handed on the way in. Gradually the room filled up: members of the cabinet began to file into the seats on the podium and a general air of expectation prevailed. The music began and to what sounded distinctly like 'Hail to the Chief' Mr Haughey entered from the back and procecded to the podium, followed by a trail of minders and photographers. He glanced to the right as he passed my row and l instantly saw the thought that popped into his mind: female, seated alone, photo oppor- tunity. Moving rapidly along the row, he sat beside me and took my hand. With the memory of the Iveagh House lunch fresh in my mind, I smiled nervously. 'Well, Eileen and how is tourism? You're having a good season I hope?' He lingered, his eyes mischievously glancing around, his minders hovering anxiously in the background. Suddenly he glared, not at me thank- fully, but at Ben Briscoe, the Lord Mayor of Dublin and Fianna Fáil T.D., scurrying down the centre aisle. The Taoiseach bent his head close to mine: 'Will you look at the little fucker,' he genially remarked, 'trying to get one up on me – himself and his fucking chain!' With that he rose to his feet, shook my hand again and majestically completed his journey to the seat of honour. I never saw the photograph nor forgot the occasion.

I was to meet him casually thereafter, at a Great Southern Hotel function, at the annual Irish Management Conference in Killarney or at the opening of the Royal Hibernian Academy Exhibition in Ely Place, where I introduced him to Owen Walsh who had two pictures hung that year. The Taoiseach recalled opening Owen's exhibition at the Project twenty years previously, or so he said with the politician's gift for remembering people. I disliked everything he stood for politically, he ruled by fear and craved power, his cloven hoof. He was also generous, cultivated and responsible for some imaginative social and cultural innovations such as the Free Travel scheme, the establishment of Aosdána and the restoration of the Royal Hospital, Kilmainham, which in those straitened times, without his autocratic mode of government, would never have happened.

The last time I remember meeting Charles Haughey was during the early summer of 1990, when the Taoiseach agreed to attend the official opening of Club Med's first northern European resort in Waterville, Co. Kerry. He landed by helicopter in the grounds of the hotel with a dark-haired lady, who was whisked away in a waiting limousine as he graciously shook hands with the waiting dignitaries, giving me a kiss on the cheek and a complicit wink as I took my place in the pecking order at the front door.

25. Parallel Lines

I give thanks for whatever degree of peace, perspective, and parenting I managed to achieve during that busy decade to Bridie Byrne first and foremost but also to a nineteenth century cottage in County Meath bought for £4000 in the summer of 1980. Ardglasson is to be found in the midst of drumlin territory between Kells and Oldcastle, close to the megalithic tombs at Loughcrew, like them a relic of a more recent but equally bygone age. Eoghan was about five years old and we were en route to Westport when my travelling companion suggested making a detour to visit a friend living in a village north of Mullingar. The detour took us twenty miles out of our way but it was worth it on two counts. The friend was Mary Banotti, who became my friend also, and the village or, rather, hamlet was Ardglasson. By the time we left some hours later I had determined to buy the cottage opposite Mary's with the yellow door and a For Sale sign in the window.

I took out a £2000 company loan adding to the nest egg of £2000 Usitravel redundancy I had managed not to invest in O'Mara Travel – times were simpler then. Ardglasson became our bolthole, our sanctuary from intractable clients and ever-mounting piles of board papers, though these sometimes showed dusty smudges from the turf fire where they were read prior to a Monday board meeting. Driving the forty odd miles to Ardglasson on a Friday evening was escaping to the childhood of my favourite books, a mix of Patricia Lynch's *The Turfcutter's Donkey* and E. Nesbit's The *Railway Children*. Ardglasson supplied everything the most demanding of seekers after rural retreats could wish for, so my guilt that Eoghan had never run barefoot in a field or seen a cow up close was fully assuaged. The two rows of terraced cottages facing each other had been built by a local landowner as homes for the workers on his estate. No shop, pub or church was nearer than Crossakiel an uphill mile away; a pump at one end and a mighty spreading sycamore tree in the middle of the common green completed the tiny settlement, which had remained untouched for over a hundred years

The reason I paid such an inflated price for my cottage, according to Mrs Reilly, Ardglasson's doyenne and purveyor of all local lore, was that it was fitted with electric light; although like all the others without water or plumbing. Purists might have sniffed at this intrusion on authenticity but could not but be satisfied by the stone flags, high roof space and best of all the great hearth where Eoghan could stand and look up to blue sky through the chimney. Less romantic were the clouds of smoke billowing out when we lit the fire in spring-time to find the chimney blocked by crows' nests, summarily poked out with no regard to the fate of eggs or avian homestead. A smaller room lay off the main one and a ladder-like wooden staircase led up to a low attic occupying half the roof space with a tiny skylight that refused to open. A lean-to scullery outside the heavy wooden back door completed the structure. There was care-fully placed the most modern of Elsan toilets, a bucket of water, a trestle table with the large jug and basin, decorated with poppies, found in the Dandelion Market. Eoghan's status among his school pals was raised enormously on weekend excursions when all rushed in on arrival to see 'the toilet-that-didn't-flush'. Less enthusiasm was expressed by their fond parents who along with all my guests feigned absolutely no interest or enquiry as to the disposal of the magic toilet's contents at the end of each weekend. The large spade and muddy wellington boots outside the back door were worn and wielded solely by the hostess after guests had waved a fond and thankful farewell.

How I loved that Shangri-la and those precious escapes from business, my own and other people's. Even in pre-motorway days, Ardglasson was not much more than an hour from Ranelagh so it didn't have to be a whole weekend, a Saturday until Sunday could be packed full; even a Sunday outing would do, with a stop at the Headfort Arms Hotel in Kells or the Wagon Wheel in Crossakiel for sandwiches or a glass of wine at either end of the journey. Within a radius of a dozen miles lay treasures and oddities galore and as we got more and more familiar with the area, favourites became essential points of pilgrimage: the purple house en route to Oldcastle, incredibly painted entirely in deep purple, lighter shades on doors and windows, windowsills adorned with plastic mauve flowers, mauve and white garden gnomes. It was a Disney World in our own back yard and best of all we never saw sight nor sound of any human inhabitant, so we could fantasize to our heart/s content as to its possible occupants.

The graveyard up the road from the cottage was another such spot; over-grown and brambly, ragged trees entwined branches across the oldest graves, many of the gravestones had toppled over and lay flat on the ground. My niece Nancy and two of her teenage friends sallied forth one Hallow'een armed with torches in search of ghosts; they did not stay long and tales of flickering lights and eldritch voices grew more spine chilling by the hour until unable to face the climb to the dark attic they spread their sleeping bags in front of the fire and spent a far more scary night listening to the wind howling down the chimney. The local lads from Crossakiel had their best Hallow'een ever, smirking over their nicotine-stained butts as they nonchalantly passed the time of day to the girls on their way to Mass next morning.

Climbing to the top of Loughcrew was a favourite high summer event; we would have our picnic in solitary grandeur at the summit beside the passage grave looking across five counties. The more renowned tombs at Knowth and Newgrange to the north-east would be inundated with tourists, coaches and cameras – on certain Sundays including an O'Mara Travel coach load of *Arts et Vie* French clients on their archaeological tour of Ireland, a fortnightly tour series that contributed in no small way to O'Mara Travel profits for twenty odd years. Other Sundays would bring us a little farther afield to the Park Hotel in Virginia, set amidst its own woodlands and lake. On her return from Italy with her toddler daughter Tania, Mary Banotti had found a live-in job at the Park Hotel and subsequently rented a cottage in nearby Ardglasson for her weekends off work. Moving on to her social affairs job with Irish Distillers and eventually to the political arena as MEP, Mary kept up her ties with Virginia and Ardglasson and bought not only one but two adjoining cottages, the scene of many a summer al fresco feast in her sheltered back garden. It was Tania Banotti who taught Eoghan to ride a bicycle, with endless patience running behind the wobbly rider down the hilly incline from the starting point of the pump, knowing just when to let go while pretending she still had a firm grip on the saddle.

Owen Senior, as he came to be known, was a frequent visitor. The cottage in Ardglasson was the last place we ever shared a bed, sadly not a successful rekindling of the flame for either of us. Unable to sleep I crept out of the house at dawn and went for a walk past the pump, over the bridge and along the river bank. It was a quiet still morning, even the crows usually so strident were silent. I sat on a stone and gazed idly at the water, thinking of nothing in particular. It was my Alice moment, not a white rabbit but a red fox ran by me and stopped not ten feet away. He was a beautiful creature, not one of those stringy, slinky urban foxes but a handsome, sleek Monsieur Reynard. He looked at me questioningly, I looked back. Without haste he turned and trotted off. I returned and made a cup of tea, happy and refreshed. I brought a cup into Owen, he enjoyed the story and without saying anything we both moved on to a different place, together yet apart.

Over the years that followed Owen Senior often spent weeks at a time in Ardglasson, walking for miles, painting and reading. Once I asked would he freshen up the white paint on the iron slatted seat that circled the sycamore tree. He tackled it with such ferocious attention to detail that a hundred years of paint layers had to be scraped off before he would even begin to apply a new coat. I gave a picture of the tree and its seat to Mary Banotti as a housewarming gift for her Ringsend home; it has a lurid, angry look as if the painter was taking revenge for his frustrating labours on his portrayal of the blameless tree.

Eoghan's teenage years brought more enthralling weekend pursuits than Ardglasson could offer, when even the charms of the purple house palled, the periods between visits became longer and longer and weekends spent there a rarity. I sold it to a Swiss gentleman for £17,000 in the early 90s. Ten years later I found myself taking another detour from Mullingar and passed a sign saying Crossakiel 1 mile. I could not bring myself to go there, it was too tender a memory to risk. I drove on.

Eoghan must have had an odd childhood, although it didn't seem odd at the time. He had an upstairs-downstairs kind of home life with the garden wall between the Byrne's and us representing the green baize door; he spent afternoons after school doing his homework on Bridie's kitchen table and polishing the linoleum in the hall by skating up and down with dusters tied to his shoes. He was often joined in this activity by one or other of his best friends, Deirdre Kelly's son Mahon or Niall O'Driscoll whose mother Rita and I had shared many of the ups and downs of single parenthood until she met and married Aidan O'Driscoll, an up-and-coming marketing guru. They shared a great love of the arts, fine food and all things Italian, and were to remain lifelong friends and staunch allies ever after. A welcome rest from floor polishing were trips to his father's Baggot Street studio when Owen Senior collected him from school and where I hoped he would imbue through the pores a sense that home did not have to be perfect or even tidy, and that music, books and paintings made more satisfying surroundings than soft furnishings or stainless steel kitchens. Interspersed with weekends at Ardglasson were those spent in one or other of the Great Southern Hotels, and hedonistic stays in a Club Med resort, where, solely for the sake of business research, we were obliged to spend our holidays, winter and summer. By the time he was ten he was a much-travelled child, seeming to get equal enjoyment from a straw hut Club in Tuscany or winter sun luxury in Agadir, Morocco or Sandpiper Bay, Florida. Free first-class flights with Aer Lingus also helped widen his horizons as Rome, Paris and New York were added to his list of cities to be explored. Though I think we both preferred the New Year we stayed in London, following a Sherlock Holmes walking tour, taking a boat down the Thames to Hampton Court and seeing *The Mousetrap* one night and Donald Sinden in *The Scarlet Pimpernel* on another.

My son soon grew from a rosy, blond, curly-headed boy child to a tow-headed youth more interested in snooker than Winnie the Pooh. I was never forgiven for sending him to bed at midnight before the nail-biting end to the World Snooker Championship in 1985 when his hero, Denis Taylor, narrowly defeated the reigning champion Steve Davis in the early hours of the morning. His Dad and Uncle Ken brought him to rugby matches in Lansdowne Road and he became an early and loyal follower of Liverpool FC. I grew to tolerate afternoons and evenings when I had to retire to the kitchen to read and shut my ears to the whistles and boos from Eoghan and his friends commandeering the sitting room and only TV in the house. His first school was the Church of Ireland two-teacher prefab on Mountpleasant Square. I was nothing if not pragmatic in my choice of both his primary and secondary schools. Proximity was the overriding concern, both had to be within walking distance as my diary was too erratic to guarantee driving. Although Eoghan had a great grounding in the Kildare Place (as it was then known) School, its facilities were limited, no sports a distinct drawback as far as he was concerned.

When he was ten we decided to look for a local school where he could continue right through secondary level. I plumped first for Gonzaga Jesuit College on Sandford Road, Ranelagh. I applied at Easter prior to the autumn term, casually mentioning both my Uncle Joe and Great Uncle Paddy O'Mara as the secret password to gain entry, despite Eoghan's Protestant primary education. At least he had made his First Communion along with the two other Catholics in his class. My family pride along with Eoghan's chances were dashed when I received a curt rejection. It appeared that, with or without two Jesuit uncles, entry to Gonzaga was booked from babyhood and latecomers need not apply. Sandford Park was just down the road, and non-denominational with a Quaker flavour. Our application this time was successful and Eoghan spent eight happy years there ending up, like my own schoolboy hero *Teddy Lester*, not only Captain of Cricket but School Captain as well.

Some snakes crawled in among the ladders of those hectic years. In May 1986 I was in New York trying to salvage something from the wreckage of Visit Ireland Inc, a company I'd set up with an Irish and American partner in 1981 to expand our American business. It was a modest undertaking with a sole employee based in New York, the bulk of the work from print production to operation of the tours to Ireland being carried out in Dublin. Although not in the same league as big players such as CIÉ Tours and Brendan Tours, by 1986 we had established a small niche and were keeping our head above water, when, literally, out of a clear blue sky, Ronald Reagan sent his B52 bombers to rain destruction on the sandy Evil Empire of Muammar Gaddafi. Within ten days over 50 per cent of our confirmed summer season's business was cancelled; as one of our mildly cultural, mid-American, middle-aged clientele put it: 'We're gonna to stay the hell out of Europe this year.'

I was waiting to board a downtown bus on Fifth Avenue after a sympathetic but fruitless discussion with the Irish Tourist Board. Not being well versed in Manhattan's public bus system I didn't know I had to have the exact fare ready so proffered my one dollar bill to the driver. 'The machine don't take bills,' he remarked as he pulled out from the kerb, 'quarters, nickels or dimes.' I fumbled in my purse to no avail and humbly prepared to get off at the next stop. The driver, not lifting his eyes from the road ahead, said, 'Ask somebody, lady.' Jostled by the influx of new passengers, I appealed to the blank faces on either side of the passageway but 'answer came there none'. Flushed with embarrassment I pushed my way to the door. Like a ventriloquist, the driver, still with his eyes fixed ahead, threw his voice back down the bus: 'ASK THE PEOPLE,' he declaimed. A stout black lady took pity on me and dropped four quarters into my nerveless palm. I slotted them into the machine. As I finally alighted and the doors swung shut behind me, the driver shouted gruffly after me, 'Lady, you give up too easy.' Give up I did not but went back to Ireland to place the American company into liquidation and put up 56 Mountpleasant Avenue as collateral to raise enough cash from AIB to keep O'Mara Travel in business.

O'Mara Travel survived, no mean feat in the travel business of the late 1980s. The recession hit hard on the discretionary income required to buy a Club Med holiday and the ever-escalating horrors of the Northern 'troubles' were changing the image of Ireland from a green, friendly country to visit to a war zone, illustrated by my Milanese taxi driver who, eventually grasping my country of origin to be 'Irlanda' rather than 'Hollanda', turned around in his seat, pointed an imaginary machine gun at me and cheerfully shouted, 'Ah Si, Irlanda ! Dat-dat-dat-dat …', and the Californian travel agent who asked me politely if I lived far from the Front. Better times in the 1990s were reached by dint of the stubborn loyalty of people like Susanne Monks, Gillian and Lise, the Whelan sisters, Eileen Kelly and the incurable optimist, Grainne Cryan, who clocked up more than ten years each and numerous progeny between them in those finger-tip hanging years.

26. Still Waving

By the end of 1990 we were back on an even keel, both professionally and domestically and were part of the cheering crowd that thronged the Olympic Ballroom to celebrate Mary Robinson's election as President of Ireland in November 1990 and watch her Mná na hÉireann speech on the big screen. I was proud to welcome her to the Great Southern Hotel, Killarney, on her triumphal campaign trail a couple of months previously. I had played a humble part telephone fundraising and was delighted to attend the festivities wearing my campaign worker black sweater with the long-stemmed red rose embroidered on the front. My fervour was slightly dashed by the encounter with two well known 'Mná na hÉireann'. Nuala Ó Faoláin and Nell McCafferty. The latter fixed me with a scathing glance, 'What are *you* doing here? Sure aren't ye one of those Fianna Fáil feckers?' And she turned on her heel before I had a chance to respond.

I did not welcome the advent of 1991. I hated being fifty and I hated the fiftieth birthday party Cartan Finegan threw for me in his Seapoint apartment. At this stage Cartan had become a fixture in our family life. I had been beguiled partly by his dynamism, partly by his quick wit and partly by our common business and political interests. He was genuine in his care for us although I sometimes found myself resisting his wish to be involved in every aspect of my life, public and private. The birthday was a case in point. I did not want this birthday to be remarked upon and certainly not celebrated as a rite of passage, the half century reached, only the downward slope ahead. That is what I envisaged, modest success achieved, no more mountains to climb, no more children to yearn for in secret.

I filled some of the gaps by assuming, not very successfully, the guise of earth mother. We added two cats and two dogs to the family, to replace the sad loss of Sophy who died peacefully a few months after the move to her fourth home: Leeson Park to Malone Gardens to Mountpleasant Avenue and finally to 21 Oakley Road, still in Ranelagh, an elegantly restored mid-nineteenth-century house next door to Cullenswood House, the first Pearse brothers' school. It had a long, well-laid-out back garden with a flourishing lilac tree bordering the back wall. My earth motherhood phase did not stretch to gardening, so it was transformed to a Japanese Garden, with trellises, pampas grass and a few bonsai trees in stone pots. The lilac remained.

Other ventures soon presented themselves to distract me from my short-lived interest in domesticity, this time bearing the tag of Irish heritage and culture. I became an enthusiastic founding trustee of the Medieval Trust with a group of people including academics Dr Howard Clarke and Dr Anngret Simms of UCD and Dr Pat Wallace, director of the National Museum, the mix leavened by business people: myself, Craig McKinney of Woodchester Bank and Michael McCarthy of Jurys Hotels, who had a shared vision of creating an authentic yet entertaining history of medieval Dublin. We acquired owner-ship of the disused Synod Hall linked by an overhead bridge to Christ Church Cathedral and with a happy mix of funding from the EU through Bórd Fáilte, Lottery Funds and private sponsorship, *Dublinia* was opened by the Taoiseach Albert Reynolds in 1993 and has flourished ever since under the sure guidance of Denise Brophy, renewing its exhibitions every few years and proving that culture and tourism can make viable and sustainable bedfellows.

Dublinia, unique in theme and location, was not unique as a new visitor attraction opening for business in the early 1990s. A plethora of what came to be known as 'heritage centres' were developed across Ireland aided by the availability of EU funds. These ranged from the ambitious, built from scratch, technology-based Celtworld in Tramore, Co. Waterford, to the restored Strokestown House and Famine Museum in Co. Roscommon. Not all were to survive. In January 1992 I was a speaker at a conference entitled 'Heritage and Tourism' at the Royal Hospital Kilmainham attended by many of this fresh breed of heritage attractions eager to learn all about the tourism industry that was to repay their hard-earned investment. This was the beginning of the next company to join the O'Mara Travel group. We established Heritage Island Ltd to act as an umbrella company providing international marketing services to over one hundred heritage and visitor attractions across the island of Ireland. I inveigled a willing Cartan Finegan, who had recently taken early retirement from CIÉ and was on the lookout for fresh fields to conquer, to head up the company with the offer of a shareholding to sweeten the deal. It was a cosy fit within the O'Mara Travel family, the staff of both companies shared Christmas Kris Kindles and weekends away and stood in for each other in the ever -increasing round of maternity leaves that were the inevitable result of our 80 per cent female work force.

In November that year Eoghan put a full-size Labour Party poster of Ruairi Quinn in his bedroom window, which I pointed out to Michael McDowell when he called at the door to canvas for the Progressive Democrats. He graciously wished me better judgment next time round but it was Labour's turn to triumph at the polls and we joined the celebrations at the Rainbow Rooms, Sir John Rogerson's Quay, when Dick Spring swept in with his Spring tide of over thirty deputies, many of them first-time women T.Ds.

These were peaceful years in Oakley Road; our fox terrier Gypsy had inexplicably fallen pregnant to Cartan's snauser Kuni and produced four extremely attractive cross breeds, one of whom we kept and christened Horace. Eoghan weathered his teenage years without the onset of either spots or subversion and we lived together in civilized harmony, sharing some common passions, politics and films noir while tolerating the vagaries of his predilection for contact sports and mine for the novels of Jane Austen and George Eliot. We gave a surprise sixtieth birthday party for Owen Senior with gratifying success. His brother Liam and wife Pam came from Westport and old friends like James McKenna and Deirdre Kelly were there to reminisce about Baggot Street in the 60s. Could it really be thirty years ago?

One missing link in those thirty years of friendship that night was Kevin Monaghan who had died two years previously. Always debonair and gay in all senses of the word, he had survived in increasing penury and ill health in his damp basement on Dawson Street not unlike an upper-crust version of 'Rashers' Tierney, until Deirdre Kelly with Owen's help broke in after three days' increasingly desperate attempts to gain entry and found him unconscious. Badly under-nourished and suffering from emphysema, the nod-and-wink Irish system of string-pulling for once worked in the favour of real need and Kevin was ensconced in a small Dublin Corporation enclave of cottages in Ranelagh, which he packed with as much bric à brac and treasures from his shop as its two-and-a-bit rooms could hold. Deirdre stored the eerie paintings of bombed-out mansions he had kept since his days as an ex-GI wandering through the ruins of his beloved post-war France. He had steadfastly refused to allow anyone to alert his wealthy sister in California, herself a renowned watercolour artist, of his true circumstances but when he died Deirdre faithfully dispatched his entire oeuvre to California. In his memory every September for the next ten years a cortège, consisting of a couple of horse-drawn carriages, one carrying Owen's vibrant portrait of Kevin wearing his favourite yellow velvet smoking jacket, with the artist and Deirdre on either side, the other bearing a cheerful muster of supporters, were to be seen proceeding from the Dawson Lounge through Duke Street and Wicklow Street to Grogans Pub, which was to be its home for the following twelve months when the procession would set out on the return journey to the Dawson Lounge. Kevin is currently in residence in a suitably gracious drawing room at 27 Merrion Square and although we will be reluctant to part with him we plan to finally send him to join his sister Eileen, where his portrait will be displayed along-side hers at the Monaghan-Whittaker Foundation in San Diego.

In June '93 Eoghan sat the Leaving Certificate, applied for a business degree at Trinity College and took a year out to study French at the Sorbonne. His mother, reliving her youth with fervour, helped to install him in a box-like *chambre de bonne* under the eaves of 8 Boulevard St Germain just where it abuts the Seine at Pont de Sully. My vicarious enjoyment extended even to the Turkish toilet on the *palier* he shared with a neighbour. They sweltered in the heat of the Indian summer that year and froze through the winter months. Small as it was, he managed to entertain his father for a week and although they argued over the privilege of sleeping on the floor the enthusiasm of their joint postcard home testified to a more successful parental visit to Paris than Joan's to me twenty-five years earlier. By spring he had gained enough local knowledge and income from evening jobs at a Pizzeria near the Pompidou Centre to move into an apartment with a couple of Scandinavian students in the Bastille *quartier.*

I had little time for Paris visits or to brood on my new found solitary life without an energetic son around the house. I was involved with allocation of funds through the EU Support Programme for Tourism in the Mid-West; one of the more attractive by-products of this came about through a colleague in the same enterprise, Frank O'Rourke of the Bank of Ireland, an opera enthusiast who persuaded me to join the board of Opera Ireland, a refreshing venture into another aspect of the arts I was to enjoy for the next ten years.

A more challenging opportunity occurred that summer when Ruairi Quinn, now Minister for Enterprise and Employment, who almost nine years earlier had appointed me to the Chair of Great Southern Hotels, reiterated his faith in my abilities by appointing me Chair of the new government agency Forbairt [later Enterprise Ireland], set up in the wake of the Culliton Report to support and develop indigenous industry and to take over the science and technology functions of Eolas.

In spite of reservations I accepted. I had not yet learned the admirable quality of saying 'No' and I was to regret my easy acquiescence over the next few years. I was immeasurably fortunate to have a high-calibre board to provide the expertize in large-scale industry that I lacked but unlike Great Southern Hotels and Aer Lingus where I was in familiar territory, the breadth, scope and scale of Forbairt's activities found me often struggling to find my feet. My most useful contribution was to create consensus in bringing together two such vastly differing agency cultures, promoting entrepreneurial SMEs on one hand and technological innovation on the other. I was fortunate to fulfil that most essential function of a chair in appointing Dan Flinter as Chief Executive of the new Agency and found the strategy of developing added value and taking up shareholdings across such diverse business sectors as the food industry and start-up technology companies the most rewarding and stimulating aspects of my role. It was a proud day when Forbairt, the plain sister of the more sexy IDA, recorded the net creation of two thousand new jobs in its 1995 Annual Report. However, I was to find the responsibility, work load and effort to stay on top of the science and technology part of my brief stressful. It was stress that increased rather than diminished as time went on. The inflexibility of a top civil servant in the Department of Enterprise in turning down my application for secretarial assistance, with the suggestion that I could move office to Forbairt's headquarters, seemed intentionally obstructive. My indefatigable PA Geraldine Farrell absorbed and churned out immense amounts of board business, reports and correspondence, and O'Mara Travel subsidised her time and effort on the nation's business.

Eighteen months later for the first time in my healthy life I sought medical aid for an increasingly painful if unromantic condition diagnosed as a frozen shoulder. A series of injections and physiotherapy sessions failed to make inroads. By Easter '95 I was not sleeping and in continuous pain interspersed by moments of sharp agony. Finally a recommendation from a friend led me to a local GP with a reputation for 'fixing' this particular condition. His treatment gave me enormous relief, but the exhaustion and lack of energy seemed to increase in much the same ratio as I sensed my effectiveness in my professional life decreasing. One June morning having a shower I felt a gristly lump on the right side of my right breast. That evening I stripped off to check and check again, I could still feel the lump and a change I had noticed before seemed suddenly very obvious, a kind of pucker or wrinkle in the same breast that I had put down to the sad reality of being in my mid-fifties.

That was 26 June. Ten days later I had passed through a kaleidoscope of events, new words like mammogram, biopsy, mastectomy, lumpectomy, nodes, histology and chemotherapy jostling about in my overcharged mind. I had made my third visit to the only Breast Clinic then in existence, a pre-fab building on Herbert Road, Ballsbridge, adjacent to St Vincent's Private Hospital, a scene of tranquil chaos where somehow with no apparent structure the multitude of women were moved in and out with an admirable degree of speed and efficiency. We sat in rows, maybe fifty in the large room and chatted as we waited our turn, old and young, rural and urban, middle and working class – all we had in common was our womanhood and the spectre of breast cancer.

This third visit was to receive the report of the biopsy. Waiting to be called the bricklike mobile phone I had in my handbag shrilly demanded an answer: ten Club Med clients had been off-loaded on their return flight from Morocco and were refusing to budge from their £100 a night hotel until the next return flight five days later. My feeble attempts to broker a compromise fell on staff's jaundiced ears: 'what meeting was she at this time ... nothing in the diary ... no contact number ... will call later ... not good enough...' An hour later young Dr McDermott, who I was to get to know well over the next few months, confirmed what I already knew. I required immediate surgery to remove a malignant tumour and surrounding nodes. I hardly listened to the details as my mind immediately jumped to practicalities. I could clear the diary in two weeks. How long would I be in hospital, what post-operative treatment would I need? I was informed tersely that it was the surgeon's diary, not my own, that would dictate the schedule and the Registrar of St Anthony's ward would contact me as to admission and operation timetable.

Out in the car park I suddenly found myself shaking all over, an onrush of tears blinded me. I drove to nearby St Alban's park, Sandymount, where Mary was living alone after Ken's death in June 1994. I managed a jaunty, 'Hi – I need a drink ', before breaking down – all Mary could say when I told her was 'Fuck', a graphic summing up of the situation. My next thoughts were for Eoghan, four weeks into his first job in a Club Med resort in Switzerland. I had collected his Trinity first-year exam results the previous day – honours all the way and had difficulty keeping my overweening pride and love to myself – mustn't smother him, bore others or indulge myself. As it transpired I had to make do with ten days to put my house in order. At least I was able to properly account for my recent lapses and now was the time to be thankful for my powers of delegation. Eileen Kelly would run the travel agency, as always quietly competent, and Susanne Monks, my rock, would carry the incoming business. They were the first to know and with them I plotted the best strategy for staff and public consumption. Retaining confidence in O'Mara Travel's highly personalized business was of primary importance. The decision was to be upfront and upbeat. Yes I was lucky to have an early diagnosis of breast cancer, involving a partial mastectomy, the prognosis was positive and treatment likely to be brief. I also confided in Dan Flinter and held the monthly Board meeting as usual on 12 July; the next was not to be until mid September – surely two months would see me through.

Two weeks after the operation on 17 July I made an appointment for a private consultation with Dr John Crown, the abrupt young oncologist who had swooped down upon me in St Anthony's Ward to inform me that he was putting me on a radical nine-month programme of high-level chemotherapy followed by radio therapy as I '*was young enough and strong enough to take it*'. Lying there in my nightie attached to a drainage utensil I felt totally inadequate to respond and decided that a one-to-one interview, dressed more suitably in a business suit, would be a better forum to discuss my immediate future. I explained I had business commitments, a company to run and a son to put through university, I was now cancer free so why the need for such a scale of post-operative treatment. He gave me a succinct answer – recent research showed that with this treatment there was a 30 per cent chance cancer would re-occur within five years; without the treatment there was a 70 per cent chance of re-occurrence – and invited me to take my choice. He was a new boy on the block, oncologists being a rare breed in the Irish health system of the early 90s. He was fresh from the cutting edge of cancer treatment and research in the USA, and was to be at the forefront of reform of breast-cancer treatment in Ireland. I knew he had no time for comfortable platitudes, respected his honesty and accepted his word.

The nine months of chemotherapy to follow became a process I thought of as gruesomely analogous to that of gestation but in reverse. In July I was relieved of a living but deadly substance growing within my body. From August until the following April poisons were introduced regularly to prevent any possibility of further progeny arising from that unwelcome incubus. Like many cancer sufferers I found the optimal way to deal with the long months of treatment stretching ahead was to get back to 'business as usual' and schedule the chemo sessions into the diary as just another out-of-office meeting.

Life resumed its regular pattern of juggling with O'Mara Travel and Other People's Business albeit at a slower pace with admittedly a few dropped balls, missed passes and occasional farcical interludes, my wig often providing the cause for hilarity or drama. My five-year old grandniece Aisling, whose sleepovers we both looked forward to, ventured to ask me one evening – eyes big in her small face – if I was a real witch? She had come upon my second best wig on its stand on my dressing table and remembered only too vividly that according to Roald Dahl a witch could be immediately identified by the wearing of a wig. It took some persuasion to regain her confidence in my mere humanity. Owen Walsh came in for some of the drama when he came for dinner one evening and found me wearing a red turban, a welcome relief from the sticky heat of the wig and I thought an attractive alternative. '*My God, woman, what's that thing you've got on your head – you're the spit of your mother!*' The inevitable straw snapped – I tore off the offending headgear, threw it at him, burst into tears and stormed off to bed. Abashed he cooked the dinner and sent Eoghan up to me with a drawing of himself in a chef's hat and me with a head like an egg wielding a threatening ladle, with the inscription '*Dinner is served.*' So peace was restored.

Almost a year to the day after my first chemo session, 4 August 1996, my full recovery and Eoghan's twenty-first birthday were cause for a double celebration as I stood in the back garden of 21 Oakley Road arm in arm with Owen. We raised a glass of champagne and drank a toast to our past and our son's future.

Epilogue

2002

The new millennium had begun well. I now lived in a small house on the unfashionable end of Dalkey behind the Cuala GAA Grounds, where soccer hero Paul McGrath had begun his football career and where Jemima, beloved if undistinguished black labrador/collie mix, could run free when I took her on her evening walk. We were often followed on these outings by Misery, meowing as piteously as her name implies. My second cat, Caesar, so called ever since as a scrawny kitten he had marched, uninvited, into our previous home at 21 Oakley Road and taken over the household, sat at the door of 13 St Begnet's Villas awaiting our return.

Eoghan had joined O'Mara Travel the previous year, having worked for Diageo in London and Dublin following a business degree in Trinity and a year in Paris. O'Mara Travel and its younger sister company Heritage Island had occupied a narrow three-storey building in Donnybrook since 1990 and with a complement of twenty-five staff, were beginning to burst at the seams. My early skill of delegation had developed into a fine art. My co-directors formed the nucleus of a management team that had learned to manage very well without me. Perforce, some said, as my absences on other people's business had become almost *de rigueur* and were hardly to be remarked.

Turning sixty in 2001 and having recently stepped down from my second term as chair of the Irish Tourist Industry Confederation I looked forward to what I called a 'doss' year in 2002, beginning by taking January off, renting a studio apartment in Cannes and seeing if I could make a start on writing. One nagging worry marred those three weeks of winter sun in the *midi*: Owen Walsh, still stubbornly clinging to his studio in Baggot Street, had had two hip replacements and more recently been in severe pain in his left shoulder and arm and was on a waiting list for an orthopaedic consultant's attention. The bad news came about a week before I was due to fly home. Owen was in Beaumont Hospital for tests. Eoghan had met the consultant to be told his father had a malignant tumour on his lung and the prognosis was poor. With little regret I cut my stay short and got back to Dublin a couple of days later.

There was no sign of Owen on St Kevin's ward when I called in to Beaumont Hospital on the evening I returned from Cannes. 'You'll probably find him in the smoker's den', a nurse said. Smoking was not allowed on the wards but on each floor, opposite the lifts, a small room was allocated to those patients whose craving demanded solace at regular intervals. The door opened into a choking blanket of smoke, through which I could dimly see a dozen people sitting on hard benches along the walls, Owen, at the far end, waved a casual hand and stumped out on his stick. I got a hug and a scold simultaneously. 'What the fuck brings you back to this God-awful dump?' Walking back to the ward I could see he was thinner than before, if that was possible, but cheery and full of chat. The 'lads' on the ward were grand, the nurses 'bossy bitches'. Delighted with my traditional gift of filterless Gitanes, the horse having well bolted at this stage his only complaint was, 'The pain in this bloody arm ... I can hardly use my fingers.'

The consultant was brief and to the point. Mr Walsh's tumour was deeply embedded on the lung and the growth was now affecting the muscles of his shoulder and arm, hence the pain and increasing immobility. He had also a form of arterial sclerosis, specifically in his right leg and foot. Chemotherapy was not advised, would not be effective and be too onerous for the patient. Radiotherapy on the other hand would be beneficial as a palliative treatment but would not alter the outcome. The cancer was inoperable and terminal with a life expectancy of between three and six months. He explained that there was no further treatment the hospital could provide Owen as an inpatient. Arrangements would be made to have him undergo radiotherapy at St Luke's Hospital in Rathgar as an outpatient. When would be convenient to have the patient moved home?

'Home' was the studio in 108 Baggot Street where Owen, in dour sole occupation since the last tenants left twenty years earlier, had been resisting all attempts, legal and otherwise, to force him out. When he had had his first hip replaced, Owen had reluctantly come to stay with me in Dalkey, where at least the bathroom was adjacent to my second bedroom. After an increasingly testy few days, not helped by the narrow confines of my bijou residence, he stormed off in a taxi, brandishing his crutches, shouting 'stuff you and your charity' to resume his solitary but independent life up two flights of unlit stairs, a third flight required for sanitation purposes. He survived then but three years later it was an unthinkable option. For some weeks we resisted the hospital's insistence of releasing his much-needed bed: he was ferried by ambulance to and from St Luke's for radiotherapy. Owen responded well to the treatment, seemed in less pain and his general health and strength improved. By now his brothers and family in Westport were fully aware of the situation and anxious to help. The solution when it came seemed obvious – Mayo it would be, but not Westport, and in March 2002 we headed west to Louisburgh.

In 1999 I had fulfilled a long held ambition to own a house in Mayo. For many years in Eoghan's childhood and adolescence we holidayed in a rambling Edwardian house about three miles outside Westport belonging to Stephen and Brigin Walsh. Successive years were captured in the annual photograph on the front steps of Kiladangan House with whatever house guests were in residence at the time. A favourite, circa 1986, has Mary and Owen smiling across Ken and myself in blue jumpsuit, Eoghan in the centre, poised with rugby ball, our dogs, fox terrier Gypsy with offspring, Horace and Bogey, looking virtuous in classic pedigree stance at our feet. After many false dawns and with surplus cash from the sale of Oakley Road after downsizing to Dalkey, I plumped for a nondescript 1970s bungalow five minutes walk from the main street of Louisburgh and ten minutes in the other direction to Carrowmore beach. What it lacked in character it made up for in an unre-stricted vista, south to a glimmer of sea, north to O'Malley's white farmhouse, fields and ridge of wind-blasted trees, and west to open meadows climbing gradually to the hillside that hid the Atlantic but warned you of the sunset in time to rush down to the harbour as the gold rim sank behind the dog's back of Clare Island, a seeming stone's throw away.

It was Owen who cast the deciding vote; often mocking my bourgeois desire to own property, usually derisive about my preference for quaint over practical, when I tentatively drove him out to Louisburgh he was uncharac-teristically positive: 'Liveable, far enough away from Westport so you won't be bothered by visitors, decent stretches of countryside, and walkable to the pub.' By Christmas that year we were in possession – that is to say we had the front-door key but had never spent a night there. Owen was staying with Liam and Pam Walsh in Westport, this time convalescing from the second hip operation. The O'Maras and the Mulvanys had spent Christmas together at the Great Southern Hotel in Killarney in a brave but pointless effort to find comfort among strangers. Mary's son David had died six months previously in London after a massive asthma attack, leaving his partner Jo and two little girls Lily and Rosa bereft. Nancy's children were young, the youngest barely two years old. Santa was still expected and Mary went along blindly with whatever was planned. It passed, perhaps more peacefully than we expected and while the rest of the family travelled back to Dublin, Eoghan and I drove northwards to spend New Year in our new house, picking up Owen en route from a much-relieved brother and family.

We spent three days getting the feel of the house. No matter how much we let the heating run, the old-fashioned radiators never seemed to get properly hot. Draughts whistled through the many windows diminishing the value of the 180-degree views. The plastic shower dribbled and it was too cold to dream of taking off enough clothes to have a bath. But the two fireplaces in front and back sitting rooms blazed merrily and the Oakley Road couches looked great and regained their old cosy contours. Jemima, plebeian successor to Gypsy and recent stowaway of hotel bedrooms, was a contented black blob in front of the hearth and a racing blur on the Carrowmore shoreline.

In the intervening years 'Follwell' in the townland of Caher, Louisburgh, had been an open house to family and friends in need of a break, mainly to assuage my own guilty feeling of neglect towards the house where I was an infrequent visitor, caught up in my self-made treadmill of business and commitments to urgent but soon forgotten causes. Gradually Owen Walsh became its most faithful occupier and care-giver, neutral territory where he felt at home and unbeholden. He oversaw the installation of new radiators and draught-free windows, the kitchen extension that opened up the Lilliput life of the O'Malley farmhouse and outbuildings on the hill. He painted inside and outside the house, both emulsion on walls and oils on canvas, and transferred his neat housekeeping habits from Baggot Street to Follwell's back sitting room, floored with newspaper, bedecked with brushes, paints, canvases, travelling easel, the entirety imbued with nostalgia and linseed oil.

Owen renewed his love of Mayo during these extended stays in Louisburgh, regaining trength and vigour, as well as two new hips to spur him on. It was as if, having lived in the city for so many years, he was discovering the day-to-day life of the countryside afresh. He walked the roads for miles around, tracking the townlands like the joyful mysteries – Askelaun, Falduff, Kilgeever, Killeen, Old Head, Bunowen, Carrowniskey, Killadoon, Thallabawn, Roonagh – watching the sky and weather changing. He developed a lively interest in nature and birdlife and acquired an old pair of binoculars and a small book on Irish birds, permanently kept on the kitchen table. One spring he reported gleefully on the masses of hares he could see lolloping about the O'Malley fields. I suspected him of wild embroidery of the facts until I woke up early one Sunday to see a brown hare, the size of a large cat, squatting motionless, its ears pricked high, on the grass not ten yards from my window.

Spring and autumn saw him in residence – the summer he left to us 'tourists' Gradually we managed to share the space and regained the ease of being together I had thought long lost: he in the back, pottering or painting, me in the front, reading or watching the despised telly. Sometimes he would yell out 'Any chance of a cup of tea, woman?', sometimes, 'Come here quick and have a look at this.' This could be swallows or swifts ducking or diving over the hedges, or the minuscule figure of Pat O'Malley striding across the upper headland driving the sheep to a new pasture with the dog loping and lurching behind the scampering strays. I had the best view of the farm from my bedroom at the back. I loved to wake early enough in summer, when the cows were in the large field directly beyond the fence, in time to see their leisurely sway upwards to the milking shed, hardly needing the dog's niggle at their heels, and then an hour later, fortified by tea and toast, watch their return, tails swishing, udders limp. How sad I was when, like most of the other local farmers, Pat O'Malley went out of dairy farming altogether to raise sheep and keep a few fattening cattle to replace those other bovine beauties. Thankfully Owen was not there to experience that same regret or to be enraged by the construction of two 'winsome' bungalows, built cheek by jowl directly across the fence, adroitly blocking views to Follwell's west and north where he used to watch the sun and shade move across the hill and accurately predict the coming change in the weather. The view from Owen's bedroom on the front of the house remains unchanged. A late and unfinished oil portrays the winding road, sagging telephone wires, stone walls in the foreground, marshy fields at the water's edge, the rushing brown of the Bunowen, a distant hillock of trees hiding a clutch of cottages and the spire of the old Protestant church in the background.

Owen's illness during March and April appeared to be in remission and he himself evinced no fears of – or indeed much interest in – the future. Before leaving Beaumont Hospital I had asked Dr Barrett if it was his intention to inform Owen of his prognosis. 'Only if I am asked a direct question – the patient himself decides how much he wants to know. I will tell him there is no further treatment we can provide for his condition.' Eoghan and I were permitted to sit in on the last consultation but Owen was the patient and his attitude would lead the discussion. Dr Barrett gave a straightforward account of the tumour: it was malignant, deep seated, radiotherapy had reduced the mass but could not remove it. There was no cure. Separately, he was suffering from progressive arterial sclerosis, mainly in his right foot and leg, due to severe hardening of the arteries. Owen listened attentively and asked a number of questions. They all related to the use of his arm and fingers: when could he expect an improvement? He demonstrated how essential his left hand was in holding palette and brushes, how he must have grasp of both, as he plucked from a fistful of brushes, the precise one to use and which tint to use, in the seamless progress of putting paint to canvas. The question hovering in the air above our heads, as visible as a cartoon balloon, remained unasked and unanswered. He asked when he could return to Baggot Street but accepted that he needed time to rest and that stairs would prove difficult for him. We were charged with a litany of medication and monthly renewable prescriptions and left with a handshake and good wishes from the busy consultant already moving on to the next file on his piled-up desk.

On St Patrick's Day, Mary drove us to Wicklow for lunch in Hunters Hotel where we sat outside for coffee in the old-world gardens, enjoying the early spring sunshine and arguing whether there was a missing comma in the instructions 'Ladies and gentlemen will not, and others must not pick the flowers'. A major row with the formidable Mrs Gelletlie was barely avoided when Owen was sharply reprimanded for smoking in the restaurant. Old grouch that he was, he quailed under her steely gaze. I would have preferred him to tell her to 'Fuck off' and march out, fag on lip: signs of weakening were proliferating. The very fact Owen had agreed so readily to the Louisburgh project was out of character. He was unnaturally disinclined to resist or question decisions made on his behalf. I approached each discussion in a crablike manner, getting to the point by way of detours and digressions, all of which he would normally see through or dismiss before I could get into my stride. But the extended stay in hospital, the talk of nurses and other patients had brought him to imagine and dread prolonged hospital or nursing-home care The proposal of independent living with its unspoken message of hope came as repeal, a permit of release, resulting in his unusually tranquil and cooperative mood.

It lasted through the journey west, until we had arrived and decanted all his paraphernalia. It was a relief to hear his familiar rant about 'blasted messers' who had indiscriminately packed his 'good stuff'' with worn-out rejects and who didn't know crayons from pastels, all boxed together, and where the hell was his Stanley knife, how was he to work without it? More serious was his robust denial that he needed anyone to stay with him: certainly not me. I had a business to run, I couldn't take off for weeks at a time just to vegetate and look after a crock like him. I was a lousy cook in any case and he would do far better on his own. It was time to call in the cavalry in the person of Dr Rossa Horgan.

Rossa was a son-in-law of Liam and Pam Walsh, married to Siobhan, also a doctor. They had set up a joint practice in Westport two years before, in the months before Liam's death from cancer. Rossa had generously agreed to take on Owen as his patient. He had already been in contact with the doctors in Beaumont and had Owen's medical files transferred to Westport. An extremely handsome young man, he had gravitas, spoke in a soft Kerry accent and, though respectful of 'Uncle Owen', took no prisoners when it came to straight talking. Owen's condition was serious, he must accept the parameters he would lay down, otherwise he would have no choice but to refer him to residential care. Thus a routine of sorts was begun, flexible and adaptable.

For the next six weeks a steady and not unpleasant pattern of existence evolved. I spent three days a week in Dublin, usually Monday to Wednesday evening, then travelled down in the lengthening spring evenings to Mayo, my heart always lifting, as was its habit before and after this period, when I topped the Sheeaun, the ancient hill overlooking Westport, to see mole-hilled Clew Bay, Croagh Patrick and in the distance Clare Island, mapped out below. Eoghan usually followed on Friday or Saturday for the weekend. For a young man of twenty-six, he showed empathy and subtlety in dealing with his often crusty parent. As time went on and the illness progressed, Eoghan quietly took over responsibility for O'Mara Travel as my trips to Dublin became more and more infrequent. Although we kept our discussions about Owen to the purely practical, I could see that some frontier had been crossed: their previous interchanges, based on sport or beer or girls mutated to a more trustful, if quieter, closeness. Owen would often dismiss my ministrations, calling for Eoghan. 'He's the only bloody one who doesn't mess me about,' he would mutter, a shade apologetically.

Jemima became a fixture in Louisburgh when I was away in Dublin. Quiet and undemanding, Owen became very fond of her. She kept her pace to his when he was able to walk as far as Kenny's for the newspaper and tobacco. Frank Kenny, the local curmudgeon who barely nodded to me, was always ready to engage Owen in chat. Misery and Caesar, as cats do, survived very well without me, fed and petted by Eugene Smith of Begnet's Villas, who kept his own menagerie of strays. On the days I was away, one or other of Owen's three senior sisters-in-law, Pam, Kay and Brigin would pay him a visit, laden with food, much of which found its way into my already-burdened fridge. But what bliss to find a succulent chicken, rich casserole, fresh soda bread and apple tart all ready to be heated up on a Friday evening. Even an occasional half salmon appeared, mysteriously provided by brother Cathal, whose fishing expeditions were now international, tales of catches in Argentina, Alaska and Nova Scotia replacing the Moy or Achill in his repertoire of tall fishy tales. Owen's fourth and youngest sister in-law, Mary MacBride, came often with her troves of golden daughters to tease and laugh with and at him while he muttered and bellowed at the invasion of 'all these bloody women'.

By some mysterious process I found we were now on the local health-service list and were visited by a specialist cancer nurse from Castlebar Hospital. Owen was eligible for 'carer' support to help with housework, dressing or shopping. Initially this came from my near neighbour Angela McGuinness, whom I had previously known only to chat with in passing; she was a great supplier of local intelligence, soon to become an intimate friend. Be it a leaky tap or a more catastrophic empty oil tank in the middle of a Bank Holiday weekend, Angela would chivvy and scold some cowed man into arriving, cap in hand, to do the business, get paid and get out as fast as he could. As Owen's condition worsened, Angela was replaced by a team of two trained carers whose twice daily visits provided not only the essential props but the security of mind, which kept our frail self-support system going for the bad times ahead. However, right through April, Owen's illness seemed in abeyance. He could get about, athough slowly, with the aid of his stick. He still worked a little every day and there was always something on the easel, although gradually that was replaced by the more easily held drawing board for sketches in his favourite pastels.

Two small self-portraits of the time: one begun in Baggot Street is more carefully executed and shows the sitter, palette gripped in left hand; a sad, puzzled gaze fixed on a point far beyond the viewer. Another painting can be seen in the background, abstract shapes with a vibrant streak of red positioned above the artist's head, reminiscent of the dove hovering above the head of Christ in a Renaissance painting. A later self-portrait, also a small canvas, is painted in a thinly applied wash of colour, giving a sense of dreamy, almost hypnotic brushwork. The sitter here is attenuated, almost spectral, in tones of deep mauves and weedy greens. He is looking straight at the viewer, almost challenging him to speak, the eyes behind his spectacles huge, and it is difficult to break his gaze. It is clear by then Owen knew and accepted he was dying.

During the month of April Owen gave the lie to this re-imagined, perhaps revisionist, interpretation of his last painting. He lived very much for the moment with little talk about the future and even less about the past. He enjoyed trips in the car, the drive through the Doolough Valley most of all. Often we drove just to the beginning of the dark lake itself, a discreet spot on a curve of the road where the car was safely tucked out of danger, and the water lapped up on a narrow stretch of pebbles where he could walk a little or sit on the low wall looking across at the back of Mweelrea, grazed bare by multitudes of EU-subsidized sheep. Brigin Walsh took him on a great adventure one day. He loved telling and re-telling of the wildness of the twenty-mile drive across the mountains, through bare miles of treeless plateaux, no human habitation to be seen, Brigin's cheerful bravado when it seemed they had lost their way, and their final triumphant emergence in Drummin on the Leenane side of Westport.

The gradual coming together of Owen, his brothers and extended family was a precious, if poignant, consequence of this time in Louisburgh. Although the relationship, so troubled and laden with bitter memories, had mellowed during recent years, when tolerance had superseded animosity, there was always wariness, a certain unease covered by jocularity by the men and busy chat from their wives. Over these weeks the barriers came down, concern replaced wariness and warmth overcame reserve. Many sun-filled afternoons were passed reminiscing about sporting prowess at Blackrock College, about childhood holidays in Lecanvey, all of ten miles, but a different world, from above the shop in Bridge Street, Westport; even broaching the forbidden subject of their beloved mother, Delia. The head of the family, ninety-year-old Uncle Padraig,

Delia's youngest and only surviving sibling, made a state visit on the arm of his son Cathal Hughes. Most importantly of all, Owen's daughter Sharon, a beautiful woman, unbelievably in her late forties, became a regular visitor to Louisburgh. Not only did she and her father reach a new intimacy after years of very infrequent and unsatisfactory contacts, but she quickly became an invaluable member of the care team. Her brother Ronan also visited on a couple of occasions. He and his father had been on good terms ever since as a young aspiring artist he had sought his father out in Baggot Street. He found dealing with his ailing father more difficult, especially when the increasing pain of his illness caused him to rail and curse any clumsy if well-intentioned attentions. It was a strange conflict of feelings for the invalid himself. On the one hand he blossomed under the palpable warmth and love he was now experiencing, after so many years of solitary living and real loneliness. At the same time his physical decline was hugely abhorrent to him, both because it forced him to accept help and because it frustrated his overpowering need to paint, for so long the only thing that gave meaning to his life.

The May Bank Holiday weekend was a watershed. It marked the change from semi-independence to total dependency, from discomfort to severe pain, only intermittently responsive to medication. It had been a delightfully warm weekend. Eoghan had been down with my grand-niece and nephew, twelve-year-old Aisling and eight year-old Cian. The children had arrived in some trepidation of meeting Owen again. Dire parental warnings of how ill he was and how quiet they had to be at all times were coupled with their already well-ingrained dread of his well-known dislike of all small children. Their mother Nancy had often regaled them with horror stories of her own childhood when she hid behind the door in Leeson Park as he arrived drunk and boisterous on occasion or when she was unwillingly persuaded to sit for a portrait only to find herself dismissed and the result described as 'fucking awful'. Admittedly he did make up for it in a very fine crayon drawing, eerily prescient of her adult self. But the new Owen neither shouted nor roared at them and sat in a chair in the front garden, wearing a sun hat and waving genially with his stick as they walked up the road from the beach.

In the days that followed his condition worsened; he could no longer walk unaided, even from room to room. A new and more regimented way of life took over the household. Either Breeda or Regina, our nursing care assistants, came morning and evening to help get Owen up and dressed and change the bandages on his leg, now the greatest manifestation of his deteriorating state. Dressing the suppurating ulcers on his foot and leg was a dreaded daily torment for him, no matter how gentle and professional the handler. It now took two people to move Owen from bed to chair, or room to room. Our local health visitor turned up at the door one morning, like a summer Santa Claus, answering one of our most pressing needs, how to get

Owen easily from bedroom to sitting room: not in a wheelchair but better, an old hospital winged armchair on wheels. He was sleeping a lot during the day, either because of restless nights or increased medication. His left hand, useless now for wielding brush or pencil, still managed the nonstop practice of rolling cigarettes. It would have taken a harder heart than mine to forbid him his remaining pleasure. I often wished I had cannabis to mix with the tobacco and had sent out an appeal to Dublin to source a supply, so far without success. A side effect of this ceaseless fiddling with cigarette paper and matches together with nodding off every half hour was the fear he would set himself and the chair on fire. Nothing quite so dramatic occurred but his clothes were increasingly dotted by tiny holes as were all the sheets and pillow-cases in the house. For many months after his death, my heart would give a little twist when I came across the telltale marks in the folds of a sheet or if a visitor teasingly asked if there were mice in the hot press.

Nights were increasingly difficult to manage as Owen woke frequently in pain and needing to be moved or propped into a different position. He was now on a breakthrough morphine-based supplement to his daily dosage for severe episodes of pain. Mary began coming down from Dublin for longer and longer periods, an ideal helpmate, no awkwardness in sharing the task; her own early nursing experience meant a pragmatic, no nonsense ability to deal with the day-to-day moods of the sick room. She kept a diary at the time:

> May 13: Shocked at change in Owen. Very frail but in good humour. Out for a small drive to beach. Insisted on going for a drink.
>
> May 14: Owen drops off to sleep very often – with cigarette in hand – nerve wracking to watch.
>
> May 15: Eileen headed back to Dublin at 7am ... visitors called: John Staunton, Cathal and Kay. Found it difficult to get Owen into bed ... he fell during the night. I didn't hear him.
>
> May 16: Poor Owen – bad day for him I had to help get him up and dressed. Spent a lot of time trying to stop him dropping off and falling ... Visitors: Audrey, Kay and Brigín Nurse and Doctor ... 2 falls during the night ... I heard and was there immediately.
>
> May 22: Owen weaker – carers in – all kinds of aids now to hand. Eileen went into Castlebar for commode. I was on my own. Owen had epileptic seizure whilst asleep. Scared the shit out of me!

The crisis came the following night. All day Owen had been unusually quiet and peaceful. He seemed reluctant to get up or move out to the sitting room so I spent a good deal of the morning with him in the bedroom while Mary walked the dogs and pottered about in the kitchen. He dozed off while I battled with the Simplex crossword. Suddenly he was wide awake and

Left: The wedding of Mary O'Mara and Ken Mulvany (St Stephen's Green, spring 1973). *Right:* Owen Walsh with Liam O'Flaherty (Dublin, 1974).

Eileen (Mont St Michel, Normandy, May 1975).

Left: Owen, Eileen and their son Eoghan, with Ruth and John Brown (Leeson Park, Dublin, August 1975). *Right:* Eileen and Eoghan (October 1975).

Princess Grace with O'Mara Travel Garden Tour
(Mount Usher Gardens, Wicklow, May 1978).

Left: 'Can this woman work miracles?' (April 1984). *Right:* Ruairi Quinn, Minister for Labour, with Eileen and Brendan Pettit (Dublin, April 1984).

Ken Mulvany, Eileen, Eoghan, Mary and Owen
(Kildangan, Westport, Mayo, August 1986).

Charles Haughey, Taoiseach, with Eileen and P.V. Doyle (Royal Hospital, Kilmainham, December 1987).

Bertie Ahern, Minister for Labour, with Eileen and Eamonn McKeon (Dublin May 1988).

Eileen with Sonny Looney, Tom Doyle and Jacky Moriarty, the 'Three Wise Men' of The Great Southern Hotel, Parknasilla, Kerry (spring 1992).

'Kevin Monaghan' in transit from Grogans to The Dawson Lounge, with Deirdre Kelly and Owen Walsh (Dublin, 1992).

Left: John Bruton, Taoiseach, with Eileen (Dublin Castle, 1994).
Right: Albert Reynolds, Taoiseach, and Eileen at Dublinia (May 1993).

Eileen on the publication of the Forbairt Annual Report (summer 1996).

Left: Eileen and Owen at Oakley Road (Ranelagh, Dublin, 4 August 1996).
Right: Cathal Walsh, Enda Kenny and Owen with 'Self-Portrait'
(Westport, Co. Mayo, September 1999).

Eileeen, Eoghan and Owen with 'Girl Reading' at
Westport exhibition (September 1999).

Left: Eoghan's Conferring at Trinity College, Dublin (October 1998).
Right: Eileen as Chairwoman of the Irish Tourist Industry Confederation (Dublin, April 2001).

Owen, with friends Zelda and Jemima (Louisburgh, Co. Mayo, April 2002).

talkative: 'We should have married you know,' was his conversational gambit. Useless as ever at opening up to emotional issues, I gave an awkward riposte something along the lines of: 'Weren't we fine as we were … we could never have lived together … too much water under too many bridges …'

He persevered: 'You were the only woman I could ever have lived with … but you were better off without me … still it would have been nice for the young fella … you did a good job there.'

Desperate to change the subject I asked what had put all this into his head.

'I get frightened sometimes,' he replied. I took his hand and asked was it death he feared? No, it was the dying he was scared about. I made some banal remarks about how we would be there for him, we wouldn't let him down, wasn't it fantastic how much the family cared about him, we'd have to put a limit on the visitors, we couldn't afford to feed them all – and came to a lame halt.

'Will you do something for me?'

'Anything you like,' I rashly responded.

'Get my notebook out of the drawer – I want to give you a list.'

I sat pen in hand, awaiting instructions.

'Well, I want you to go through all the stuff in the studio and I want you to share out all my work between you – Eoghan, Sharon, Ronan and yourself.'

'This sounds like your last will and testament,' I tried to joke.

'That's about the size of it.'

I dutifully took down his detailed and obviously much reflected upon list of special bequests, ranging from the large studio easel to his son Ronan, to his collection of LPs to Mary, to specific paintings for family members, and a treasured watercolour he believed to be of an early Venetian master for myself (sadly Adams judged it a mere Victorian pastiche some months later). Owen never actually signed the will but I kept the notebook and carried out his wishes as instructed. Later he asked me to take off the ring he always wore on his little finger – looser than I remembered, it needed a warm soapy cloth to get it over the knuckle. It was a man's signet ring, his mother's wedding gift to his father, with a gap in the middle where a tiny diamond used to sit. 'Take it now,' he said 'and get the stone put back, I'd like to see you wear it. I wore it with pride next to Joan's wedding ring until a fateful day three years later when I returned from a walk on Carramore beach with Jemima but without the ring. The sea did not give up its treasure in spite of useless scouring along the shore. It was another two years before Eoghan gave me the idea and some symbolic comfort in getting another ring made in its exact design and weight, but without its much-worn history. But I wear it nonetheless and sometimes even forget it is not the real thing.

That night Mary was on duty. Owen did not stir but she became concerned at his harsh breathing as morning came and woke me before six o'clock. He was sweaty to the touch and we could not rouse him. I phoned Rossa Horgan who drove straight out from Westport. He told us Owen was dying; he had given him an injection to ease his breathing but believed it was a matter of hours rather than days and the family should be informed straight away. Time passed in a flurry of phone calls and comings and goings throughout the long day. Mary said her own goodbye and drove back to Dublin, feeling the Walsh family needed this time in privacy. There was much discussion about calling a priest, in which I did not join. A family friend and well-known Jesuit and Gaelic scholar, Fr Micheál McGréill, spent some time with Owen in the afternoon but had little response. One by one, various members of the family went in to sit with him for a few minutes. I was especially touched when Pam Walsh arrived in the pouring rain. She had found it impossible to see Owen over the last few weeks, the death of her husband Liam still too raw to bear reliving the experience in another brother's all too similar circumstances.

By late afternoon the house was full. Eoghan had arrived and Sharon was expected on the evening train. A sudden influx, causing a certain amount of tut-tutting, came with Mary MacBride Walsh and three of her children, all of whom gathered around the deathbed. Abruptly the sitting-room door burst open, 'Come quick, come quick, Uncle Owen's awake and shouting at us!' Awake he amazingly was, querulously demanding 'Where are me fucking teeth?' Where indeed? While others scattered to make tea, call Rossa, tend to Owen, I made a desperate and fruitless search for the missing dentures. I distinctly remembered Rossa telling me to remove them early that morning and carefully wrapping them in tissue paper, but where and how they had vanished in the meantime had me in frantic dread of the recriminations shortly to be hurled at my head by their angry, now revitalized, owner. My friend Audrey Breslin, with great presence of mind, decided to search through the black plastic sack of rubbish but to no avail. Finally St Anthony came to my rescue when I opened the top drawer of the kitchen dresser to find them nestling in a pristine cellophane wrapper, carefully put in a safe place by my ever-efficient sister before departure. The evening took on a festive air. It was a case of Walsh's Wake, when the dead man rose to join the party. I was soon to wish he *had* died that morning, peacefully and at home.

Over the next week Owen rallied but remained very weak. Relatives and friends went back to their normal lives – the waiting game went on. But by 4 June the situation had changed. The previous weekend had been difficult: I had developed a septic throat and was on antibiotics. Some expected night cover from Owen's son Ronan had not proved possible. Eoghan made his third journey down from Dublin within a week. He was the only one who could now manage to shift his father's position in the bed and Owen trusted him so did not tense up with ensuing exacerbation of his pain. It had become patently obvious that our system of home care was not adequate. Rossa

Horgan advised admitting Owen to Castlebar Hospital. Getting Owen into the ambulance was a nightmare. No matter how gentle the ambulancemen were, and they were extremely so, the manoeuvring of the stretcher out of the house seemed never ending as was the twenty-five mile drive to the hospital, bumping over country roads. On admission, the duty doctor gave Owen an immediate morphine injection to bring blessed, if temporary, relief.

Owen clung tenaciously to life for another interminable nineteen days, most of the time amidst the busy cacophony of a six-bedded ward, families coming and going on visits to uncles, brothers and fathers, doctors and their retinues sweeping by, meals being served and medication dished out. Nurses were, as always, heroic, humorous and tender in their care of him, applying morphine dressings to his sores, lifting and changing him, monitoring his vital signs. The family devised a roster to ensure there was someone with him throughout the long days. It seemed impossible he could survive the series of mini-deaths that followed, like the day I drove back to Dublin, or as far as Lucan, only to receive a call saying Owen had had a seizure and was dying. Turning back, I reached Castlebar again within three hours, Eoghan following close behind. He awoke about midnight and was able to eat a little yoghurt and enjoy a cup of tea. I could have told them it would take more than an epileptic attack to finish him off!

On my return, I found Owen mercifully transferred to a side ward, in essence a private room, where we would also be with him during the night. I fervently hoped it was near the end. It was a peaceful week. I sat with him reading for long hours at a time, and it seemed hardly worthwhile driving back to Louisburgh. How well I knew every curve and pothole of those twenty-five miles, the enduring beauty of the Louisburgh to Westport stretch in either direction, the weary hedgerows of the Westport to Castlebar section, where tired eyes could droop too easily into sleep. Owen slept most of the time now receiving most of his sustenance through a drip, also serving to keep the morphine level high. He hardly spoke and it was difficult to make out the words. Once he opened his eyes and said 'Is it you?' in a very clear voice.

One last torment and one last pleasure were still to come – was Jehovah up there in the clouds, weighing out the penances and the rewards one against the other like a child playing a macabre game of Snakes and Ladders? The pleasure came first. I had a call one evening from a good friend, Mary Banotti, MEP and recent presidential candidate, also companion of happy years in the 1980s in our neighbouring cottages at Ardglasson, Co. Meath. She told me she had come across a poem in a new collection *Cries of an Irish Caveman* by Paul Durcan, which she felt might refer to Owen Walsh. Passing through Westport next day, I stopped in Seamus Duffy's bookshop to enquire. 'Of course we have it, isn't he one of our own?' said Seamus. I sat in the car and turned to page 36. There was no might about it. It was Owen at his bravest, boldest and bravura best. I drove the rest of the way to Castlebar, brimming with delight, and read it to Owen. His eyes were closed. Then a wavering smile and a slight pressure of his fingers: 'Read it again', and this is what I read.

Portrait of the Artist

At closing time on Saturday nights in winter,
Off Grafton Street in Dublin in the 1950s,
He was a young creamy bull stamping his hooves
On pavements, goring, butting, bellowing, bleeding,
Straining at the neck and being restrained
By stringy maidens in waist-length plaits.

Monday mornings he'd appear in the District Court,
Eyes closed, lips swollen violet to the cheekbone.
Thursdays he'd draw a beauty with charcoal
And with crayon he had the nerve of Degas.
We watched and waited
While he chose New York or Paris or Rome.

He stayed at home and he never joined
Any coterie coy or callous;
Never licked the buttock of any clique.
He was so political he was anti-political.
Wild red deer. Extinction!
He became a creature of the Forest of Nothing.

This August morning – the first morning of autumn –
Warm, moist, smoky, leaf-splattered –
Rowing his stick across Baggot Street Bridge –
A simulacrum of Pollock in old age:
Lean the meat of the old bull of Wyoming;
Debonair, puckish, streetwise countryman.

Limp roll-up stuck to his upper lip;
Sporting a spotless cream linen jacket,
A canary yellow shirt open at the neck,
Olive-green pressed trousers and a pair
Of polished, spit-in-your-eye, tan, laced brogues.
Disinterested in clichés of recognition.

Blarneyless, he invites me
To have 'a jar' with him in the Waterloo House,
Whose proprietor Andy Ryan – he imparts to me –

Has sold the House for two million.
'I see him in the street smiling like a hen –
An ould hen sitting on two million!'

Over glasses – Heineken for him, Ginger Ale for me –
In response to a query from myself, he smiles
That there was none handier in our time than Paul Klee.
He is quiet with glee about the light in Mayo
But also, he mutters, the quality of its dark.
He drawls: 'I miss listening to the dark in Mayo.'

Artist knowing what he wants and does not want
He is as nonchalant as he was
Fifty-five easel-courting years ago;
He whom now no trend-editor can identify.
Leaning on his stick he growls 'Goodbye'
And steps away to work another year alone.

7 AUGUST 1999

Twenty-four hours later I was sitting with him while he slept. He had hardly woken since I had come in. Abruptly, frighteningly, he began flailing about, his eyes staring, his mouth open in a soundless rictus – somehow the morphine drip had become detached from the cannula in his arm. I ran into the corridor shouting for help. A nurse bustled in, then hurried away. For an endless number of minutes I tried to calm his pleading eyes, hold his clawing hands. The drugs cupboard was locked, Sister was on another floor. I raged helplessly at this last, gratuitous cruelty. An injection directly into the blood stream sent him into blessed unconsciousness.

For the next two days he lay in a coma and finally died. It was 7 am on 23 June 2002. Eoghan and I had left for home and sleep at 5 am, assured there was no immediate danger. It was a glorious dawn. Stephen and Brigín Walsh were at his beside as were his daughter Sharon and son Ronan who had arrived that night. The comforting Irish rituals of death and mourning took over. With Cathal Walsh's assistance as to the niceties of the language, and deference to family, I composed the Death Notice for *The Irish Times*:

> WALSH Owen (Artist) Louisburgh, Co. Mayo and formerly of Baggot Street, Dublin and Westport. June 23 (peacefully), at Castlebar General Hospital: Deeply regretted by his loving friend and partner Eileen O'Mara Walsh, their son Eoghan, daughter Sharon and son Ronan, children of deceased wife Beryl, brothers Stephen, Cathal and Seamus, sister Mary, sisters-in-law, grandchildren, nephews, nieces and many friends. R.I.P. Reposing at Navin's Funeral Home, Westport this (Monday) evening from 6.30 o'c. With

removal at 8 o'c. to St Mary's Church, Westport. Burial tomorrow (Tuesday) after 11 o'c. Mass in Aughagower Cemetery.

'Gra agus beannacht leat'

Eoghan and I decided against bringing Owen home to Louisburgh to be laid out for the twenty-four hours prior to the removal to St Mary's Church, Westport. Our instincts, inheritors of Joan's Puritanism, flinched at the prospect. The house was still replete with the smells and utensils of illness. I had not the energy to play the role and hold state for the many hours it would take for callers to pay their respects.

In the event, Owen's home town of Westport gave him a magnificent send off. The family escorted the hearse from Castlebar to Navin's Funeral Home, where the open coffin laid for two hours while an endless stream of mainly unknown faces nodded and unknown hands were shook to the murmur of 'Sorry for your trouble, Ma'm.' It was a public statement of affection and respect, not for the dead man, who was unknown to most of those present, but for the Walsh and Hughes families, their stature in the town and the traditions they represented. From this point, at the clock dissecting Bridge Street and Mill Street, the cortege set forth, headed by the hearse, immediatly behind which carried aloft by his nephews was a large self-portrait of Owen, followed on by throngs of people. With the Garda diverting the traffic, we walked, a straggling line abreast, the short stretch to the Octagon overlooked by the stone statue of St Patrick (commissioned by Liam Walsh, by the sculptor Ken Thompson, and subject of much ireful debate with his brother Owen). Down James Street we strode in the bright June sunlight, me clutching on to Eoghan all the way, partly for support, partly in sheer exhilaration. At the Mall, so familiar a subject matter in Owen's landscapes, we turned right and entered the church. A few prayers said and another procession of respectful mourners filed up and shook hands with the two rows of direct family members at the top of aisle.

The funeral next day was choreographed by the younger Walsh generation headed by Willie Walsh, Owen's favourite nephew. The self-portrait, showing Owen at his most flamboyant in multi-coloured robe, was set on an easel beside the coffin and Fr Mícheál MacGréill S.J. gave a wise and generous homily on the man, his art and spiritual core. I was surprised at the depth of his understanding based on the few short meetings he had had with Owen in the last few weeks. After Communion I read *Portrait of the Artist* from the altar – for me a word painting I could neither add to nor better. Then the coffin was shouldered out to the waiting hearse, Eoghan among the bearers.

The final graveyard ceremony at Aghagower I saw, like Alice, through the wrong end of a telescope, the crowd of people trailing up the long hill to one of the three cemeteries of this tiny hamlet, whimsically known as 'the *dead* centre of Ireland', the group standing around the Walsh family grave, where Owen joined William J. and Delia Walsh and their infant son, Liam, under the granite Celtic Cross. Suddenly I felt light as air, unsubstantial, transparent. I looked around – everyone else looked reassuringly normal. Solemn faces turned to smiles as we turned away to walk back down the hill. We spoke about the beautiful day, the clear sight of the cone of Croagh Patrick, for once not wreathed in its usual cap of cloud; how Owen would be looking forward to a pint after all the solemnity. For tradition's sake we stopped at Scott's Public House, at the bottom of the hill; bear hugs from Owen's Westport 'coveys' and some contemporaries from the art world; kisses and tears from my Dublin friends. Stephen and Brigín Walsh held open house in Altamont Street, unending supplies of cold meats, salads, sandwiches, scones, and cream-filled delicacies.

My dreamlike state continued on the drive back to Louisburgh. It was late evening, the sun was going down. On an impulse I took out the car again and drove down to the harbour. 'Red in the evening a shepherd's delight; red in the morning, a sailor's warning.' Then I knew the sense of lightness was happiness. I was not sad, I was glad. It was over.

In June 2012 a Retrospective Exhibition of the work of Owen Walsh entitled 'Colour and Light', curated by Dr Niamh Nic Ghabhann, opened in The Linenhall Gallery, Castlebar, and transferred to The National College of Art & Design Gallery in Dublin, where it ran from July to September.

Appendix

THE RUSSELL—FOLLWELL LETTERS

APRIL 1927–22 SEPTEMBER 1929

31 Sydney Street
London SW3
Thursday

My dear Joan (may I call you so?)

I am telling the booksellers to send you a volume of Tchekov and also a tiny volume of my own. If you like the former, there are 11 more like it. I haven't much time as I go to Leicester today and Bristol tomorrow, but then my public jobs are done.

Saturday of next week I go to Cornwall for the whole summer – then to America for oct and nov. After that I shall live in Petersfield, where my wife and I are starting a school – but from there I shall come to London about once a week. If you think it worthwhile I should like to keep in touch with you by letter, so that when the time comes I can see you again. And I shall wish to know about your career, if you have time and inclination to tell me. Like other people I am not a free agent as regards where I live – but I shall keep the recollection of my visit to Salisbury, not without hopes for the future.

Yours
BR

Carn Voel
Porthcurno
Penzance
5.4.27

My dear Joan (but this should be mutual)

Thank you for your letter and for the nice things you say about 'What I Believe".

When you have time I should love to hear the more you say you could write about it.

I am not so busy down here as I am in London – at any rate there is no telephone. I write books here, which is not so insistent as meetings and visitors.

You ask what I should like you to write about – First of all anything you feels an impulse to write about – Then anything autobiographical, past, present or future. Adventures in thought and feeling, adventures in love, ambitions, etc. And if course anything about your plans when they are definite – more particularly if there were a chance of another meeting.

Have you read 'Elmer Gantry' by Sinclair Lewis? It is very good. I recommend it.

Yours BR

---

302 Clapham Road
London S.W.9
June 11 1927

Dear Mr Russell

It is a long time since I received your last letter. But I have always intended to write you again and I hope a faint interest in me still remains, which this letter may revive. As you see I am now in London. There is nothing to say about it, because I have only been here three days and I have, as yet, no sensation of permanency, and the prospect of three months or three years and perhaps always, almost frightens me. Everything is quite awful – my work and my digs – and there is nothing else. I am now a slave to a machine, which is a symbol of monotony, and I am sharing a most horrible flat with another girl and her father, who is a widower. Sitting in this room I feel like a shipwrecked mariner in a sea of green wallpaper, carpet and tablecloth (I nearly forgot the aspidistras). Outside are tall, dingy houses with mournful people peering from the windows (I'm sorry about all these adjectives, they will happen). But the worst thing of all is that here I can never be alone. I have not been by myself for one minute since I arrived, except in the lavatory, which is not very salubrious. You see, I share a bedroom with this girl and she has not even the merit of being nice to sleep with. I must sometimes be alone, or I cannot think or write or be myself at all. And London is so indifferent. Even the hours in the office are preferable to those after 5 p.m. I cannot even see any dangers or temptations which it would be amusing to avoid. Just existing and youth is simply rushing past me. I have been re-reading

Arnold Bennett's 'Lillian'. It is incredibly clever, only things like that don't happen to typists in real life, however beautiful.

I think now of Salisbury, and the green and greyness of it, and the friends I had there, and my father and brother, and my room with its hard, narrow bed and low pillow, (here we have a beastly feather bed) and my books – and I am astonished at my acceptance of these things and yet I did appreciate them. I never became used to adorable things, like the view from Harnham Bridge (where we stood that night) and the sensation of closing my door behind me and being quite alone in my own room.

I am not happy (and this is true) it is only because I have learned to wait, and to endure things, that I can carry on at all. If I did not realise the futility of it I would feel like Lillian, that it is wrong and unnatural to live like this. Because it is true also of me that I am made to please and to make someone happy. I have that instinct, and I shall never be the altogether admirable, independent, self-sufficient woman -

You asked me to be autobiographical, and I inflict a lot of my troubles on you. But I think you will understand that it helps me, it is almost necessary for me to write like this to someone and perhaps you will be 'sympathique'.

I hope you will find time to write me – one is almost pitifully anxious for letters, and I shall be glad to write again, if I know you are still interested.

Yours very sincerely
Joan Follwell

Carn Voel
Porthcurno
Penzance
13.6.27

My dear Joan

I was very glad to get your letter, as I was worried by not hearing. I am a person of quick impressions, and I do not mean to lose sight of you if I can help it. If you drop me altogether I shall be sorry.

Your letter is sad and I can realize how utterly horrible it is to have to endure the hideousness of London, especially in June, when the country is so heavenly. It is quite awful to have to share a room with a person you don't like. Will that have to continue ? I suppose you are free to change your lodgings if you can afford to. I wonder if there is any way in which I can help you. It occurred to me that you might be able to write for the Bermondsey Book, a magazine which specializes in South London talent. If you like, I will give you a letter of introduction to the editor, Frederick Heath. If you could make an occasional fiver by writing, you could be more comfortable and private. Let me know if your lodgings are unescapable or not. If you had the money you ought to join the 1917 Club. I wonder if your father would stand it you. It is a Labour club; you would make friends there. Don't despair. London takes time, but it gets alright after a time. Let me know if there is any way I can help you. I would gladly give you the subscription to the 1917 Club if you would let me, and write to people to get you elected. It is a nasty place but would give rise to acquaintanceships. Goodbye for the moment, my dear Joan, you need never doubt my interest in you.

Yours
BR

Museum 148
Nonesuch Press
10 Francis Maquell
16 Great James Street
WC1

Wednesday

My dear Joan

I am unexpectedly in town for a few nights. Would you like to dine with me in a restaurant tomorrow (Thursday) ? If so could you ring me up here some time during the morning, not before 10 ? I could manage lunch, but I imagine that time would be short. If dinner suits you I suggest you should come here as soon as your work is over and I will take you wherever you like. I want to see you again very much, and those are my only free times.

Yours
Bertrand Russell

If you can't phone a letter posted early would do or a wire.

---

302 Clapham Road
London S.W.9
Sunday. June 26 '27

I want to write to you, and yet for the first time I experience a certain difficulty. I envy you the apparent ease with which you write the most adorable letter – the unexpected one I received on Friday night. It made me very happy, because I think it was sincere. Shall I be candid? I left you on Thursday evening with a sensation of surprise. Things had happened differently from what I had expected. I had expected you to make love to me. I did not expect you to love me. I thought I should resist, but I did not want to resist. And so as I undressed in the dark. so as not to wake Dorothy, and as I lay in bed I was happy, but I was most conscious of surprise. Everything seems so unreal, but I shall carry the memory of it with me through the next six months until I see you again. I know you will not forget me, and it is sweet to know that you, in your busy, important life, will sometimes think of me, and perhaps write to me.

I will write you a longer letter soon.

Joan

The beginning and the end are difficult, so I have left them out.

---

302 Clapham Road
London S.W.9
Sunday July 17 27

I think this is going to be a very long letter, because I have such an accumulation of thought to express. I expect you have wondered why I haven't written before. I didn't even thank you for the books. There was one night when I could have written. I had been reading your book in bed, and as always with you, it caused an extraordinary clearness of thought in me. I forget now – that's the pity of it – what those thoughts were, but if I had got up and written you then, you'd have had a wonderful letter.

Since then I have been away for a fortnight with my family – at Bexhill. It is, I suppose, quite an ordinary place, but it seemed like heaven to me after London. While I was there I read Rose Macaulay's '*Dangerous Ages*' and found your name in it, and you were discussed at dinner, and all the while I had my secret thought of you. Then in the train yesterday, returning, I read the chapter in your book on marriage, and it said so many things I've always thought and not been able to define. And so I determined to write you again, and explain the reason for my silence. I have always remembered what you said about always telling the truth. The difficulty and the danger lies in the fear that people will not understand. But I am going to risk it – I hate to dissimulate with you.

You see soon after I saw you I spent a week-end with my lover and I reverted to the state of mind in which I sometimes find myself. A romantic state I suppose it could be called, which is all feeling and where 'love' and 'faithfulness' and an obscure sort of 'goodness' assume a supreme importance. After that week-end it seemed to me that it didn't matter how much I suffered, or how lonely I was, until the next one. I could live in the past and in the future and for the present I could just exist – carry on in the solitude and monotony of easting, sleeping, working, with books and cigarettes as a drug. But now, with the intensity dimming a little, and the disappointment of letters that try and fail to reach my standard, (the inferiority I told you of) I am thinking again. And I want you to tell me that 'faithfulness' is only a word without meaning, a tradition that no longer holds.

I want to know you better, and people like you whom you can help me to meet. People who think as I do, so that I can develop, instead of being cramped as I am now. You do not know the vulgarity of the people with whom I live – I couldn't explain it in a letter. I never see anything beautiful, or have any of the intellectual stimulation I delight in. A phrase in your book describes life exactly as it is for me – 'and life becomes no longer a whole with a single movement, but a series of detached moments, some of them pleasurable, most of them full of weariness and discouragement.' And the pleasurable ones are so few! Sometimes when they are happening, I think they are worth all the weariness, past and to come – they are so very pleasurable. But living like this makes life so short, a few days, a few nights in each year.

And yet the fact remains, I am in love. And I am loved, more truly and more devotedly than I have ever been, I think. I don't know why I love, the inferiority is there, always hurting me. I have to limit myself to his understanding, yet he pleases me in some indefinable way. I am sick and heavy with love when I am with him so that I would do anything, give up anything, forego my individuality, if I could. But I cannot – it persists in spite of everything. That is why I am writing to you, asking you to help me, to explain me to myself so that I can thin k clearly and see things in their true perspective. Don't think that other men are distasteful to me. They are not. I am not faithful by instinct, I never have been before, but he lays such stress on it that it seems there must be something in it.

Now I have told you the truth, and perhaps even you will not understand. I have wanted to write you but I couldn't without telling you these things, and I was half afraid to. I am not going to apologise for the length of this letter, because you told me to write and said that you would be interested. And yet one feels somewhat small and naked, having said so much and having revealed oneself so plainly. Am I after all, quite ordinary and young and gauche?

Forgive me if I am, but try to understand and write soon.

Joan

I know it will take a long letter to answer this and that you are busy. Talking is so much more satisfactory. But if you have not time to write at length, send me a few lines soon, so that I know you are still 'sympathique'.

Carn Voel Porthcurno
Penzance
July 19 1927

My darling Joan – I was glad to get a letter from you, as I had been wondering and feeling worried about you. You need not have had any hesitation in telling me the exact truth about your feeling – you never need have. One's feelings are facts of nature, and it is as absurd for another person to be hurt by them as by the rain. In any case, your feelings are most natural. May I set out the whole thing in its skeleton? On your lover's side is jealousy, which is the source of all conventional sexual morality, and therefore has at its beck and call all that you have been taught or have picked up about 'goodness'. On your side, while you are with him, is the desire to please, which requires that you should aim at faithfulness; and then and for some time afterwards this seems easy, because sex hunger is satisfied. As sex hunger revives, you mood begins to change. That is, on both sides, the basis of the intellectual and emotional superstructure.

Well, now comes the question: would you be wise to keep yourself for your lover wholly? Or ought you to assert your right to have other men at times when you can't be with him? I am an interested party so you must only believe what I say if it commends itself to your reason; at the same time I have said it in print, where I had no motives of self interest to affect me, so at any rate it is what I genuinely believe.

First: the belief, which sometimes you have, that it is in some way morally better to live for one lover, is merely the rationalisation of your desire not to hurt his jealousy, as you will find if you try to think it through. Secondly, you are young, you have a very good but undeveloped mind, you have strong passions, and you are amazingly attractive, both physically and mentally. You are very young and if you do not tie yourself up, you can emerge, within a year or so, from the atmosphere in which you are now immersed, and live among intelligent people whom you will like. But your development will depend upon men, and men will not be able to do much for you without wanting you – at least certainly I can't.

Third: Faithfulness to an occasional lover is not in your nature; if you attempt it, you will fail, and perhaps blame yourself, which would be a mistake.

Fourth: to damage your mind for love is, to me, the Sin against the Holy Ghost; one should never, as you say, limit oneself to another's understanding. I would not win the most beautiful woman in the world by pretending to agree with her when I thought her silly. But on this point I am something of a fanatic. One must, however, believe something, and I think you would feel what you owe to your own mental capacities. Love should open gateways, not close prison doors. And love which demands possession has a canker at the core, 'He that binds to himself a joy, Does the winged life destroy'.

If you have not read my wife's book 'The Right to be Happy', I should advise you to do so. It talks about many things that are in the line of your problems. She and I have the most completely happy marriage I know of, but we are neither of us physically faithful. If we were, we should be less happy in each other, since each would come to seem the jailer of the other's impulses – and, moreover, of impulses which make for life. I want to live and to give life – that is my deepest impulse.

And now to God the Father ...

The sermon is over –

Remember that I am very fond of you and very anxious to help you, and very anxious for a chance to be your lover. <u>Please</u> write again as soon as you possibly can. It worries me when I don't hear. Goodbye, my lovely darling.

B.R.

PS I am writing to Dr Maurice Newfield to ask if he will put you up for the 1917 Club, No 5 Gerrard Street, Shaftesbury Ave. He is a young and intelligent Jew. He may want to meet you first.

My darling Joan

Do write to me. I look for a letter from you every day, particularly after the week-end; when it doesn't come I am disappointed. I want to know the state of your thoughts and feelings. The memory of our one evening is so vivid to me and I long to be with you again. I do really feel a great deal for you. If you were willing, I could see you at the end of August or the beginning of September, but this time it must be more complete than last time or else I should mind dreadfully. Do you ever have a holiday or a week-end when you can get away? Do please write and let me knows you are not angry with me. I kiss your dear eyes.

BR

My darling Joan – Such a lovely long letter for you today! It must have crossed mine from you begging for a letter. I am very glad of everything you say. Yes, I know the feeling of having suffered to the utmost through love, and then resolving indignantly to have done with it. When this happened to me, I have been glad afterwards. I do not in the very slightest degree dislike anything you say in your letter about sex. Do you know that you write wonderfully good letters? This one, especially, is really remarkable. I want most dreadfully to be with you. There will be a chance for me at the end of this next month, about August 1 or Sep 1 – I shall know the exact date in a few days – I shall be going from here to Telegraph House in Sussex, and shall be a night in town on the way. I should awfully like to know if you would be willing to come to me for the night then. My only fear is lest you find me inadequate sexually, as I am no longer young, and not so satisfactory as a younger man; but I think there are ways in which I can make up for it. And I do want you dreadfully and I am sure I can help you in ways you will like, to know people, to come across books, to think out your problems and so on.

I am glad to know you are thinking of changing your lodgings. You ought to have a place to yourself – if possible, not as part of a household – a detached studio, or something. Here is a delicate question: would you allow me to help you out with the rent? If I added 10s a week to what you could otherwise afford, you could get a much nicer place – don't hesitate to say I may; I have been earning much more than usual lately and could easily manage it.

As to how you are undeveloped: I meant only through not having lived with people who are your mental equals. You have considerable literary talent and you could write well; but a little association with the right sort of people would help you. Remember your ambition is the best part of you, and must not be denied. I have come to the conclusion that the business of the 1917 Club ought to wait till I come to London – I want to go about it so that it will run smoothly.

My dear, I really do believe that you will like me, though that sounds fatuous. As I told you before, I can only be an occasional episode, and I shall never have any wish to interfere with the rest of your life in any way whatever, except when you want my opinion. I think however that you would make a mistake to go back to Salisbury now. Give life a chance first. Goodbye for the moment, Joan dear. Write again soon. I <u>love</u> your letters.

BR

---

302 Clapham Road
Tuesday, August 9. 27

Forgive me for not replying sooner to your letter. You have been continuously in my thoughts since I received it and I had an impulse as I read it to answer right away. I wish I had because I should have said the same then as I shall now and spared you this uncertainty, or, do you like me, recognise the inevitable? I told myself that what you asked and suggested required thinking about, but I knew all the time what my answer would be.

And yet, even now I am undecided. The truth is that I am afraid. It seems to me that it is a very important decision I have to make, not the fact of sleeping with you, I want to do that to please you and make you happy; and I have so much to give that I cannot lose by it. But I am afraid because I am tempted by the things you offer me – such as helping me financially. But I think it is better to leave that until I see you when I can explain how I feel about it. Most of all I am afraid of risking the happiness I have – which is foolish because I am not happy at all in my daily life and sometimes I feel that I cannot bear it any longer. But I have a secret happiness, the knowledge that I am loved and needed and that I am the only thing that matters in one person's life. I know that in your philosophy this is all wrong, but all the same it is true, and I could not bear to hurt him.

You must understand this because you say you feel the same about your wife, so that you would not do anything tactless or indiscreet.

I don't know how you feel about this, whether you dislike my speaking about him. Perhaps in this respect I am being tactless. If I hurt you, I am sorry, only I want to make you understand that he must never, never know. He would most certainly leave me. He is like the lover in The Red Lily – you remember? 'Je vois toujours cet autre.'

It has been very difficult to write this and even now I have only said a very little of what I really feel. But I will see you and talk to you and things will happen inevitably and perhaps I shall find that my fears have been groundless and there will be no apparent change in me.

If you knew how confused my desires are – I want to come to you – I feel a sort of curiosity and excitement at the thought, and of course I shall like you. That part of your letter seemed quite sad to me. I do like you, I want to love you – it would make things much easier. It is so difficult to write about things like this and yet it is wonderful to know that I can and that you will understand, or do I expect too much from you? Perhaps I have been too candid and after this letter you will think it better to let me go. In any case write me as soon as you can and tell me what to do. I will make any arrangements, practical ones, that you suggest – and one thing more I must say. I am sorry now that I wrote so much about sexual (horrible word) pleasure. Please don't think I'm one of those people who like to make love all night. Truly I am not like that, and don't please worry about inadequacy or being able to satisfy me. You will find it quite easy, in fact you may find me disappointing, I am not awfully clever or experienced in the arts of love. I hate writing about this but I don't want you to have a wrong impression.

I am not pleased with this letter. I wish you were here so that I could talk to you. Perhaps I shall write better in my next letter. But you will try to understand, won't you?

Joan

Carn Voel
Porthcurno
Penzance
11.8.27

My darling Joan – I <u>love</u> the honesty of your letters. Apart from your physical attractiveness, it is chiefly your honesty that draws me to you.

I don't see anything for you to worry about, though. As you know, it will be very seldom that I shall be free. I can see you one night, possibly two, at the end of this month, and once a week from the middle of January to the middle of March – after that I don't know whether I shall be able to be in London. And you commit yourself to nothing by the experiment.

As for love, what I feel for you hardly as yet deserves that name, though I feel it soon may. What I feel for you at present is a strong attraction, both physical and mental, and a very insistent desire to know you better. Where there is a strong physical attraction, it is impossible for a man and a woman to get to know each other well without sex, as the strain is too great. I think it is a mistake to resist sex attraction unless there is already a really serious passion; the best love, I have found, grows up after sex has been allowed to have its way. But of course one accepts one's risk of the opposite.

I do not in the least mind anything you say about the man you love. I don't want to possess you exclusively; how could I, in fairness? I am sure that, with your temperament, you will not long continue to refuse all other men that your one occasional lover; if his attitude is such that you have to deceive him, that is a pity, but the fault is his, not yours.

All extraneous factors, such as finance, can wait till we meet. But as regards helping you with your rent, that would cost me nothing if you got a place where you were independent and I could come. The alternative is a hotel, which is not so nice, and cost just as much as helping with the rent. But all that can wait. For this next time, it had better be a hotel, unless by chance you find an apartment you like before the end of the month, which seems unlikely. (Have you tried Clapham Common?). It will be probably the 0th and 31st August that I shall be in London-arriving Paddington 4.45. We can arrange details later.

It is not wrong in any philosophy that you should have the secret happiness you speak of. To me equally that happiness is essential, and I have it. But my wife and I agree that there is no need of physical faithfulness. This requires a little self control, since one feels jealous at times; but being mutual, it is not really very difficult, and it means not being shut in a prison.

I don't even want (with the rational part of me) that you should love me deeply, because I cannot give you enough – I am tied by work much more than by marriage. But of course the instinctive part of me wants you to love me. But the feelings of a man of my age are a little different from those of a younger man. I want you to trust me psychologically, I want to help you, I want to know you intimately, physically and mentally. Your feelings are very much what I should expect in your circumstances. I don't think you need ever worry for fear I shan't understand you or shall be annoyed. Of course, if you break with me after one trial, I shall be sad – but such things happen, and one takes one's chance. And I cannot promise, any more than demand, future emotions.

I had not a wrong impression about sexual pleasure – but of that no more till we meet.Goodbye for the moment, dear Joan. Write again as soon as you can. And don't think you are going to offend or hurt me, whatever you say.

Yours B

Penzance
18.8.27

My darling Joan – Each letter you write me seems better than the last; you letters are really wonderful in their quality of exact truth. When, in my last letter, I said I did not, strictly speaking, love you, I was reflecting how little I know you; but I feel for you the utmost that is possible with so little knowledge. At first, the attraction I felt was almost wholly physical, and I think you have quite an extraordinary physical charm, the sort that is irresistible, but now, through your letters, I have come to care for you mentally, which is a more important way. I believe you to be capable of doing things that are of value, probably in the way of writing. I long to help you find yourself and get some purpose that will satisfy your ambitions and fill your time – for you ought not to stay in an office for ever.

I know from my own experience the different moods you describe, finding religion, knowing how others feel and feeling sorry for them, then the gradual fade of that intensity. You will find the mood at its height expressed in an essay I wrote 25 years ago, called 'The freeman's worship', in a book called 'Mysticism and Logic'. Something of that has remained with me in an incapacity for cruelty and ruthlessness, an ability to endure misfortune, and a kind of active love which prevents me from being oppressive to those I live with. But of course the intensity fades.

For you I should have thought the best sort of work would be not one inspired by philanthropic motive but rather the quest after perfection as one can have it in writing. The most intense and the best kind of life, in my experience, is the pursuit of a phantom – a kind of vision of life and the world, exact and beautiful and impersonal – I get glimpses of the phantom in mathematics, in physics, in love, in poetry, in natural beauty. I believe you have it in you to live the same way. But, as you say, we have only met twice. Yet I am writing out my whole soul to you. It is strange. It is not quite an ordinary thing. I believe that I am on the threshold of something that will be extremely important to me – only it is unwise to feel sure, and I keep warning myself how little I know you. But that shall be remedied.

As for practical arrangements: could you bear two nights, or would you be too tired? I feel that there will be so much to keep us awake that we shan't sleep very long, and you may feel a second night would be too much. I am not sure what would make you happiest. If it is 2 nights, it will August 30 and 31, as I have to go to Petersfield on Sep 1. I wish it could have been a week-end, or that you could have got a day off for the funeral of a grandfather or some such purpose; in that case we would have gone into the country. As it is, we had better go where you can get to your work easily. I suggest Charing Cross Hotel, dining first at a restaurant. I shall reach London (Paddington) at 4.45. What time do you leave your office? When I know that I will tell you where to meet me. We must arrive at the hotel together. O my dear, I do want you.

B

Carn Voel
Porthcurno
Penzance
Saturday

My darling Joan

Our cook has gone queer, and I cannot (as I had intended) leave the children and their governess with her, nor can I at this season get another cook at a moment's notice, so I have to take them all to London with me and then down to Petersfield, where my wife is already getting our school ready. That dashes my hope of having Wednesday free. It is very vexing but there is nothing to be done.

No time for more – I have to do masses of things.
                                        Yours sorrowfully
                                        BR

My dearest Joan

You must have been wondering at my long silence, and perhaps been angry. A most unpleasant thing occurred. Our cook, a wild Irishwoman, got a vehement and half insane hatred of the governess, who was to have stayed in Cornwall with the children while I came here. The result was that I had to come with the children here, just when I had meant to be with you. There were very difficult times coping with the situation and I am now almost a nervous wreck. It was hard to protect the children. It also took up the little spare time I had for preparing this school and finishing my work for America, and it has involved infinite work trying to get a new cook. I am too tired now to feel anything but a wish for sleep, which I shall be able to indulge on the Atlantic. I sail Sep 21. I am very sorry indeed about you. I had already engaged a room at a hotel. But Providence willed otherwise.

Please write to me – after Sep 21 my address is: c/o Wm B Feakins Inc, Times Building, New York, USA
                                        Yours as ever
                                        BR

My dear Joan

At last I have summoned up courage to ask for news of you. When you didn't answer my letters a year and a half ago, I assumed that you thought you had reason to be angry with me. I was at the moment so discouraged and disheartened that I gave up in despair. But from that time to this I have been constantly wishing things had turned out otherwise, and perhaps by this time you will be willing to let me know something about you. Don't answer if you would rather not; but I do hope you will.
                                        Yours
                                        Bertrand Russell

My dear Joan

I cannot find words to express the joy I felt in seeing your handwriting after I had given up all hope of your answering my letter. And when I read what you had written, I found again that exciting quality that I remembered – a quality that I find it hard to define, but that makes me invariably convinced of your great potentialities, in spite of present confusion and temporary lack of achievement. You do not in any way fall short of 'my memories and imaginings'. I feel, as I did before, that I come to know you well, I shall probably love you deeply. This is a prophecy; but it is present fact that I desire ardently to see you. And it gives me a very intense joy that you say you will not be unkind when we meet; and whatever the difficulties, we <u>must</u> meet.

As to ways and means: I do not know your possibilities, but here are mine. I spend Saturday to Wednesday at home, at Petersfield; Wednesday to Saturday, alone in London. Therefore every Wed to Sat till the end of June is in some degree possible to me. I am in London to get quiet to write a book which must be finished by the end of June; but I could miss some days without disaster. I imagine your work ties you; but I could come down for a night to some place not too far from your work, if that would suit you. You could in the morning get back to your work by car if necessary. Of course if you could ever come to London, it would be easier, but I imagine you can't. If no other way is possible, I will manage a week-end; but for domestic reasons, that is difficult. However I will manage somehow whatever is necessary on your account; only it must be before the end of June, as after that I shall be immovable in Cornwall.

Will you let me know what you think possible would like within this framework?

I quite agree with you in hating London. It is a beastly place. I am glad you are out of it, and where the spring has beauty. I long to hear all the rest, that you say you cannot write. Do <u>write</u> soon.

I <u>am</u> glad you wrote. Bless you, Joan dear.

Your
B.

---

25 May 1929

My very dear Joan

Your letter came today. Like all your letters, I find it strangely exciting, and it makes me want you very much indeed. It is not only your body – that is essential, since otherwise mental companionship is impossible – but it is your particular kind of passion, above all, that I want to know and feel. I understand intimately and profoundly what you say about killing; I have felt the same way when I have been deeply stirred. If I knew you would kill me at the first light of dawn, it would not make me wish less to be with you through the previous hours. It is true, I think, that in my judgements I am sane and balanced; but that is only because I know the wildness for which one must find some outlet.

You are right to wish to be 'recognized'; there is a quality in you that deserves it, and it is this that holds me to you. I want to bring the great things in you to birth; I have the feeling that if we saw much of each other, I could do much for you. I would in time give you the power of self expression in some way that you would feel important; and that would make you happy. You ought not to waste yourself wholly on people who do not know what there is in you. And from your letters I feel convinced that you could write. But some taste of happiness is necessary to prevent your writing from being too self-centred.

It is true that I'm by no means completely free. My lack of freedom has its source in my affection for my children, which has become the most important thing in my life. For their sakes, I must avoid causing their mother too much unhappiness. Neither she nor I make any pretence of conjugal fidelity, but she is still fond of me, and so certain decencies have to be preserved. If I failed in this, difficulties would arise between us, and the children would suffer. It is also for the sake of the children that I think it necessary to earn a good deal of money, which, of course, takes up much of my time, and involves occasionally going to America. All this lack of freedom is self-imposed, and is not quite absolute. But it means I have to plan some way ahead to get free time.

I am sorry my last letter was too practical. The truth is that past events have made me afraid of protestations, for fear you should distrust them. I feel that I <u>must</u> see you to put things right. If I may be practical again, I think much the best plan is for you to come up on a Saturday for the day, as you suggest, and go back by the excursion train. Then you will see what you think of me and whether it is worth your while to attempt a week-end at the end of June. So please come the very first Saturday you can – 10 days from now, I hope. I don't know if you are G.W.R. or S.R., nor when your excursion train leaves, nor when you could arrive. Do please let me know these things.

I am sorry you are worried by ill-natured gossip; that is bound to happen in a small place. The only way is to ignore it.

Of course if you come to London I will refund you your expenses. Come straight here from the station, and ring the bell that has my name. I live up innumerable stairs, but it is not so bad when once one arrives

I want to see you and talk. It seems to me quite likely that you and I might have a relation that would be of real importance to us both; oddly enough, this makes me more patient. Nothing very important can happen till next January because I have to be away. But if we agree that it is possible psychologically, we can devote the intervening months to making it possible geographically. To decide all this we must meet.

Do <u>please</u> write soon. If you write before Monday afternoon, address Telegraph House, Harting, Petersfield; after that here.

I really think I have something to give that is worthy of your acceptance in the way of understanding and recognition. Passion you could get from any adult male, but the other things are rarer.

Your

B

238

30 Barnard Street
WCI
5.6.29

My very dear Joan

I found your letter waiting for me when I got here this morning, and it made me very happy. All day long, through my work, I have had a song in my heart. I feel that once we have time to talk all will be well. It will be wonderful if you can stay till Sunday when you come; but in any case we shall meet, and something very vital will happen, I believe. – How well I know the feeling you had on election night! It is one that can bring great happiness. – I must not write more now, as I have masses of work to do. This is just a line to take you my love and gratitude.

Yours
B

Telegraph House
Harting, Petersfield
Sunday

My very dear Joan

I have just learned that my wife has to be in London this next week-end for a meeting of the women's advisory committee of the I.L.P. Consequently, I have to be here, as we can't both leave the school at once. So I hope the week-end after next will be alright for you. I haven't heard yet which you had chosen, so I hope that will be all right.

No time for more

Your
B.

Telegraph House
Harting, Petersfield
Friday

My dearest Joan

No letter has come from you this week. I do hope Saturday of next week is going to be all right for you; if not we can't meet till After Xmas, and I want very much indeed to see you. I am keeping Saturday and Sunday night of next week free, but it is very inconvenient not knowing, so I hope you can let me know soon. If you write Saturday or Sunday, send the letter to Petersfield; after that to 30 Bernard St.WCI,

I shall be in London Wed night, then in the country on a visit Thurs and Fri, and I shall come back to London Sat morning if you are coming; otherwise I shall go home Sat. My Darling, <u>do</u> come if you can.

Must stop.

B

1 Sandridge Road
Melksham
17.6.29

Dear Bertrand

I received your letter this evening and I have read it several times. I am sorry that I didn't write earlier last week. I am afraid I am very vague and impractical. Even now I can't tell you at just what time I shall arrive in London on Saturday. I don't understand timetables very well, but I shall find out and let you know by the end of the week. I expect as I said it will be about 6 o'clock and I can return at any time on Sunday, although not too late. I expect I shall lunch in town and get back here in the early evening. I think I had better write you again with these details; if I address the letter to Russell Square so that you get it on Saturday, will that do? You can, of course, count on my coming and staying the night, which is the important thing isn't it?

As to where we shall stay – I'll tell you what I think, but you had better decide. Hotels rather embarrass me, I find it difficult to look married and respectable; but if you think you can steer me through that part of it, and if you yourself would prefer it, we will go to a hotel. But I think the disadvantages of your flat can be easily over-come. I like nothing better than grapefruit for breakfast, and although I can't cook I can make tea. As for going out in the early morning, do you think we shall want to? I can't tell from your letter which you would prefer – as long as the bed is comfortable – and may I hope for a bath? – I shall be content. It has taken me a long time to write this and perhaps my shyness has made me rather crude) I expect you will understand how I feel and you will be able to decide.

Please don't worry about being able to satisfy me physically. I shall be happy in pleasing you; and all I ask is that you will listen to me and advise me what to do. I feel this letter is very badly written, I am very tired. It is half-past eleven and I am writing this in bed. I have only nice thoughts of you but I cannot express them to-night. Soon I shall be with you.

Yours
Joan

My very dear Joan

Your letter came yesterday evening and I was overjoyed to get it. I want very much to have you come Saturday and am passionately anxious that you should stay till Sunday. You say you hope we shan't be disappointed in each other. Of course we can't really tell as we hardly know each other. You may find me disappointing from a physical point of view: I can no longer be sure of being as potent as I could wish, although in feeling I am as passionate as I ever was. I think it very unlikely that I shall be disappointed in you. Although I know (or think I do) the outline of the things you have to tell me: that you love one man, and wish you were faithful to him, and believe you cannot love anyone else deeply. But you can get from me certain mental things that I think you will feel worth having; at least that is what I am hoping. I believe I can give you understanding and encouragement and an atmosphere in which all your shyest thoughts can expand. – One practical question: shall we stay at my flat, or at an hotel? You would come first to my flat in any case. Of course i shall pay your railway fare, taxi, etc. The advantages of the latter are that you can have breakfast in bed; if you come to me we can have only what we can prepare ourselves, or else we must go out to breakfast. Also we must, in my flat, pay some slight deference to the landlady's scruples, by going out separately (if at all) in the early morning. (She is quite friendly, and only wants not to <u>have</u> to know. She lives on the ground floor, and I am on the third.) Send me a line as to what you prefer; also, when you know, what time to expect you, and what time you have to leave on Sunday. I shall be in town on Wed, night, and return to town on Sat morning; I shall stay in town on Sat night in any case.

I am feeling much more than a 'mild' excitement. I am nervous for fear I may disappoint you; you will find me more satisfactory on subsequent occasions, as I shall be shy at first. Goodbye fore the moment – and bless you.

B.

THE AVON INDIA RUBBER CO LTD
Head Office and Works
MELKSHAM
Wilts., England

21.6.29

Dear Bertrand

I am writing this in the office and have only a few minutes to spare. I haven't had a letter from you in reply to the one I sent you on Tuesday, but perhaps I shall get one this evening.

This is just to say that I shall get to Paddington Station at 6.15 on Saturday. I can't be earlier because I don't finish work until midday and the train service is not good.

I'm beginning to feel very nervous, so you must be brave for both of us. I shall be with you between 6.30 and 7 to-morrow. To-morrow.

Yours
Joan

I shall have to get the 3.15 on Sun

Telegraph House
Harting
Petersfield
Monday

My dearest Joan

Only a moment remains before the post goes – I have been rushed every moment since we parted – but I do want to tell you how happy I am in the memory of the hours during which you were with me – it was even more lovely than I had expected; and you were so kind and dear!

Write a word to say how you are and how the time composes itself in your memory.

Must stop. Goodbye, my love.

B.

My dearest Joan

End of term and end of book coming together, and interviews with new parents and new teachers, have kept me unconscionably busy; only now I have time for a real letter. The memory of the little time we were together remains one of pure joy, and I want to keep some place in your thoughts so long as you are not completely happy and settled. When that happens, it must be my part to fade away.

I long to be with you in the country, where we both feel we can breathe more freely. I have been looking up places possible for us both, and I incline to Loos in Cornwall. We could meet at Plymouth and go by car from there – July 27? But on studying Bradshaw I think this is too difficult a journey for you and we had better meet at Taunton and go into the Quantocks. Do you know any place in the Quantocks that you particularly like? Let me know what you think you would like best.

Must stop – post going. My dear, I do want to be with you again – it was heavenly.

Your
B

Carn Voel
Porthcurno
Penzance
9 July 1929

My dearest Joan

Do write me one line to reassure me. I have heard not a syllable from you since we were together, and I don't know whether you hate me, or repent of me, or find me a tiresome complication, or what. For my part, you have become important to me and I long to be with you again. Please write. This is my address until Sep 8 except for 10 days on the Continent, Aug 14–24.

B.

Carn Voel
Porthcurno
Penzance
24.7.29

Dear Joan

Not having heard from you, I conclude you don't want to see me again. I am sorry but I dare say you have good reasons.

Yours
B

On board S.S. 'HOMERIC'.
22 Sep 1929

Dear Joan

This is a last time to say: Do write just once more, if only to tell me why you have been silent, all this time. If you write before December 1, my address is:

c/o Mr Wm. B. Feakins
Times Building, New York.

I should like your news and your reasons for silence.

Your
B.R.

If you don't answer this I shan't write again.

Index